MACHIAVELLI AND GUICCIARDINI
Politics and History in Sixteenth-Century Florence

MACHIAVELLI AND GUICCIARDINI

Politics and History in Sixteenth-Century Florence

BY FELIX GILBERT

PRINCETON, NEW JERSEY
PRINCETON UNIVERSITY PRESS

ACKNOWLEDGMENTS

The writing of this book has extended over a long period and during these years I have received advice and help from many individuals and organizations.

The bulk of the work for this book was done while I was a member of the History Department of Bryn Mawr College. Friends and colleagues on the faculty of Bryn Mawr College showed a stimulating interest in the progress of my work. I want to express my gratitude to Miss Katharine E. McBride, the President of Bryn Mawr College, for granting me leaves of absence for research abroad. A Guggenheim Fellowship permitted me to spend the year 1952/53 in Italy and a Rockefeller Grant enabled me to stay six months in Florence in 1956; I am thankful for this support.

I have very much appreciated the friendliness with which Italian archivists and librarians responded to the numerous requests of the foreign scholar. In particular, I want to thank the officials of the Florentine Archivio di Stato for many kindnesses and useful advice. I am grateful to the Guicciardini family for having granted me the use of their family archives.

Interest in Florentine history creates a common bond among those sitting around the table in the Study Room of the Florentine Archivio di Stato; I have many personal acquaintances among the authors whose books or articles I quote and I have benefited greatly from discussions with them. I owe a particular debt of gratitude to Dr. Nicolai Rubinstein who read the entire manuscript of this book and whose careful observations and criticisms enabled me to eliminate a number of mistakes. Likewise I am grateful to Professor Lauro Martines for reading

v

the manuscript and suggesting improvements; Professor Martines was also kind enough to undertake a number of inquiries on my behalf in the Florentine Biblioteca Nazionale. I also wish to acknowledge the help of Dr. Gino Corti in checking quotations of my manuscript.

Mary Raymond Gilbert has actively collaborated in every stage of the composition of this book. She took part in the research and repeatedly worked through the manuscript sentence for sentence and word for word, making suggestions for achieving greater clarity of presentation and improvements in style. The book became a common enterprise.

For the tedious job of typing and retyping the manuscript I am obligated to Mrs. R. Forster.

It was a pleasure to have the assistance and advice of Mr. David Harrop in preparing the manuscript for publication. The interest which for several years the Princeton University Press, particularly its Managing Editor, Miss R. Miriam Brokaw, has shown in the progress and the completion of this manuscript was a great encouragement.

I fear that despite good advice and friendly help, the book might contain errors and mistakes. I want to conclude therefore with a statement which can be found in a manuscript written in 1512; the writer had copied a lengthy political treatise which his father had composed, and he stated at the end: "*Si aliquis error apparuerit, mea, non illius causa fuit.*"

The Institute for Advanced Study　　　　Felix Gilbert
Princeton, New Jersey

CONTENTS

CONTENTS

EXPLANATIONS

ABBREVIATIONS:

A.S.F., Archivio di Stato in Florence
B.N.F., Biblioteca Nazionale in Florence
Bibl. Marc., Biblioteca Marciana in Venice
Prov., Registri delle Provvisioni in A.S.F.

TERMINOLOGY:

"Republic" or "republican regime" in Florence refers to the political system existing in Florence between 1494 and 1512; a few references to the "renewed republic" refer to the Florentine government from 1527 to 1530. Formally, Florence was a republic also under the Medici between 1434 and 1494 and between 1512 and 1527, but the Florentines drew a sharp distinction between the government system existing under the Medici and the "free governments" (*governo libero*) of 1494 to 1512 and of 1527 to 1530. Thus it seems appropriate to reserve the term "republic" for the periods of "free government."

The law of December 22/23, 1494, which established the Great Council, is frequently referred to as the "fundamental law," the "constitutional law," the "constitution" of Florence. These expressions seem justified because the Florentines were conscious of the revolutionary changes brought about by the establishment of the Great Council. However, it might be well to state that this law was not a "constitution" in the modern sense of organizing the entire government system, but a quite limited and technical law (a regular *provvisione*), restricted to arrangements regarding the new "Great Council" and the election of officials.

In the sixteenth century as well as in modern scholarly literature a great variety of terms are used to designate the members of the Florentine upper group: oligarchs, *Grandi*, patricians, *optimates*, etc., etc. I have used most frequently the term "aristocrats"; the reason is that this term is vague and the vagueness seems therefore to evoke less precise political or sociological associations than other terms.

Technical terms—like the names of magistracies—have been given in English, although, when the word first appears in the text, the Italian term is given in brackets. A few of these terms—like *Gonfaloniere*—for which there is no English equivalent have been left in Italian.

The Index contains brief data about the life of persons mentioned in the text.

TRANSLATIONS:

Quotations from sources have been given in English, but the original Italian text can always be found in footnotes.

For the English version of Machiavelli's *Prince* and *Discourses*, I have used the translations given in the *Modern Library* edition of these two works, as well as the translation of the *Discourses* by Leslie J. Walker; sometimes I have made slight changes when they seemed to be necessary for a precise rendering of Machiavelli's text.

The English text of the quotations from Guicciardini's *Ricordi* has been taken from a new translation of this work by Mario Domandi; this translation is to appear as a paperback in Harper's Torchbook series.

MACHIAVELLI AND GUICCIARDINI
Politics and History in
Sixteenth-Century Florence

INTRODUCTION

It may seem foolhardy or superfluous to add another book to the existing literature on Machiavelli and Guicciardini. Machiavelli has been a center of discussion and dispute for centuries and new studies about him appear every year. Outside Italy, Guicciardini has aroused less interest but the Italian literature on him is considerable and steadily mounting. The lives and minds of few personalities of earlier centuries have been so carefully and intensively investigated and analyzed as those of these two Florentines.

The importance of Machiavelli as a political thinker and of Guicciardini as an historian has raised these two to lonely eminence. Consequently, the students of Machiavelli and Guicciardini have used primarily a biographical approach: the explanation for the genesis of their ideas has been sought in the investigation of their careers and in the development of their minds as it could be reconstructed from their own writings. I have tried to proceed by a somewhat different route. This book begins with a description and analysis of the prevailing trends and tendencies in politics and history, and after the contemporary scene has been outlined, I attempt to place the ideas of Machiavelli and Guicciardini in this context. Only the fourth chapter is entirely devoted to Machiavelli; in the first three chapters his name hardly occurs. Guicciardini appears more frequently throughout the entire book, but again, only one chapter, the last, is exclusively centered on him.

Thus the emphasis of this book is placed on determining the relationship between the ideas of Machiavelli and Guicciardini and those of their contemporaries. My aim has been to establish clearly Machiavelli's and Guicciardini's distinctive contributions to the development of political and historical thought and, insofar as possible, to define what constitutes their originality. In this sense I hope the book furthers the understanding of Machiavelli's and Guicciardini's position and influence in the development of political and historical thought. A necessary consequence of this procedure is that Machiavelli and Guicciardini are treated together. For in the sixteenth century political and historical thinking belong together; the new approach to political science and the new approach to history represent different, but closely connected stages in the attempt to gain comprehension of a changed and changing social world.

Although this book is directed towards an analysis of Machiavelli's and Guicciardini's ideas, its conception demands a detailed description of the political, social, and intellectual developments in Florence. Thus the contents of this book can be described no less by its subtitle "Politics and History in Sixteenth-Century Florence" than by its title "Machiavelli and Guicciardini." The interrelationship between the achievements of Machiavelli and Guicciardini and the political fate of the city whose sons they were has been emphasized by Jacob Burckhardt. This book is an elaboration of the famous passage in which he characterized the role of Renaissance Florence in politics and history: "That wondrous Florentine spirit, at once keenly critical and artistically creative, was incessantly transforming the social and political condition of the state, and as incessantly describing and judging the change. Florence thus became the home of political doctrines and theories, of experiments and sudden changes . . . and, alone and above all other states of the world, the home of historical representation in the modern sense of the phrase."

4

PART I

Politics

Chapter 1 FLORENTINE POLITICAL INSTITUTIONS, ISSUES, AND IDEAS AT THE END OF THE FIFTEENTH CENTURY

• I •

In 1494 the Medici regime, which had lasted for sixty years, collapsed, and the citizens of Florence were confronted with the task of replacing the control which the Medici and their close adherents had exerted over Florentine politics with a government which would be directed by the entire citizenry. In the words of the city's greatest political thinker, the Florentines were faced with the question, "whether in a corrupt state it is possible to maintain a free government."[1]

The Medici had ruled behind a republican façade.[2] That the citizens of Florence were the rulers of their city was a fiction which the Medici had carefully preserved.

[1] "Se in una città corrotta si può mantenere lo stato libero," Machiavelli, *Discorsi sopra la prima deca di Tito Livio*, Book I, Chapter XVIII (*Opere* [Biblioteca di Classici Italiani-Feltrinelli Editore], vol. I, p. 179).

[2] For the structure of the communal government in the fourteenth century, see Gene A. Brucker, *Florentine Politics and Society 1343-1378*, Princeton, 1962, particularly pp. 57-71; for the changes under the Medici, see L. F. Marks, "The Financial Oligarchy in Florence under Lorenzo," *Italian Renaissance Studies*, ed. E. F. Jacob, London, 1960, pp. 123-147. See also the literature discussed in Appendix A.

7

The magistrates of the city had to submit their proposals to a number of councils which were supposed to comprise the various groups of the citizenry. Some of these councils—the Council of the Commune and the Council of the People—had originated in the earliest times of the city's history; the latter had been added to the former, when, with the growing economic importance of Florence, new social groups had demanded a part in the government. Other councils—the Council of the Seventy and the Council of the Hundred—had been established by the Medici. Composed largely of Florentine patricians friendly to the Medici regime, the Councils of the Seventy and of the Hundred guaranteed strict observation of the Medici interests. This complicated juxtaposition of different councils had fragmented power in such a way that it had been easy for the Medici to impose their will upon the people. And so when the Medici regime was overthrown in November 1494, the need for a more centralized system of government was evident if the citizens themselves were directly to conduct the affairs of Florence. Consequently, the councils which had been established in Medicean times were abolished and, by the famous law of December 22/23, 1494,[3] the government was reorganized. The Florentines intended to return to the form of government which had existed at the time of the foundation of the city. The Council of the Commune and the Council of the People, as time-hallowed, original institutions, were left in existence. However, they were

---

[3] *Prov.*, vol. 185, ff. 9r.-13v.; only sections of this law have been published in Francesco Guicciardini, *Opere inedite*, ed. Giuseppe Canestrini, vol. II, Firenze, 1858, pp. 228-232. Its contents and significance have been analyzed by Nicolai Rubinstein, "I Primi Anni del Consiglio Maggiore di Firenze (1494-1499)," *Archivio Storico Italiano*, Anno CXII (1954), pp. 151-194, 321-347.

combined into one body which was called the Council of the People and of the Commune.[4] This body was larger in size than any previous council had been, and was soon generally referred to as the Great Council. In the years of the republican regime, this Great Council was regarded as "the soul of the city."[5]

The Florentines borrowed the concept of the Great Council from Venice. The power, stability, and prosperity of Venice was ascribed to the perfection of its constitution, which was believed to have realized the ideals of classical political wisdom. When Savonarola preached to the Florentines, in December 1494,[6] about the need for political reforms, he referred to the Venetian Great Council as an institution which the Florentines ought to adopt. In following this advice the Florentines expected the establishment of a Great Council would yield the same benefits which Venice enjoyed: internal harmony and external strength.

The influence of the Florentines' belief in the paradigmatic character of Venetian political institutions found visible expression. Since there was no available building

[4] "si dichiara che decto Consigl[i]o Magiore si chiami el Consiglio del popolo et comune. . . . ," *Prov.*, vol. 185, f. 11r., see Rubinstein, *loc. cit.*, p. 156.

[5] Examples: "come l'anima è forma del corpo, così questo consiglio è forma della cictà. . . . ," A.S.F., *Consulte e Pratiche*, vol. 62, f. 380v., or Francesco Guicciardini, *Dialogo e Discorsi del Reggimento di Firenze*, ed. R. Palmarocchi, Bari, 1932, p. 225, "anima di questo corpo." There was one other council, the Council of Eighty, but the limitation of the term of membership to six months and, still more important, the method by which its members were elected, made the Eighty a smaller edition of the Great Council. The Council of Eighty did not become a special defender of aristocratic interests nor did it play an independent political role.

[6] The reference to Venice was contained in Savonarola's sermon of December 14, 1494, printed in Mario Ferrara, Savonarola, vol. I, Firenze, 1952, p. 166.

9

in Florence large enough to accommodate the Great
Council, a special hall had to be built; the work was done
with an almost religious fervor and the building was completed so quickly that it was thought that it could not
have been accomplished if God's angels had not taken a
hand.[7] In its size and proportions the hall, which the arch-
itect Antonio da San Gallo erected, was an exact repro-
duction of the hall of the Venetian *Consiglio Maggiore*
in the palace of the Doge.[8] Yet the Florentines were not
satisfied with mere imitation of Venice; they wanted
their hall to surpass in splendor the government buildings
of all other cities. Inside the hall of the Great Council the
wall along which the ruling magistrates sat when they
presided over the meetings was decorated by a painting
of the Madonna. On the opposite wall two frescos representing famous Florentine victories, the battles of Anghiari and Cascina, were to be executed by the two men
regarded as the greatest artists of the time: Leonardo and
Michelangelo. The hall of the Great Council was the embodiment of Florentine republicanism. When the Medici
returned to Florence in 1512, their first step was to end
the existence of the institution of the Great Council and
to demolish the hall in which it had met. "This deeply
pained all Florence, I mean the defacement of this beautiful and expensive structure—almost more than the overthrow of the regime"; with these remarks a Florentine
shopkeeper commented on the end of the republican
regime.[9]

[7] See Benedetto Varchi, *Storia Fiorentina*, ed. Gaetano Milanesi,
Firenze, 1888, vol. I, p. 141; see also Pasquale Villari, *La Storia di
Girolamo Savonarola*, new edition, vol. I, Firenze 1930, p. 436.

[8] See J. Wilde, "The Hall of the Great Council of Florence,"
Journal of the Warburg and Courtauld Institutes, vol. VII (1944),
pp. 65-81.

[9] "E in questo tempo piacque a questo governo nuovo di guastare

Because the Great Council was the one institutional innovation which was brought about by the revolution of 1494, its functions and political significance require some explanation. Like so many other institutions of the city-states of the Italian Renaissance, the Great Council of Florence had some features which seem modern and others which are alien to our concept of a modern parliament. Florentine laws required the approval by vote of the Great Council and taxes could be levied only if the Great Council agreed. But here the resemblances to a modern parliament end. No speeches were made in the Great Council and no debate took place. Only when a legislative proposal had been rejected and was re-submitted for a second vote were the presiding officers entitled to designate a person to make a speech explaining and justifying the proposal. There was great astonishment once when Francesco Ambrogini, who had been called up to defend a tax proposal, rose and opposed it. When Luigi Mannelli used such an opportunity for attacking other citizens he was severely punished for this daring break with tradition.[10]

---

la sala del Consiglio maggiore, cioè el legniame e tante belle cose, ch'erano fatte con tanta grande spesa, e tante belle spalliere . . . la qual cosa dolse a tutto Firenze, non la mutazione dello Stato, ma quella bella opera del legniame di tanta spesa," Luca Landucci, *Diario Fiorentino*, ed. Jodoco del Badia, Firenze, 1883, p. 333.

[10] Piero Parenti, *Storia Fiorentina*, Ms. B.N.F., II.II.130, f. 74 (Ambrogini); II.II.133, ff. 90v.-96v. (Luigi Mannelli). According to Cerretani, *Historia Fiorentina*, Ms. B.N.F., II.III.74, f. 307r., Mannelli said: ". . . gl'homini potentti colle graveze co' giuditii in afanno grandissimo et ruina manifesta hanno questo povero popolo condocto. . . ." It ought to be said that, at certain very rare occasions, a general discussion was permitted (*ringhiera libera*). The demand for open discussion was sometimes brought forward by elements opposed to the Florentine patricians, but one of the difficulties was that when the Signoria permitted a *ringhiera libera* nobody dared to talk. See Parenti (printed by J. Schnitzer, *Quellen*

The Great Council was not meant to be a deliberative body; its principle function was to vote and to elect. Its most important task was to choose the men who were to sit on the various executive boards. Thus there was a close relationship between the Great Council and the part of the government which determined policy and executed it.

In Florence, executive tasks were carried out not by individuals, but by a number of boards. All policy decisions were taken collectively. Indeed, executive officials, in the sense of a single individual having a special sphere of competence and responsibility to the government, did not exist in Florence. The reforms undertaken in 1494 did not touch the existing bureaucratic structure. It was a complex and cumbersome legacy which the republican regime accepted. Just as, in the course of time, one council had been added to another when circumstances had demanded, so also executive boards had been created in an unsystematic and almost haphazard way. Some of these boards had been established when new tasks had been forced upon the government as a result of the growth of the city-state in population and territory. Other executive agencies had been instituted as a result of changes in the social composition of the city. Whenever a corporate organization or a social group gained sufficient strength to attain a position of prominence in the economic life of the city, it forced the government to recognize its importance by creating a new board which would represent its interests in the formation of policy

---

und Forschungen zur Geschichte Savonarolas, vol. IV, *Piero Parenti*, Leipzig, 1910, p. 167): "Onde si rende per opera del gonfaloniere massime la ringhiera libera, laqual cosa molto piacque al popolo. . . . Nondimeno per costumatezza nessuno del consiglio ardi parlare. . . ."

decisions. Thus the executive boards mirrored the various corporate organizations and social groupings of the city. Each of the boards was made up of a prescribed number of members. Although some of these boards had fewer members than others, the more important of them tended to be sizable because in accordance with the corporate structure of Florentine society members had to come from different quarters of the city and from both types of guilds: *arti maggiori* and *arti minori.* An example is the chief executive board, the Signoria; it was composed of nine members—eight Priors of Liberty (*Priori di Libertá*) and a *Gonfaloniere* of Justice (*Gonfaloniere di Giustizia*). From each quarter of the city came two Priors of Liberty. Seven members of the Signoria had to belong to the *arti maggiori,* two to the *arti minori.*

The *Gonfaloniere* was the presiding officer of the Signoria and the official head of the Florentine Republic. The Signoria made the final decisions on all questions of policy. It received advice from two boards: the board of the Twelve Good Men (*Dodici Buonuomini*) and the board of the Sixteen *Gonfalonieri* (*Sedici Gonfalonieri di Compagnia*). These two boards had been established in the thirteenth century, and at that time, they had been the ruling magistracies. The antiquity of these boards gave them great prestige although they no longer exerted any particular governmental function. The Signoria prepared, deliberated upon, and agreed to all legislative proposals before submitting them to the Boards of the Twelve Good Men, of the Sixteen *Gonfalonieri,* and then to the Great Council for approval.

The most important fields of government activity were supervised by the following boards: the board of the Ten (*Dieci*) managed the conduct of foreign policy and of wars, the board of the Eight (*Otto di Guardia*) was in charge of the administration of justice, and the officials of the *Monte* (*Ufficiali di Monte*) handled finances. The latter, as their name indicates, had originally been instituted for the purpose of overseeing the public debt, but their functions soon ranged over a wider field: the raising of loans and of taxes. These boards, either singly or in cooperation with other agencies, administered the affairs of the city and determined its foreign and domestic policy. In addition, there were other political positions which offered prestige and distinction, but whose functions were purely administrative. These were the officials through whom the Florentines controlled their Tuscan territory. A Captain and a *Podestà* were sent to Pisa, Pistoia, and Arezzo, Captains to Volterra, Cortona, Leghorn—to name only the more important places under Florentine domination. Besides these positions of high standing, there were a large number of minor officials: superintendents of prisons, supervisors of the markets, administrators of economic monopolies (such as salt), guardians of morality, directors of hospitals, and others who managed the public business.[11]

The most characteristic feature of the system by which executive business was conducted in Florence was the short tenure of office. The members of the Signoria held office for only two months; the terms of members of other boards were somewhat longer. Only a few officials, primarily those who held a position outside the city, served for an entire year. The purpose of this arrangement was to rotate offices as quickly as possible among all the

[11] For a complete list of the various Florentine governmental agencies and offices, published by the Chancellery late in the fifteenth century, see B.N.F., E. 63.38.

citizens who had paid taxes and were resident in Florence for a required period. This system had originated when Florence was a small town. In those times office-holding was a duty to be shared by all the citizens; the limited term of office guaranteed that no individual would, by virtue of holding office, be kept unduly long from earning his livelihood. In the course of time, brief tenure of office gained a new and different meaning. It was seen as a safeguard against tyranny, for which the long occupation of an office might prepare the ground. Moreover, as the city grew its administration was enlarged, and the attitude to holding office changed. The highest offices remained unsalaried but the influence on political and economic affairs which could be exerted by the holders of these offices gave them evident advantages. For the holders of less prestigious offices, salaries were introduced and graduated according to the importance of the office. Considerable material gains could be acquired by public service, and thus earlier reluctance to take on the burden of office-holding was replaced by eagerness for office and insistence on getting one's share.[12] Laws openly stated that all citizens of the republic should receive benefits through the circulation of offices.[13]

[12] Parenti, ed. Schnitzer, *loc. cit.*, p. 291: ". . . [because of economic difficulties] molto piu che per l'ordinario s'attendeva alli ufici, maxime a quelli, donde qualche utile si traeva. . . ." Unsalaried were the members of the Signoria, the Sixteen Gonfalonieri, the Twelve Good Men, and the Ten, see Guido Pampaloni, "Fermenti di riforme democratiche nella Firenze medicea del Quattrocento," *Archivio Storico Italiano*, vol. CXIX (1961), pp. 42-43. Pampaloni explains that, when the Florentines spoke of the "onori e utili" of government service, they meant by "onori" the unsalaried offices, by "utili" the rest of the administrative positions.

[13] "dare benefitio universalmente a tutti e cittadini della nostra repubblica et maxime circha alla distribuzione degli ufici et dignità di quella . . . ," *Prov.*, vol. 186, f. 140r, November 26, 1495.

In order to insure the rotation of offices among the citizens, a number of prohibitions (*divieti*) were established. A person who had held office was ineligible to hold another office for a certain length of time; and members of the same family were not permitted to hold office simultaneously. Moreover, for each of the more important offices certain minimum age requirements existed.

The concept that every citizen had a right to hold office lay behind the method used to fill the offices of the city. For each board or position a list was put together of the names of all those citizens who met the requirements for this office. Each name on this list of eligible citizens was written on a slip of paper and these slips were then thrown into a red leather bag. When an office or position was to be filled (and this, because of the short tenure of offices, happened very frequently), a slip was drawn from the bag containing the names of those entitled to serve in the particular office which was vacant, and if the citizen whose name was written on that slip of paper had paid his taxes and was found to have no *divieto*, he received the office. But because there were many prohibitions which barred a citizen from taking office the number of those whose names were drawn was always much larger than the number of those who became office holders.

These lists of possible office-holders had to be revised repeatedly because of the constant changes in the qualifications determining the eligibility of a citizen. This job was done in different stages. First, there was a scrutiny, and then special officials, the *Accoppiatori*, distributed the names which had passed the scrutiny among the bags for the various offices. Of course, the *Accoppiatori* had many opportunities for manipulating the Florentine officialdom, and the temptation of abusing their power was great. In the times of the Medici the *Accoppiatori* had been an essential factor in maintaining the Medici regime. By placing only the names of adherents of the Medici in the bags for the various offices, the *Accoppiatori* assured the subservience of the executive agencies to the will of the rulers.

The stability of the Medici regime had been based on two factors: the division of the citizenry into different councils which served to keep the various strata of society apart, and the reservation of government offices for those who supported the regime. The creation of the Great Council in 1494 provided the citizenry a means for common action. An even more important aspect of the Great Council was its part in the process of allotting offices to the citizens, thereby destroying the monopoly of a small group.

Membership in the Great Council was granted to all those whose names, or whose father's or grandfather's names, had been drawn for the three most prestigious executive boards—the Signoria, the Twelve Good Men, and the Sixteen *Gonfalonieri*, whether they had received the office or not. The Medici policy of preventing opponents from receiving offices was undone. All members of the Great Council possessed the right to hold office. These men—members of the Great Council and concomitantly, potential office-holders—and these men alone possessed full citizen rights.[14] The identity of membership in the

---

[14] It is more or less a question of definition whom one ought to call a "citizen" of Florence. After 1494, full rights of citizenship (including the right of holding office) were possessed only by those whose fathers' or grandfathers' names had been drawn for the three highest magistrates (Signoria, 16 Gonfalonieri, 12 Buonuomini); these were the *statuali beneficiati* and comprised the Great

Great Council with the right of holding office constituted the unique character of the Great Council. Its members were not representatives of the Florentine population; rather the Great Council encompassed the entire Florentine citizenry.

However, the establishment of the Great Council not only increased the number of men who might enjoy the benefit of office; the law of December 1494 provided a safeguard against the danger that a tyrant or an oligarchy might consolidate its power by manipulating the system of allotting offices to the citizens. This safeguard was the introduction of a provision which entrusted to the Great Council the election of some officials.

The traditional method of distributing offices by lot was not abandoned; it was maintained for most of the minor offices. The number of offices filled by straight elections was small: the captaincies of fortresses and castles in the Florentine empire were given to those who received the largest number of votes in the Great Council. For the most important offices a complicated system which combined election and allotment was adopted. This system guaranteed that the members of the Great Council had a part in determining those who, from their

---

Council. Then there were Florentines who paid taxes, and whose family members had in earlier times held some office; of this group, every three years 60 were selected and voted upon by the Great Council, to which they then were admitted. Then there were inhabitants of Florence who paid taxes, but could never hold office; they had certain privileges such as exemption from certain tolls and duties. Finally there were those who paid no taxes, and had no rights whatsoever. See Amadeo Crivellucci, "Del Governo Popolare di Firenze 1494-1512," *Annali della R. Scuola Normale Superiore di Pisa*, vol. III (1877), parte II: Filosofia e Filologia, pp. 266 et seq. But see also Nicolai Rubinstein, *loc. cit.*, pp. 343 et seq., where the conditions of office holding are more sharply defined.

midst, would fill the positions on the executive boards of the city.

The entire citizenry of Florence, not just a small privileged group, was to approve taxes and laws and supervise their execution. That was the meaning of the law of December 22, 1494 by which the Great Council was established. This law was the fundamental law of the republican period. It was taken for granted by the Florentines that this law established a stable regime in which all the citizens would work together harmoniously for the "common good" of Florence.

• II •

The opposite occurred. The eighteen years of the republican regime in Florence were full of unrest, dissensions, and bitter internal struggles that contributed decisively to the inglorious collapse of the republic in 1512.

In this period two different, fundamental antagonisms existed in Florence. One was the basic animosity between social groups within the Great Council; the other was the enmity between those who were excluded from the Great Council and those who were members of it.[15] It has sometimes been said that this latter antagonism was the main reason for the instability and insecurity of the republican regime, but such a statement is probably based on an overestimation of the importance of those inhabitants of Florence who did not fulfill the requirements for membership in the Great Council. The number of men living in Florence who were not members of the Great Council was considerable, indeed. Around the year 1500, Florence is thought to have had a population of about

[15] See previous note.

seventy thousand,[16] whereas the Great Council had a little more than three thousand members.[17] Yet this disproportion is not as great as these figures might suggest. The estimate of seventy thousand inhabitants includes women and children; membership in the Great Council was limited to males who had reached the age of 29. It might be estimated, therefore, that one out of every four or five adult males in Florence was a member of the Great Council, and this amounts to a significant part of the Florentine population.

Nevertheless, the fact remains that the presence of a group which had no part in the government was a threat to the republican regime, particularly in times of difficulties and crises. And the republic slid continuously from one crisis to another. The last years of the fifteenth century and the first years of the sixteenth century were marked by economic distress caused by poor harvests and incessant war, which restricted trade and forced a reduction in industrial productivity. In these years, the masses, hard hit by unemployment and rising prices, near starva-

[16] After Karl Julius Beloch, *Bevoelkerungsgeschichte Italiens*, vol. II, Berlin, 1939, p. 139; Enrico Fiumi, "Fioritura e decadenza dell' economia fiorentina" *Archivio Storico Italiano*, vol. CXVI (1958), p. 467 seems to assume a lower figure, others higher figures. All these estimates are very rough.

[17] See Rubinstein, *loc. cit.*, p. 181, who quotes a register of the Great Council of April 1496, which lists 3300 members of the Great Council. This does not mean that all those who were entitled to attend the meetings of the Great Council were always present. Those who were in arrears with their tax payments were not permitted to attend; moreover many Florentines did not want to lose time by attending. Thus one of the concerns of the government was that too few attended and no quorum (2/3 of those entitled to attend) was reached. Thus the plan of dividing the Great Council in three sections, each serving a limited time, was abandoned; from 1496 on, all the members of the Great Council assembled together, and the quorum was established as 1000. For these developments, see Rubinstein, *loc. cit.*, pp. 160-194.

tion, and without a stake in the government, were visibly restless and dissatisfied. The citizens feared that every attempt to change the government would find willing supporters among the masses. When, in 1501, Cesare Borgia marched his troops towards Florence, it was believed that he could count on an inside revolt which would open the gates to him and permit him to take the city.[18] The existence of masses, all too eager to be seduced with promises of better times, gave every rumor about the formation of opposition groups or conspiracies a fearsome aspect. There is no proof that any serious attempt was ever made to organize the malcontent and politically excluded for a coup d'etat, and such a danger was probably more imaginary than real. However such apprehensions loaded the political atmosphere with suspicion and distrust.

The discontent of the masses might not have mattered if, as it had been hoped and expected in 1494, the members of the Great Council had worked together in harmony. But from the outset there was competition and conflict among them. Despite the large number of positions in the Florentine government, and despite the use of a system of quick rotation among the office-holders, there were more members in the Great Council than offices to be filled. It was unavoidable that disappointment set in among those who did not receive the "benefit of office." More important still, the creation of the Great Council had not only widened the ruling group in Florence, but it had also changed its composition by the addition of men who came from the middle classes. Two groups, disparate in their interests and economic standing, faced each other within the Great Council.

[18] Parenti, *op. cit.*, II.IV. 170, f. 173v.; Cerretani, *op. cit.*, II.III., 74, ff. 280-282.

The wealth of Florence was concentrated in the hands of a very small group of men. This can be shown by the following statistic: in one district of the city there were 660 taxpayers, of which 30 people (less than 5 percent) paid more than 50 percent of the taxes imposed on that district.[19] In the times of Lorenzo Magnifico positions on the government's policy-making boards had rotated among a few hundred men, all of whom were loyal to the Medici regime.[20] With few exceptions these men had come from the same closely knit and socially coherent group. They had been men of wealth—bankers, merchants, and cloth manufacturers. They had business all over Italy, and they bought and sold in France, Spain, the Netherlands, and England; the position of Florence as a power of European significance depended on the economic activities of this class. A wide economic and social gulf divided these men from the much more numerous Florentine middle class: the shopkeepers, local businessmen, and artisans. In the times of Lorenzo Magnifico, Luca Landucci, the owner of a pharmacy opposite the corner where the grandiose Strozzi palace was erected, characterized the building enterprises of the members of the Florentine ruling group with words which seem to combine awe and detestation, as "things typical of great men."[21] After 1494 Landucci was a member of the Great Council, sitting alongside those whom he had formerly seen at

[19] Based on L. F. Marks, "La crisi Finanziaria a Firenze dal 1494 al 1502," *Archivio Storico Italiano*, vol. CXII (1954), pp. 50-51 and on the document quoted by Marks on p. 50, note 32.

[20] On the Florentine ruling group under Lorenzo, see F. L. Marks, "The Financial Oligarchy . . . ," *loc. cit*. The prominent figures of the Florentine ruling group under Lorenzo Magnifico were the members of the Council of Seventy and the Council of Hundred.

[21] "Cose da signori . . . ," Landucci, *op. cit.*, p. 59.

a distance as "great men." Landucci's attitude provides a striking illustration of the change in the character of the Florentine ruling group after the establishment of the Great Council. Previously the wealthy merchants and bankers had enjoyed a monopoly of government power— holding the most important offices and making the political decisions. After 1494 the rich and socially prominent Florentines had to share the government with men from the middle classes, men whom they considered inferior.[22]

The Florentines themselves were fully aware that the membership of the Great Council reflected two distinct interest groups. It was not realized in the sixteenth century that each political society was a unique formation whose individual characteristics had to be precisely analyzed in order to define the nature and number of its components. Men are more inclined to try to fit the object of their investigations into a traditional scheme.[23] And so when the Florentines distinguished the various elements of their city's population they applied to their analysis either the tripartite scheme which Aristotle had formulated or the dualistic scheme which Roman historians had employed. The terms most frequently used by the Florentines who followed the tripartite scheme of Aristotle were "poor," "middle classes" (*mezzani*), and "wealthy."[24] Usually "poor" referred to the masses out-

[22] Probably most of the members of the Great Council had possessed the right of office-holding also under the Medici, but this was a purely theoretical right; actually the Medici—by means of scrutinies and *Accoppiatori*—reserved offices to a small group.

[23] On this problem, see F. Zweig, "The Theory of Social Classes," *Kyklos*, vol. XI (1958), pp. 390-401.

[24] Instances from Parenti, *op. cit.*, II.II.134, f. 44v. ". . . ricchi . . . mediocri . . . poveri . . . ," f. 90r.-v.: ". . . primati . . . mediocri . . . infimi . . . ," II.IV. 170, f. 96r. "huomini di mezzana qualità. . . ."

side the Great Council, whereas "middle classes" and "wealthy" designated the social groups within the Great Council. But in chronicles and diaries a number of other names were employed. Expressions applied to that part of the population which did not belong to the Great Council were "plebs" (*plebe*), or the "lower plebs" (*infima plebe*), or "mob" (*vulgo*).[25] Characteristically, these expressions have a derogatory connotation and imply that this element was of little significance. For some other writers who used the tripartite scheme, this part of the population is almost non-existent, because to them the membership of the Great Council made up the entire population of Florence. When they used the expression "mass" (*moltitudine*) or "bulk" (*universale*), they meant not the inhabitants of Florence who lacked political rights, but the least influential part of the Great Council, its economically weakest members.[26]

In general, however, Florentine writers who proceeded in their analysis as if the Great Council was identical with the entire Florentine population applied a dualistic scheme to the description of Florentine society.[27] This dualistic scheme seemed particularly appropriate because of the view which the Florentines had of their own his-

[25] Instances from Cerretani, *op. cit.*, II.III.75, f. 534r.: "nel popolo e tra la plebe si diceva che c'era consapevoli molti nobili cittadini . . ."; f. 82r.: "[Valori] fu afrontato d'alquanti del infima plebe."; Francesco Guicciardini, *Storie Fiorentine*, ed. R. Palmarocchi, Bari, 1931, p. 338: ". . . non solo nel vulgo, ma ne' cittadini principali e ne' collegi. . . ."

[26] Examples: Parenti, *op. cit.*, II.IV. 170, f. 126v.: ". . . e grandi desideravano farsi X di balìa . . . la universale li ricusava . . ."; Guicciardini, *op. cit.*, p. 273: ". . . perché la moltitudine ed el consiglio grande non curava e non attendeva a queste cose. . . ."

[27] Giovanni Cambi, "Istorie," ed. Fr. Ildefonso di San Luigi, *Delizie degli Eruditi Toscani*, vol. XXI, Firenze, 1785, p. 175: "[uomo] non di molta riputatione apresso agli uomini grandi, ma di credito, effede grande inverso el popolo."

tory. In the thirteenth century the "people" (*populo*) of Florence had engaged in a long and bitter struggle against domination by the magnates (*magnati*). The triumph of the *populo* was followed by a split within the victorious group; the "great" and the "rich" on one side confronted the men of moderate means (*populo minuto*) on the other. The two groups within the Great Council were regarded as the successors of these factions which had opposed each other in the past, and therefore in the time of the republic they were described in terms which characterized the previous struggles. Thus the newcomers to the ruling group were called "common men" (*populari*) or "tradesmen" (*mercatanti*) but sometimes they were termed "the people" (*populo*) or "men of moderate means" (*populo minuto*). The men of the old ruling group were the "nobles" (*nobili*), or the members of the "great houses" (*case*), or the "great" (*grandi*) or the "rich" (*ricchi*), sometimes the "first citizens" (*principali*) or the "wise men" (*uomini savi*).[28]

The criteria used for distinguishing these two groups indicate that wealth was considered significant, yet other factors were also taken into account: the antiquity and reputation of a person's family, as well as the knowledge and education which a person possessed. In the minds of the Florentines, personal qualities, quite as much as eco-

---

[28] All these expressions were so frequent that particular references are not needed. I shall give a characteristic passage from Guicciardini, *op. cit.*, p. 241: "Allo universale della città, che erano gli uomini di case basse e che conoscevano che negli stati stretti le case loro non arebbono condizione, erano gli uomini di buone case, ma che avevano consorti di piú autoritá e qualitá di loro e però vedevano che in uno vivere stretto rimarrebbono adrieto; a tutti costoro, che erano in fatto molto maggiore numero, piaceva molto el governo, nel quale si faceva poca distinzione da uomo a uomo presente e da casa a casa."

nomic resources, determined the status of a citizen. The Florentines were aware that great differences of experience, wealth, and knowledge existed among the members of the Great Council, but they failed to understand that economic differences among the members of the Great Council would create an irreconcilable conflict of interest. On the contrary, it was believed that the establishment of a popular regime (*vivere populare*), as the government introduced in 1494 was called,[29] would place at the disposal of the Florentine government the experience and knowledge of the upper classes, who would serve the government while being unable to oppress the other citizens. It was thought that if the *vivere populare* did not function smoothly, it was the result not of deficiencies in the institutions which had been created in 1494, but rather stemmed from the mistakes and misbehavior of individuals. Those who were dissatisfied with the popular regime were in the eyes of one of its enthusiastic supporters, "evil men."[30] Remarks such as, it is a pity that the "great men" are not always wiser, are often to be found.[31] These were the views not only of passionate defenders of the popular regime; a moderate man like Piero Parenti also judged the political struggle in moral terms. He was convinced that the "people" would bestow upon the "great men" all the honors and positions which

[29] Landucci, *op. cit.*, p. 110: "Ogniuno s'accordava che questo fussi el vero modo del vivere popolare fiorentino, più che fussi mai." But there are many very similar expressions; see the law of April 20, 1498, *Prov.*, vol. 189, f. 5v.: "ad conservatione et augumento del presente populare governo."

[30] Cambi, *loc cit.*, vol., XXI, p. 232: ". . . se non fussino stati e' chattivi ciptadini Fiorentini . . . ," or see also Landucci, *op. cit.*, p. 149: ". . . e tristi e gli Arabiati. . . ."

[31] For instance, Cambi, *loc. cit.*, vol. XXI, p. 155, or see below, note 33.

they could rightfully claim; if the "great men" were not satisfied with their situation in the republican regime, the reason was that they were "ambitious";[32] and ambition was a sin.[33]

One man objected. Francesco Guicciardini wrote scornfully of the men from the middle classes who sat on the Great Council: they are "poor and ignorant," they have "little capacity." Usually he described the members of the upper group as "wise men," "men of experience," "noble and intelligent men."[34] To Guicciardini, ambition in politics was a virtue,[35] at least, ambition among the

[32] Parenti, *op. cit.*, II. IV. 170, f. 158r.: "Mai dishonorò e primati: anzi sempre li hebbe ne' primi luoghi honorati, benchè qualche volta alcuni popolari con loro insieme mescolassi, ma raro. Nondimeno non contenti essi stare alla discretione dello universale. . . ."

[33] Landucci, *op. cit.*, p. 317: "Se gli uomini grandi e ricchi fussino savi, e' fuggirebbono el volere dominare quello che à essere comune a ogniuno, perchè si tiene con troppo grande odio, e che si stessino con la loro ricchezza e stare contenti al bene comune e farsi grande nelle mercanzie e nello onesto vivere da cristiani, e dare molti guadagni a' poveri di Dio e amare la sua patria con retto cuore." Condemnations of ambition were frequent; for instance, Cerretani, *op. cit.*, II.III.75, f. 286v: ". . . erono in un mare d'ambizioni . . . ciascuno voleva essere il primo, non pensando al danno o degnità della cittá."

[34] Guicciardini, *op. cit.*, p. 209: ". . . uomini spicciolati e di poca qualitá"; p. 225: ". . . uomini da pochi ed ignoranti"; contrast p. 30: "nobili e prudenti"; p. 239: ". . . cittadini savi ed esperti. . . ."

[35] The characteristic passage comes from the *Discorso di Logrogno* of 1512, printed in Guicciardini, *Dialogo e Discorsi del Reggimento di Firenze*, p. 239: "E' quali oltre a avere amore della cittá, è bene, acciò che li operino piú ardentemente, che abbino uno sprone di ambizione, uno appetito di grandezza e di condursi in qualche sommo grado . . . chi può dubitare che questa ambizione è laudabile ed utilissima? La quale chi non sente è in una certa freddezza e li manca uno certo stimulo di gloria, che da lui non esce mai cose generose ed eccelse. È adunche bene per eccitare questa onesta ambizione nelli spiriti grandi. . . ." Also in the earlier *Storie Fiorentine*, he characterized, without derogatory implications, leading personalities like Piero Capponi, etc., as ambitious. However, Guicciardini, in the *Storie Fiorentine*, indicated that in general the Florentines held it

men of the upper classes; it gave them the right to rule.[36]
But the writings of Guicciardini which contain these
ideas—unusual for the time—were composed when the republican period was drawing to its end and hopes for
cooperation among the Florentine citizens had been shattered. Guicciardini's opinions, rejecting the suppositions
on which the republican regime had been founded,
pointed towards a new departure in political thinking.

• III •

After the overthrow of the Medici the Florentines
tried to establish a government based on the presupposition of a harmoniously integrated society, striving co-
operatively for the common good of the community.
The Florentines expected to achieve this aim by restoring the institutions which they believed to have existed in
the city's past. But a highly complex and differentiated
society had developed in Florence, and the reform of the
government according to an idealized memory of the
past only sharpened tensions and conflicts. The political
struggles in Florence during the republican regime were
of decisive importance for the development of a new approach to politics and history because the basic issues underlying the continual tensions of Florentine political
life could not be resolved within the framework of tra-

---

against a man if they believed him to be ambitious (see, for instance,
p. 284). Guicciardini was opposed to "ambizione infinita, la quale
non si saziassi degli onori consueti ed ordinari, ma desiderassi una
potenzia ed autoritá estraordinaria...." (*Storie Fiorentine*, p. 284);
see also in *Discorso di Logrogno:* "È stato origine di questo male
una ambizione venuta in ognuno di volersi ingerire a tutti li
onori..." (*Dialogo*, p. 229).

[36] *Storie Fiorentine*, p. 240: "... in effetto quando gli uomini di
qualitá non hanno, io non dico la tirannide, ma quello grado che si
conviene loro, la cittá ne patisce."

ditional assumptions. The achievements of the Florentine political thinkers and historians of the sixteenth century derived from their attempts to make the conceptual framework adequate to the political reality; their efforts engendered a new way of thinking about politics and history. But this new approach to politics and history was not simply the result of the impact of events on the minds of the thinkers. Rather, it also implied an adjustment of traditional political concepts and assumptions to the problems of the contemporary world.

The subject of this book is the genesis of a new way of thinking about politics and history. In order to investigate this process we shall have to move between a description of what happened and an analysis of the way in which these events were seen by the Florentines of the early sixteenth century. The narrative of the political situation which existed in Florence after the overthrow of the Medici must therefore be complemented by an anallysis of the prevailing mode of thinking. In Florence the Signoria and other executive boards were accustomed to call together influential citizens for a consultation—a *pratica*—whenever the government of Florence was faced with a difficult problem.[37] Protocols of these meetings have been preserved in the Florentine archives, and they permit us an insight into the traditional assumptions with which Florentines approached political decisions in the first years of the republican regime.

[37] *Pratica* is the singular form, *pratiche* the plural. For a more detailed description of the working of the *pratiche* see below, pp. 65 et seq. and for the role of the *pratiche* in Florentine politics, see my article, "Florentine Political Assumptions in the Period of Savonarola and Soderini," *Journal of the Warburg and Courtauld Institutes*, vol. XX (1957), pp. 187-214, particularly pp. 187-195. Section 3 of this chapter is an abbreviation of this article to which I refer the reader for more extensive documentation. My notes

During the republican regime there was an obvious need for frequent debates on foreign policy. Florence's traditional alliance with France, of unquestionable value in the times of the Medici, had become a doubtful legacy after the actual appearance in Italy of the French armies, first under Charles VIII and then under his successor Louis XII. By adhering to the French alliance Florence came into conflict with those Italian powers which led the resistance against France, mainly Milan and the rulers of the Church State. The Florentines were forced to consider whether Maximilian, the German Emperor, and Spain—whose support the enemies of France were seeking—could be inveigled to intervene in Italy, and if so, whether or not their strength was comparable to that of the French. The urgency of this problem was heightened by the revolt of Pisa in 1494 and the war which Florence waged from 1494 to 1508 to regain this vital seaport. At various occasions, the Florentine conflict with Pisa gave to France as well as to her opponents the opportunity of using pressure tactics on Florence. Each of the powers competing for a Florentine alliance tried to force the Florentines' hands by supporting Pisan resistance and by promising withdrawal of this support if Florence would decide in its favor.

The discussions in the *pratiche* on foreign policy were permeated by a profound feeling of the weakness of Florence. The Florentines took pride in the cultural superiority of Italy over all other countries of the Christian world, and in their own city in particular which was "the heart of Italy."[38] But the central importance of Flor-

here are chiefly limited to give the Italian text and to indicate the place of direct quotations from the volume of the A.S.F.

[38] "essendo noi nel quore di Italia," A.S.F., *Consulte e Pratiche,* vol. 65, f. 205v.

ence in Italian life only heightened the dangers: "When Italy is agitated by great new forces, we are in the middle, which is most violently affected."[39]

The concrete basis from which these feelings of weakness arose was the economic situation of Florence. Her prosperity—almost her existence—depended on trade, and in the case of war, commerce might come to a standstill. These considerations made it almost impossible for the Florentines to make a choice between France and the Church State. The chief business of the Florentine merchants was with France, and an abandonment of the French alliance would mean an end of Florence's most profitable economic enterprises. On the other hand, conflict with the Church State could be equally damaging, for the Popes could employ the weapon of the interdict which the Florentines feared for material rather than for spiritual reasons. When a state came under an interdict, its citizens lost all legal protection everywhere in Christendom; an interdict therefore would permit the "robbing of all the possessions of Florentines wherever they were—in Rome, in Naples, in England or in any other place."[40] When Pope Alexander VI, infuriated by Savonarola's vehement attacks, demanded that the Florentine government silence the impertinent Frate, Florentines who were opposed to obeying the Pope's request were told by their fellow citizens that they would use a different language if they had goods outstanding all over Italy.

---

[39] "Preterea totam Italiae fluctuare novis et magnis rebus, nos autem esse quasi in centro quod magis vexari potest," vol. 61, f. 5r.
[40] "dare in preda tucte le robe de' mercatanti fiorentini in qualunque luogo si trovino o ad Roma o a Napoli o in Inghilterra et in qualunque altro luogho," vol. 70, f. 36r. And for the following see meeting of March 14, 1498, vol. 64, ff. 27r et seq.

The Florentines regarded their city-state as rather small and insignificant in comparison to the great territorial states which had grown up outside Italy. So inexhaustible and far-reaching seemed the power of the large states that the Florentines saw the hand of France and Spain behind every move which was made on the Italian scene. Even when Pisan resistance was clearly at its end, the Florentines believed they could not strike the final blow before negotiating with France and Spain: "As things stand in Italy, one can't have Pisa without the two kings."[41]

The great states outside Italy were not only superior in strength; the awe which they inspired was compounded by the inscrutability of their political moves. It seemed to the Florentines, who were not able to calculate the permanent interests behind the policy of these great states, that all their actions were determined by the arbitrary will of the ruler. Consequently, whenever discussion in the *pratiche* turned to questions involving these great states, a kind of psychological guessing game developed about the personal qualities and inclinations of their rulers. For example, there was a debate on the question whether or not King Charles VIII, after he had been driven out of Italy in 1495, would set out on another Italian expedition. Some Florentines believed that Charles VIII felt so strongly about honor that he would certainly return in order to "revenge himself on his enemies." To others, the French King appeared as a weakling "led by his advisors"; "they did not want him out of France," and so he would not come.[42]

[41] "Stando le cose come stanno in Italia hora, non si possa havere Pisa sanza dua re," vol. 69, f. 149v.
[42] Some said that Charles VIII would want to "vendicarsi de'

The Florentines believed that their city was not strong enough to allow them to take the initiative and to shape events according to their desires. In the conduct of foreign policy the aim of the Florentines was much more moderate: "Wise men take what is least bad instead of what is good."[43] They were anxious to play safe and to avoid a premature decision which would make Florence the ally of that group which at the end would be defeated. "One ought not to take risks without the most urgent necessity or without being sure of victory."[44] Thus the customary recommendation was to delay making a decision and to avoid taking sides until a situation was clarified. For this policy of delay and postponement the Florentines had a characteristic expression: "to enjoy the benefit of time."[45] The policy of waiting became so much of a panacea for the Florentines that as late as July 1512, when the troops of the Spaniards and of the Pope—who were to re-install the Medici in Florence and to end the life of the republic—closed in on the city, the postponement of decisive action, in the hope of gaining time, was regarded as the best possible advice. A consequence of this policy of "enjoying the benefit of time" was that, whenever a conflict had broken out, the Florentines sought to remain neutral. They were not unaware that such a policy might involve the risk of falling between two stools, and they tried to remain as long as possible on

---

suoi nimici"; Bernardo Rucellai insisted that the King "sia menato da' suoi" and they "non lo vorebbono fuori di Francia," vol. 62, ff. 154r, 158v.

[43] "E savii hanno il men male in luogo di bene," vol. 65, f. 24v.

[44] "Non si mettino ad pericolo o sanza gran necessità o manifesta victoria," vol. 69, f. 36v.

[45] "Nelle cose dubie è manco periculo godere el beneficio del tempo," vol. 69, f. 116r.

good terms with both sides. Their preference was for the "middle way"—another favorite expression.[46]

Although the Florentines were well aware that their city was weak and inferior to other states they did not feel helpless. The policy of delay, of waiting, of benefiting from circumstances, was not purely an expression of political impotence but a consciously adopted method of conducting politics. The Florentines used a weapon with which they believed they could compensate for the lack of military strength. This weapon was reason (*ragione*) and the Florentines considered themselves as experts in its use. In 1496, when the other Italian powers took up a threatening attitude because of the Florentine loyalty to France, it was said that two ways were open to Florence: "to resist either with force or with intelligence. And it does not appear possible that we can resist the whole of Italy relying on force. We must take the alternative: intelligence."[47] There was an almost religious conviction in this Florentine belief in the triumph of reason; one finds coupled together: "trusting in God, in reason."[48]

Despite differences in recommendations on practical political steps, a common outlook can be found in all the discussions in the *pratiche* on foreign policy. Domestic affairs, on the other hand, were viewed in two distinctly different ways. The need for seeking the advice of a *pratica* arose usually from the failure of the Great Council to accept legislative proposals, particularly those which were to raise new taxes; the *pratica* was expected

[46] "Via di mezo," for instance, vol. 69, f. 76r.

[47] "difendere colla forza o collo ingegno. E con la forza non si vede che noi lo possiamo fare contro tucta Italia. Bisogna torre l'altro, cioè l'ingegno," vol. 62, f. 205r.

[48] "sperando in Dio, nella ragione," vol. 64, f. 105r.

to indicate ways to overcome a deadlock. Thus the debates frequently turned to an evaluation of the constitutional arrangements which had been made in 1494. For a number of the speakers in the *pratiche*, the measures which had been taken in 1494 were not an innovation, but a reform in the original sense of the word—a re-establishment of the "old republican way of life," as it had existed in the earliest times of Florence.

Thus changes, attempts to make institutional improvements, were inappropriate. "Any change diminishes the reputation of the city."[49] The only important question to be asked was whether or not the existing institutions corresponded to those which had been established when the city was founded; a satisfactory government could be realized only by "going back to the beginnings." The original institutions were believed to have been given to Florence by God: "We feel deeply grateful to God and express to Him our thanks for having deigned to lead us to a true form of social life. And it is equally our duty to accept and preserve in its entire and unchanged form the gift which God's grace had given us. . . ."[50] Behind this assumption lay the view that there was only one true task of government: administration of justice—"justice includes everything."[51] A constitution given by God would provide society with a just government and create the foundations of a harmonious social life. Discontent and unrest, it was thought, were not the result of de-

[49] "ogni mutatione togli[e] reputatione alla cicta," vol. 62, f. 380r.

[50] "Nos debere maximas immortali Deo gratias et agere et habere qui ad vere civilem nos vitam perducere dignatus sit. Et ideo debere nos quod Dei beneficio acceperimus munus inviolatum et integrum velle conservare, nec quicquam minuere ex dominantis auctoritate ac dignitate," vol. 61, f. 6r.

[51] "La iustizia ha in sè ogni cosa," vol. 65, f. 164r.

fects in the city's institutions, but rather the result of human failure; internal conflict was the fruit of "sins." Difficulties which had arisen in Florence had originated because men pursued "private passions" instead of the "common good," because men succumbed to the particular vice of politics—"ambition." If there were factions in Florence, they were the result of this sinful and egoistic behavior; factions were evil, incompatible with good government. If the malfunctioning of government was the outcome of immoral behavior by the citizens, the remedy must be a strict enforcement of laws. In times of tension those who held these views suggested that the government order the priests of the city to preach love and unity and that reconciliation committees be formed to admonish the citizens "to act in concord."

Opinions were divided on this issue of the need for reforms. In contrast to those who regarded the constitutional setting as definite and inviolable because of its divinely ordered nature, there were others who regarded the institutions as man-made and therefore in need of adjustments and improvements. A characteristic argument was that Venice had required centuries to attain that constitutional stability and perfection which she had reached by the beginning of the sixteenth century, and for which she was widely admired; the Florentines could not expect that their constitution could be perfect at one stroke. Willingness to make changes and improvements is not the only interesting aspect of this remark. It shows that the advocates of such measures considered Florence not as an entirely unique political formation but rather as a city-state similar to other city-states; Florence could profit from the experiences of others. Venice and Rome were the two examples most frequently mentioned. The discussions in the *pratiche* show that the Florentines had intimate knowledge of the functioning of the Venetian constitution which, some believed, Florence should imitate even in formal details like calling the citizens to the meetings of the Great Council by the ringing of bells. The favorite example, however, was republican Rome. For instance, when Cesare Borgia stood threatening before the gates of Florence, it was recommended in a *pratica* that full power and authority be handed over to a few men. The justification for such advice was that "the ancients in dangerous times gave authority to one man."[52]

Although the protocols of the *pratiche* show that some Florentines applied to the political order a criterion of rational efficiency, while others regarded the institutions as God-given and therefore unchangeable, these differences in attitude were not as great as they might seem, for they were gradual and relative rather than definite and absolute. Hardly any of the speakers in the *pratiche* held firmly to the one attitude or to the other in his argument. In the minds of most of the speakers both attitudes had value. The reason was that almost all the participants of the *pratiche* held identical views about the nature of the forces working in the world of politics and about the limited extent of the influence which men could exert on events. All the speakers believed that there was a narrow realm in which man's reason could be effective, and that non-rational forces also held sway in the world of politics. The expressions used to designate these two forces—usually viewed as adversaries, struggling with each other—were *ragione* and *Fortuna*. These two terms

[52] "li antiqui ne' tempi pericolosi davano auctorità a uno solo," vol. 66, f. 51r.

are full of associations and they are rather ambiguous; they have no precise counterparts in English.

The meaning of *ragione* can perhaps best be clarified by a negative definition. Actions directed by *ragione* were the opposite of actions directed by "desire" or "will." If a decision is made "guided by will and not by *ragione*, the outcome will be bad."[53] Thus *ragione* was the instrument which enabled man to steer a straight course between illusionary hopes and exaggerated fears to arrive at correct decisions. However, *ragione* was useful to man not only by guiding him on his own course of action, but also by providing the means for anticipating how others would act. At all times and all places, man had responded to the same motivating forces. There was a recurrent pattern behind man's behavior which made his actions calculable. *Ragione* enabled man to deduce general rules of human behavior and to apply them to the individual case under deliberation.

The opinions expressed in the *pratiche* suggested that the Florentines did not assume the existence of special rules for political behavior; every known rule of human behavior was also applicable to politics. Thus the age-old wisdom reflected in proverbs was frequently used for arriving at judgments on the possible behavior of an opponent and for making political decisions. When Piero Medici loudly announced his immediate return to Florence, the proverb that "dogs which bark don't bite"[54] was cited and this was regarded to be sufficient assurance of the futility of Piero's threats.

The sources most assiduously tapped in this search for

---

[53] Decisions "indutti dalla voluntà et non dalla ragione, fanno mali effetti," vol. 69, f. 41v.
[54] "Cane che abbaia non morde," vol. 61, f. 38v.

general rules which could be applied to present-day problems were experience and authority. "Experience is the greatest teacher."[55] Experience was not only what people themselves had seen, but everything known about events in the past; the entire field of history was experience. The speakers in the *pratiche* referred frequently to the lessons which could be drawn from events in Florentine history, but their favorite source was the history of ancient Rome. The speakers took enormous pride in their knowledge of the classical world, and they seemed to delight in displaying it. When Savonarola had been imprisoned and it was debated in the *pratiche* whether he should be physically forced to reveal the names of all his associates and connections, one speaker warned against such a prolonged and extended investigation because it would increase tension and bitterness in Florence. Caesar, after his victory over Pompey, had refused to look at Pompey's correspondence. This argument was sharply contradicted: if Caesar had studied Pompey's correspondence, he might have found out who his enemies were and might not have been assassinated.

There was a reason for attributing particular importance to the rules of human behavior taught by classical history. The story of these events was handed down in the books of great writers, and references to classical history, therefore, combined the weight of reasoning from experience with the weight of reasoning from authority. The quotation of the view of an acknowledged authority was regarded as the most telling argument. The statements of a famous author about human behavior were regarded as valid without questioning. Even if speakers could have justified an opinion by common sense or by

[55] "experientia, que rerum est magistra," vol. 61, f. 6v.

reference to experience, they preferred to cite an authority. The recognized canon of authorities comprised classical as well as Christian authors; St. Paul and Demosthenes were quoted side by side, and references to classical and Christian writers were equally frequent.

The Florentines delighted in the use of *ragione*. They prided themselves on their cool and objective attitude in making decisions and on their capacity to discover in the apparent chaos of arbitrary moves a pattern which made the actions of other states and rulers foreseeable and calculable. They considered *ragione* and force as equally efficient weapons. Nevertheless, it should not be assumed that the Florentines conceived of the world and of politics as being a rational order, moving according to laws. *Ragione* was not yet the bright and dazzling sun of the eighteenth century whose rays dispersed the few clouds which had been casting dark shadows on some corners of the world. On the contrary, the Florentines' pride in their ability to act according to *ragione* was so great, and their emphasis on the need for *ragione* was so passionate and shrill, because they were oppressed by the feeling of being exposed to arbitrary and uncontrollable powers. The Florentines clung to *ragione* as to a candle which creates a small circle of light in the surrounding darkness. The cry for *ragione* was the corollary of a feeling of helplessness in the face of non-rational forces.

The term symbolizing the world of non-rational forces was *Fortuna,* and this again was a concept of many facets. *Fortuna* was responsible for those events which happened against all rational calculations and expectations. Man was powerless to do anything about those things which were "in the hands of *Fortuna*."[56] In this respect,

[56] "in mano della fortuna," vol. 61, f. 165v.

the meaning of *Fortuna* was almost identical with the meaning of another concept frequently used in these discussions: *Necessità*. Both *Necessità* and *Fortuna* make rational calculations superfluous. "When *Necessità* chases us, we don't need to deliberate."[57] "*Necessità* knows of no laws." "*Necessità* dictates."[58] Yet to the Florentines, there was a distinction between *Necessità* and *Fortuna*. Whereas *Necessità* entered when the accumulation of adverse circumstances was so great that no choice was left to man and human calculations were reduced to automatic reactions, *Fortuna* could permit room for human choice and initiative. She could place unexpected chances in a man's way; it was his task to recognize and to make use of them. "When there are favorable opportunities and man then does not try his luck, *Fortuna* will leave him."[59]

Thus to the Florentines *Fortuna* had preserved many of the characteristics of a pagan goddess. She is a personality, she has her whims; she interferes arbitrarily in human affairs. Some men she dislikes, on others she smiles. In political calculations one has to take into account whether a ruler is "fortunate," a favorite of *Fortuna*. Yet at the same time this pagan goddess exerts her power in a Christian world and has to be integrated in it. God rules everything on this earth and thus it is not possible clearly to distinguish between what is done by God and what is done by *Fortuna*. Events like the salvation of Florence through the sudden death of Giangaleazzo Visconti in 1402 were sometimes ascribed to *Fortuna,* sometimes to God. *Fortuna* is God's messenger and He directs her.

[57] "Dove necessità caccia non bisogna consiglio," vol. 67, f. 63r.
[58] "La necessità non ha legge," "la necessità constringne," vol. 62, f. 221r; vol. 69, f. 47r. Of course, these are classical rules.
[59] "Quando l'occasioni sono oportune chi non tenta la fortuna, la fortuna lo lascia," vol. 69, f. 167v.

Thus God can "change fortune."[60] "When *Fortuna* gives one a chance, one ought not to miss it because this might be a sign that God wants to help."[61]

The identification of the work of *Fortuna* with the work of God shows that to the Florentines God had not retired behind laws of nature which He had established. He directly interferred in the course of events where-ever and whenever He wanted; the final limitation of human efforts and designs lay in the omnipotence of God.

This raised the question in the minds of the Florentines whether it was worthwhile to expend one's energy and ingenuity on trying to discover the plans of one's opponents, on trying to forestall one's enemies and on trying to chart a safe course for oneself, or whether it might not be more effective to concentrate on gaining God's favor so that He would direct affairs in a way which would be favorable to Florence. The discussions in the *pratiche* indicate that this was a real problem to the Florentines. It was in this conceptual framework that they looked upon the problem which we now call the relation of morals and politics.

A few of the Florentines held extreme views. One speaker, characteristically a passionate adherent of Savonarola, believed one ought to follow "the counsels of Christianity rather than the counsels of mundane wisdom because this would please God more."[62] Some took the

---

[60] "...mutare fortuna," vol. 69, f. 43v.

[61] "[one should not] lasciar passare tanta occasione di fortuna perchè pare che da ogni parte Iddio monstri di volervi aiutare," vol. 62, f. 340v.

[62] "referendomi sempre piutosto al consiglio cristiano che philosophico perchè è piu secondo Iddio," vol. 70, f. 81r. The speaker was Bartolomeo Redditi, who, in an apology of Savonarola, written in 1501, has an interesting analogous passage opposing "lume sopranaturale" and "opinione di ragione humana e naturale"; see

opposite point of view: in the Italian political world, in which all states "were eager to deceive each other in order to increase their territory,"[63] one had to act as the others were acting. "When he tries to trip us, we must try to trip him."[64] This kind of worldly wisdom celebrated its greatest triumph in the deliberations on the case of the Condottiere Paolo Vitelli. He had been put into prison because he was suspected of treasonable negotiations with Florence's enemies while being in the service of Florence. However, no proof of his crime could be found. Yet it was decided to execute Vitelli because he would never have forgiven the Florentines for his imprisonment and would have been a powerful enemy of the city as long as he lived. The reasoning which prompted this decision was clearly stated by one of the speakers: "I feel one should not proceed in this case according to the usual standards of fairness, as one usually does not proceed in such a way in affairs of state."[65]

In general, however, the Florentines were not inclined to take an exclusively religious or an exclusively mundane attitude. They might deliberate according to human reason, but the first advice was always "to turn to God."[66] In particularly critical situations, this advice was supplemented by more detailed instructions: the priests were ordered to hold processions and the government was asked to distribute alms to the poor or to bring the

---

Joseph Schnitzer, *Quellen und Forschungen zur Geschichte Savonarolas*, vol. I, *Bartolomeo Redditi und Tomaso Ginori*, Muenchen, 1902, p. 54.

[63] ". . . stanno vigilanti per ingannare l'uno l'altro al bisogno per ingrandirsi," vol. 61, f. 176v.

[64] "Quando lui uccellassi, uccellare anche voi," vol. 69, f. 26v.

[65] "Judichò anchora non si proceda secondo e termini di ragione, che così non si suole nelle cose delli stati," vol. 65, f. 116r.

[66] "Ricorrere a Dio."

miracle-working statue of the Madonna della Impruneta to Florence. Sometimes it was even suggested that deliberations be deferred for a day which would then be spent in prayer so that God might inspire the right decision. The conviction of the dependence of all political events on God's will also had practical consequences. If Florence had weathered the storms in the past and had achieved a position of greatness, this could not have been the work of man, but of God. It demonstrated that Florence, the city of San Giovanni, was a favorite of the Lord. He would not have given Florence his support if the city had been entirely unworthy, but "from its earliest beginnings their republic had been distinguished by having the habit of keeping faith."[67] Thus, in the discussions on foreign policy, questions of honor, of defending a just cause, of loyalty to commitments once entered were carefully weighed, and such questions played a significant role in the final decisions. There sometimes appears, in these deliberations of men who prided themselves on having the most subtle minds of Italy, an unrealistic, illusionary spirit. In their inner hearts, the Florentines would never believe that their situation could ever be hopeless. Often in the course of Florentine history—with the sudden death of Giangaleazzo Visconti, with the unexpected decision of Charles VIII to evacuate the occupied Florence—God had given signs that he had taken the city on the Arno under his special protection: "in many ways God has shown that He will not abandon this city."[68]

[67] "Essendo maxime questa republica sempre consueta per suo antichissimo instituto di mantenere la fede promessa," vol. 70, f. 77v.

[68] "[God] in molte cose ha dimonstro non abandonare questa città," vol. 66, f. 292r.

Florentine assumptions about politics contained diverse elements. The turbulent political events of the years of the Florentine republic accelerated the divergence and accentuated the need to adjust traditional concepts to contemporary problems.

• IV •

This analysis of the troubles which beset the Florentine republican regime from the hour of its foundation should not lead one to conclude that these problems arose suddenly upon the overthrow of the Medici. The difficulties which confounded the republic were deeply rooted in the Florentine past, and similar problems plagued the greater towns and cities all over Europe.

A major weakness of the city-state—and one which became increasingly obvious in the time of the consolidation of the territorial monarchies—was the narrow base from which it drew its political strength. By various means the cities had gained control over most of the surrounding areas, and they zealously guarded their right to exploit those whom they had brought under their rule. It is hardly surprising that whenever a city-state was threatened by foreign invaders or by internal crises the inhabitants of the dependent areas seized the opportunity to try to regain their freedom. Not infrequently a city-state was confronted simultaneously by foreign armies and by rebellious subjects, and often its resources were not sufficient to maintain both its independence and its domain.

Just as the immanent structure of the city-state was a reason for its precarious position in face of external dangers, so also the wealth and vitality of the city-state lay behind its other great weakness: internal instability. Most

45

city-states had become prominent through the growth of trade and industry, usually the cloth industry. The development of the cloth industry required a large labor force, ranging from the unskilled beaters and washers who prepared the raw material, to the master dyers and shearmen who finished the finest cloth. As a result of the increased number of workers as well as the diversity and hierarchy of skills necessary for the manufacture and finishing of cloth, new forms of organization of labor developed, and they gradually weakened the traditional forms of labor organization—independent individuals and guilds more or less equal in rank—on which the institutional structure of a city-state was based. In almost all towns sharp social tensions arose between rich and poor, between independent entrepreneurs and dependent workers, between the large trading guilds and those which produced for the local market. These tensions were aggravated when industrial activity spread from a few centers—the Netherlands and northern Italy—to other parts of Europe. With the creation of a highly competitive market the great merchants of the city-states felt more strongly the need for increased political support for their mercantile enterprises; and their demand for the exclusive control of their governments was more vehement, more urgent than in the times of easy economic expansion.

The pressure of the divergencies in economic interests and the diversities in economic and social status among the inhabitants of an urban center, the issues which, as we have indicated, disturbed the internal peace in Florence, were the roots of virulent contention in nearly all the larger cities of Europe. A particular object of dispute was the determination of the preconditions which established the right of participating in the government or of controlling it. But this question was inextricably bound up with the problem of the nature of a political society; hence the principles justifying the existence of different social groups within a political body were carefully scrutinized. Nevertheless, it was assumed that the existence of different social groups with different interests was not—or should not be—a destructive force in a political society. Thus the ideals of the unity of a political body and the legitimation of political leadership remained in existence, but there was no agreement on the means to realize them.

Awareness of the deficiencies of traditional institutions and doubt about the appropriate role of the various elements of a political society were intensified by a prevailing mood of uncertainty and discontent—again, a widespread, almost general phenomenon in Europe at the end of the Middle Ages. As economic activities and accumulation of wealth became increasingly more central concerns, it became steadily more difficult to maintain the traditional orientation of all values towards a world beyond. As a consequence of this loss of orientation, a strong reaction against the preoccupation with secular affairs set in, and although it varied in form and degree, it was most often manifest in fervent religiosity. Appeals to withdraw from the world and cries for reform were expressions of men's bewilderment and dissatisfaction with the world as it was around them.

Nevertheless, the predominant intellectual interest was to find a justification for a more secular way of life. In pursuing this aim, men would look for new authorities or they would interpret old authorities in a new manner. They were driven to study again the question of the nature of man, and the old questions of man's particular qualities, of the character of his special dignity, and of his freedom of will were raised anew.

The bearing of these social and intellectual changes on the development of political thought is evident: the form which the political body had taken no longer fitted traditional concepts, and the factor which acted in and upon the political body—man—came to be seen in a new light.

The situation in Florence after the overthrow of the Medici was the particular reflection of a general crisis existing at the time. The inevitable adjustment of traditional ideas about politics and society to the changed—and changing—political and social conditions found its first most trenchant expression in Florence, and the ideas which were advanced there came to form an important and enduring strand in the fabric of modern political thought. From the inner contradictions on which the republican regime was built, there necessarily followed a bitter struggle for political control. This struggle not only accelerated and intensified the search for a solution to political instability, but it also established the direction along which the solution was sought. The issues and tensions which troubled the Florentine republic determined the nature of the problems and concepts fundamental to the elaboration of a new—a reasoned and intellectual—approach to politics.

Chapter 2 THE REACTION OF THE FLORENTINE ARISTOCRATS TO THE REVOLUTION OF 1494

• I •

Through the constitutional changes of 1494 the middle classes became part of the ruling group. The upper group had to share the power which previously it alone had possessed. Consequently, during the entire republican period the men of the upper group led the attacks against the constitution of 1494 and pressed for changes and reform.

In distinguishing the upper group from the rest of the population the Florentines used a variety of terms: the members of the upper group were the *ricchi*, or the *nobili*, the *grandi*, or the *savi*. These terms derived, of course, from distinguishing attributes commonly enjoyed by the upper group; nearly all those counted among this group were, in addition to being wealthy, usually descended from an ancient and honorable family, and politically experienced or well educated. In some instances we find it difficult to determine the social standing of an individual or to explain why a particular man was a member of the upper group, but the Florentines themselves knew exactly who were the traditional rulers of their city. Sometimes they were called *le case*.[1] The aristocrats were members of those families who owned the great

[1] See above, note 28 of Chapter I.

palaces which towered over the narrow streets and the houses of the neighborhood, and which were the pride of all those living in the same quarter of the city. Many of these palaces—like those of the Corsini, Guicciardini, Ridolfi, and Pandolfini—although still bearing the name which they had in the fifteenth and sixteenth centuries, have been rebuilt in more recent times. Others—like those which in the fifteenth century Brunelleschi had built for the Pazzi, Alberti for the Rucellai, and Michelozzi for the Medici, or like the Strozzi palace which, at the beginning of the sixteenth century, was nearing completion, or the Guadagni palace on Santo Spiritò which Cronaca was building during the republican period—are still so similar to what they were at the beginning of the sixteenth century that the connection which existed in the Florentine mind between the dominating structure of the palaces and the pre-eminent social and political position of the families which owned them is evident. It was impossible for the members of these families, or for others, to lose sight of the leading role which they played in the cultural and political life of Florence. A wide distance separated them not only from the workers, the servants—from those whom the Florentines called "plebe" or "vulgo." The Florentine upper group was also clearly distinguished from the artisans, the tradesmen, the shopkeepers, the owners of small enterprises who in the literal sense formed a "middle class."[2]

[2] Ugolino Verino, *De illustratione urbis Florentiae,* written between 1480 and 1487, shows those whom a contemporary considered the great Florentine families to have been. For a modern discussion of "the factors that determined elevated social place" in Florence, see Lauro Martines, *The Social World of the Florentine Humanists,* Princeton, 1963, pp. 18-84. It ought to be emphasized, however, that, although a gifted individual might rise into the upper group, its dominant element was the old families of great

Although after 1494 the aristocrats no longer had a monopoly over the government, they still had to carry a heavy political burden. Because of their experience, their education and knowledge, they were entrusted with all diplomatic missions. Moreover, the aristocrats could be relied upon to have the resources for advancing loans to the government, which frequently needed extra funds to cover the expenses of an urgent enterprise. Thus the aristocrats found themselves in the anomalous position of having great responsibilities without having the possibility of directing policy entirely as they wanted. Conflict between the aristocrats and the middle classes was almost unavoidable, and, indeed, the period of the republican regime was a time of discord.

The contrast between the groups which would struggle against each other throughout the period of the republic emerged almost immediately after the fall of the Medici, but in the first four years of the republican regime this underlying conflict was obscured by bitter dissension over the immanent validity of Savonarola's message. After the execution of Savonarola in 1498 the disparity of group interests dominated the political alignment in Florentine politics. In the period from 1498 to 1502, the most critical time of the republic, contention arose over the form of government established in 1494; the focal point of this dispute was the question of reducing the power of the Great Council. This fight reached some conclusion in 1502 with a moderate constitutional reform which transformed the office of the *Gonfaloniere*

---

wealth. For instance members of these families frequently had their names placed into the voting bags on several "polizze," not only on one; see the forthcoming study of Nicolai Rubinstein on the Medicean government system.

into a life-long position. In the last ten years of the republican regime the conflict became less acute. However the aristocrats, dissatisfied with the compromise of 1502, remained in opposition and waited for an opportunity to introduce reforms which would increase their influence. Finally, in 1512, they believed their hour had come, for then they were able to carry through a constitutional reform which realized their aims. But the return of the Medici deprived them of their control of the government almost immediately.

The first four years of the republican regime were years of great internal tension, political confusion, and uncertainty. Although the establishment of the Great Council marked the beginning of a new era in Florentine history, the Florentines themselves were not fully aware, at first, of the implications of the changes effected in 1494.[3] When Piero Medici fled Florence in November of 1494 the aristocrats were glad to be rid of a ruler whose arrogant behavior and precipitate actions they had resented and feared. But the aristocrats intended to control the government. The only change which they envisaged was to give those members of aristocratic families who had been opponents of the Medici a share in the government. Thus the first step of the aristocrats after the flight of Piero Medici was to force the people to install twenty of the most prominent aristocrats as *Accoppiatori*. The *Accoppiatori* were charged with revising the lists of citizens eligible to hold office, but while they were occupied

---

[3] The authoritative treatment of these developments is that by Nicolai Rubinstein, "I Primi Anni del Consiglio Maggiore di Firenze (1494-1499)," *Archivio Storico Italiano*, vol. CXII (1954), pp. 151-194, 321-347.

with this task they acted as an interim government, filling all the offices with men of their choice. For a number of weeks the *Accoppiatori* were the real rulers of Florence. Some aristocrats believed—and they clung to their belief throughout the republican period—that such a small committee, of twenty or thirty aristocrats, was the ideal way of governing Florence. However, during these weeks of November and early December—with Pisa in revolt and the French armies in Italy—most of the aristocrats realized that such a regime would have a most precarious existence because of its limited popular support. People made the bitter joke that the rule of one tyrant had been replaced by the rule of twenty tyrants; and resentment threatened to explode in violence.

By mid-December the situation was critical, and a settlement had to be made quickly if civil strife was to be avoided. The aristocrats were not adverse to the idea of the establishment of a Great Council because an enlargement of the ruling group promised greater stability; more people would be tied to the maintenance of the regime and committed to its defence. Nevertheless, the aristocrats were aware that if they were to remain in political control, the enlargement of the ruling group must be limited. Thus their idea was to restrict membership in the Great Council to the sons and grandsons of all those who had sat on the three most prestigious executive boards— Signoria, the Twelve Good Men, and the Sixteen *Gonfalonieri*.[4] Although such a requirement would have widened the ruling group, it would have been composed of

---

[4] This results from the drafts for the law of the Great Council, mentioned by Rubinstein, *loc. cit.*, p. 154, note 13; one draft, that of Domenico Bonsi, shows that some aristocrats recognized the necessity of a broadly based Great Council.

men who shared the same outlook and interests. It is uncertain why, instead of this conservative suggestion, a more radical proposal became law: the Great Council was to be composed not only of descendants of all those who actually had held offices, but also of the descendants of all those whose names had been drawn from the eligibility lists even if they had been prevented from taking office. Through this innovation the Florentine government was opened to the middle classes, and the whole character of the ruling group was changed.[5] Although the aristocrats had reservations about including this group of men in the Great Council, they had no notion what the concrete consequences would be. No one seems to have envisaged that the Great Council would consist of as many as 3000 members. Had the aristocrats been aware that the Great Council would be so large they might have offered stronger opposition.

As it was, aristocratic opposition centered not so much on the requirements for membership in the Great Council, but on the introduction of an electoral procedure for filling some of the offices in the Florentine government. Because the aristocrats were accustomed to the system of filling offices by allotment, which in the past they had been able to manipulate to their satisfaction, they expected that any change in this method would lead to a diminution of their influence. About this they were mistaken. The method of filling some of the offices in the government by election in the Great Council turned out to be to their advantage. Whenever offices were distributed by lot, the increase in the number of those entitled to hold offices would bring in many "new men", members of the middle classes. But when elections took place,

[5] See above note 14 of Chapter I.

54

a well-known name—usually that of an aristocrat—would be chosen. Thus a strange reversal of fronts occurred.[6] The aristocrats became interested in defending and broadening the electoral principle, whereas the middle classes became advocates of distributing offices by lot. The men from the middle classes began to doubt the value of the electoral method which originally they had regarded as necessary for the preservation of a republic. The law of December 22, 1494 had precisely regulated the way in which each office was to be filled; some of the offices were to be filled by election in the Great Council, some by allotment, and some by a combination of election and allotment. The disagreement between the aristocrats and the middle classes on this issue led to frequent changes in these regulations. Sometimes the number of offices filled by election was increased, sometimes decreased. Thus in the first four years of the republic, not the function and composition of the Great Council, but the regulations about the filling of the executive boards was the only issue which indicated the existence of a fundamental division between the wealthy upper group and the middle classes.

The reason was that in these years other issues of great divisive force overshadowed contrasts of group interests. From 1494 to 1498 Savonarola was the central figure in Florentine politics.[7] Savonarola was never the ruler of Florence, and his adherents were in the majority in the Signoria only intermittently and for short periods. Nevertheless, Savonarola's sermons with their moral exhortations and political counsels dominated Florentine life. From

[6] See Rubinstein, *loc. cit.*, pp. 323-340.

[7] Roberto Ridolfi, *Vita di Girolamo Savonarola*, 2 vols., Rome, 1952 (English translation by Cecil Grayson, New York, 1959) is now the standard biography.

the pulpit of the cathedral whence the Frate directed his passionate and visionary appeals to the Florentines, a large black shadow fell over the whole of the city, subduing and muting its multi-colored life.

Savonarola's influence over the Florentines was derived from the belief of many that he was a true prophet.[8] He had predicted that a great disaster would befall Italy, and the divine nature of this prophecy became apparent to the Florentines when the French invaded Italy in 1494. Thus in the critical months following the overthrow of the Medici his advice carried great weight and his advocacy of the establishment of a Great Council was decisive. Savonarola never identified himself with any social group or class; his exhortations to moral and political reform were aimed at every man in Florence. It is true indeed that because the creation of the Great Council had allowed the middle classes a place in the government, his admirers and most loyal supporters came particularly from this group. However, in consequence of Savonarola's attacks on the Papacy and his condemnation by Pope Alexander VI quite a number of men from the middle classes began to change their minds about him.

On the other hand, Savonarola was by no means opposed by all aristocrats. The seriousness of his moral concerns, the fire of his eloquence, the impact of his personality were so great that many aristocrats accepted his leadership because they regarded him as a true prophet. For instance, one of Savonarola's aristocratic adherents was Piero Guicciardini, a deeply religious man who was attracted by Savonarola's piety. But less religious and

---

[8] On Savonarola's prophetic message, see Donald Weinstein, "Savonarola, Florence, and the Millenarian Tradition," *Church History,* vol. XXVII (1958), pp. 3-17.

more cynical aristocrats also favored him. Although such men might have doubted the divine origin of Savonarola's inspiration, they believed it might be easier to use Savonarola than to oppose him. Realizing his influence over the citizens, they befriended him and suggested to him measures which, with his espousal, might be more quickly adopted by the Great Council. This was the relationship which existed between Savonarola and Francesco Valori, who, although he had always been a protagonist of a small oligarchic regime, became the head of the Savonarolians in Florence. Valori was unable to extricate himself from this union with Savonarola. The belief of the Florentines in Savonarola's divinely-inspired prophetic powers could last only as long as he continued to make correct prognostications. When the French king did not return to Italy, in contrast to what the Frate had predicted, his reputation as a man of God declined. Finally, Valori, the leader of the Savonarola party, was assassinated the day Savonarola was put into prison.

The multiplicity of political groupings and factions which emerged in Florence in these early years of the republican regime indicate that a variety of issues obscured the existence within the Great Council of two groups of different economic interests. We hear about *Frateschi* and *Piagnoni, Mastricapaternostri, Disperati* and *Arrabbiati,* and these names reflect the extent to which the political struggle in Florence was dominated by disputes over the personality of Savonarola.[9]

[9] On the names of the Florentine political groups, see Nicolai Rubinstein, "Politics and Constitution in Florence at the End of the Fifteenth Century," *Italian Renaissance Studies,* ed. E. F. Jacob, London, 1960, pp. 170-171. *Frateschi* means adherents of the Frate, *piagnoni* suggests Savonarola's appeals to emotion, *mastricapaternostri* Savonarola's reliance on paternoster. Savonarola's enemies were *arrabbiati* (fanatics) or *disperati.*

In the four years following Savonarola's execution tension in Florence continued and even increased. Whereas the citizenry in the Savonarolian period had been split into numerous factions by a diversity of issues, from 1498 to 1502 there was one central issue: whether or not the government established in 1494 needed to be reformed and improved. On this issue the members of the Great Council aligned themselves strictly according to group interests. Because in the course of this conflict some new and important ideas on politics emerged, the events of these years must be described in some detail.

The background of the constitutional struggle was formed by external threats and dangers. Italy was thrown into new turmoil by the return of the French armies under King Louis XII in 1499 and by the subsequent appearance of the Spaniards in Naples. Florence was directly involved because Cesare Borgia used this confused situation for his own audacious plans—to establish a territorial lordship in central Italy, in the neighborhood of Florence. Moreover, throughout these years Florence was involved in a war to subject Pisa once again to its domination.

Mounting financial exigencies forged the link between these external dangers and the domestic crises.[10] Money was needed to pay condottieri, to buy off enemies, to keep the protection of the French King, and to continue

[10] For a broad discussion see Antonio Anzilotti, *La Crisi Costituzionale della Repubblica Fiorentina*, Firenze, 1912. The two articles by Rubinstein—"I Primi Anni" and "Politics and Constitution in Florence"—and the article by L. F. Marks, "La crisi Finanziaria a Firenze dal 1494 al 1502," *Archivio Storico Italiano*, vol. CXII (1954), pp. 40-72, contain a more detailed treatment of the developments. Rubinstein's articles do not go beyond the year 1499; the political and institutional developments after 1499 have not yet been treated in a thorough fashion.

the war against Pisa. Income from taxes was hardly ever sufficient, and in emergencies additional funds had to be raised without delay. The government was forced to ask the wealthy upper group for loans which were to be repaid by the income from taxes. But since the income from the existing taxes was not sufficient to repay loans made in previous times, new loans required new taxes. Yet the demand for new taxes met intense opposition in the Great Council, particularly among members from the middle classes who failed to see the urgency of reimbursing the aristocrats for their loans to the government. Moreover, Florence suffered in these years from a severe economic crisis; and this increased the unwillingness of the middle classes to approve new tax legislation.

Agreement to raise new taxes had to be bought by concessions which would strengthen the political position of the middle classes. In the spring of 1499, after several proposals for new taxation had been rejected, a tax law was finally approved. However, it would not have passed the Great Council had not the Signoria introduced at the same time a law which, by increasing the number of offices to be filled by allotment, gave the middle classes a greater chance to enjoy the "benefits of government."[11] Half a year later, when still more taxes were needed, again the agreement of the middle classes had to be purchased, this time by a change in the tax laws. A graduated

[11] For the interconnection between the agreement to a new tax (the "piacente") and the change in the electoral procedure, see Francesco Guicciardini, *Storie Fiorentine*, ed. R. Palmarocchi, Bari, 1931, pp. 178-179. On the changes in the electoral system, see Rubinstein, "Politics and Constitution," *loc. cit.*, pp. 178-179: "When this reform was completed in May 1499, all the highest offices, including the *Signoria*, were filled by an ingenious system combining election by voting and by lot, while the other offices were to be filled by lot only."

tax, increasing proportionately with the amount of wealth—the *Decima scalata*—was put into effect in January 1500.[12]

Because of the immediacy of the financial needs, the Great Council in these years divided strictly according to class lines. The aristocrats and the middle classes began to look upon each other with unconcealed distrust. Chroniclers and diarists report that political life had become polarized between advocates of a *governo largho* and advocates of a *governo stretto*.[13] *Governo largho* was the name given to the form of government which had been introduced in 1494 and which the middle classes were anxious to maintain. *Governo stretto* was the term used to describe a form of government in which the aristocrats would have control. There was much talk about the plans of the aristocrats for establishing a *governo stretto*. One of their plans was believed to be the handing over of power to a committee of twenty or thirty;[14] another less radical and therefore less risky plan was to transfer some of the most important functions of the Great Council to a council of 200,[15] to be composed exclusively of aristocrats.

[12] See Marks, "La Crisi Finanziaria," *loc. cit.*, p. 58: "La decima scalata fosse diretta contro una classe sociale e non semplicemente contro una particolare forma di ricchezza."

[13] The contrast between these two forms of government is old; and the contrast was particularly sharp in the fourteenth century. See Gene A. Brucker, *Florentine Politics and Society, 1343-1378*, Princeton, 1962, pp. 87 et seq., but the contrast was less evident during the century of oligarchic rule. However, on the existence of some tendencies towards a broadening of the basis of government in the times of the Medici, see Guido Pampaloni, "Fermenti di riforme democratiche nella Firenze Medicea del Quattrocento," *Archivio Storico Italiano*, vol. CXIX (1961), pp. 11-62.

[14] For instance, Parenti remarks on such rumours in January 1499 and July 1500, see *Storia Fiorentina*, Ms. B.N.F., II.IV.170, ff. 60v.-61r., 136v.

[15] Again Parenti, *op. cit.*, II.IV.170, f. 45v (July 1498), f. 152v (October 1500).

The suspicion of the middle classes about the intentions of the aristocrats showed itself in another conflict which placed aristocrats and middle classes against each other in the years 1499 and 1500. The center of this conflict was the Board of the Ten.[16] The members of the Board of the Ten were in charge of supervising military operations and diplomatic negotiations. The members of the Ten were almost always aristocrats because it was believed that their experience and knowledge were indispensable for the execution of these tasks. But because the Ten controlled the military forces of the city, the middle classes feared that it was the instrument through which the aristocrats might carry through their plans for a *governo stretto*. The city was full of rumors. The patricians, some said, planned to engage a condottiere in order to establish an oligarchic regime by military means; others maintained that the patricians were prolonging the war against Pisa in order to keep a military force at their disposal which they could employ for their own ends in Florence.[17] Thus when the term of the Ten expired in May 1499, the Great Council refused to make new appointments for the Ten. The aristocrats were indignant. They found themselves in danger of losing a position which guaranteed them a share in determining the course

[16] On this conflict, see Guicciardini, *Storie Fiorentine*, pp. 177 et seq.

[17] Parenti, *op. cit.*, II.IV.170, f. 89r (August 1499): "Dette presumptione a molti nostri che e primati qui fautori del Capitano, o del Conte, si fussino insieme uniti . . . per levare il reggimento di mano all' universale." Parenti, *op. cit.*, II.IV.170, f. 84v (July 1499): "Stimando che se Pisa si recuperava in questo modo, si uscirebbe delle mani de' grandi, et interaments si viverebbe alla populare et in vera liberta. . . ." See also Parenti, *op. cit.*, II.IV.170, f. 108r (February 1500). See also Guicciardini, *Storie Fiorentine*, p. 225. For the economic interests involved in the reconquest of Pisa, see M. E. Mallett, "Anglo-Florentine Commercial Relations, 1465-1491," *Economic History Review*, Second Series, vol. XV (1962), pp. 250-265.

of Florentine policy. Moreover, the aristocrats considered the failure to re-appoint the Ten as equivalent to abandoning the war against Pisa. In contrast to the middle classes, with economic interests centered around the local market, the aristocrats, who drew their wealth from export, were conscious of the great importance of the Pisan seaport for Florentine economic prosperity. The openly expressed dissatisfaction of the aristocrats generated obstinacy on the part of the middle classes; they rejected various attempts to reinstate the Board of the Ten. Only a year and a half later, in September 1500, was the struggle over the Board of the Ten brought to an end with a compromise. The Ten was reinstituted, but the freedom of its members to select condottieri, to appoint military commissioners, and to negotiate with foreign powers was curtailed.[18]

The crisis over the Board of the Ten shows the depth of the tension between aristocrats and middle classes. The compromise which ended the conflict illustrates that increasing external danger had forced the opposing groups to recognize that by continuing the internal conflict they might jeopardize the independence and freedom of Florence. From this point of view, this crisis can be considered as a prelude to the events of the following two years in which internal tensions sharpened immensely, but which ended finally with the compromise solution of the establishment of the *Gonfaloniere a vita*. In the years 1501 and 1502 the city had to fight for its very existence. The period of acute danger began in January

---

[18] The law, restoring the Ten, was accepted September 18, 1500, see *Prov.*, vol. 191, ff. 27r.-28v.; for a brief summary of the contents of this law, see Guicciardini, *Storie Fiorentine*, p. 206. The various attempts to reinstitute the Ten between spring 1499 and September 1500 are described by Parenti.

1501 with a civil war in Pistoia which threatened the Florentine domination. The revolt seemed the more ominous because of the appearance of Cesare Borgia and his troops in the neighborhood of Pistoia. In May 1501, Cesare Borgia stationed himself in Campi, five miles outside Florence, and the Florentines were thrown into a panic. In order to persuade Cesare Borgia to evacuate their territory, the Florentines agreed to pay him a large sum of money. However, they had gained only a temporary respite. In the next summer rebellion broke out in Arezzo and the surrounding Valdichiana. The Florentines suspected Cesare Borgia of instigating these revolts and of backing their leader, Piero Medici. Thus, in the summer of 1502, Pisa was still defending its independence, Pistoia was torn by civil war, and Arezzo and its surroundings were in rebellion; Florence had lost half of her empire.

The disasters which fell on Florence in the years 1501 and 1502 had the effect of increasing internal tension by necessitating great financial outlays. The wealthy citizens refused to give further loans, and as an indication of the desperateness of the situation, on January 31, 1501, the officials of the Monte resigned before the expiration of their term.[19] The aristocrats, enraged by the unwillingness of the middle classes to take a share in the financial burden, began to withdraw from governmental activities; they declined to serve on diplomatic missions, and they refused to attend advisory meetings to which the Signoria summoned them.[20] Such a political boycott had been used by aggrieved individuals in the past, but it had never been adopted systematically by a large group

---

[19] See L. F. Marks, "La Crisi Finanziaria," *loc. cit.*, p. 69, where details about the financial developments can be found.

[20] See Guicciardini, *Storie Fiorentine*, pp. 239-241.

of citizens. The attitude of the aristocrats heightened the distrust of the middle classes. When Cesare Borgia was near Florence it was rumored that he had an understanding with the aristocrats who wanted to use him to overthrow the *governo largho*.[21] The populace was so alarmed that they threatened to burn down the houses of the aristocratic leaders.[22] For more than a year, from the summer of 1501 to the summer of 1502, no new tax legislation passed the Great Council. The Signoria took recourse to temporary expedients—calling in overdue tax payments and raising the price of salt. But in the summer of 1502 it had come to the point where the government was unable to make any further disbursements.

Nevertheless, while external dangers and their economic impact increased internal tension, they had also the effect of making the Florentines aware of the need for compromise and accommodation. Both the aristocrats and the middle classes were conscious that there was great hazard in opposing each other too vehemently; a government crippled by internal strife was powerless to defend itself against its enemies. Some members of the middle classes came to the point of admitting that the revolts in Pistoia and Arezzo were "the consequences of disorder and bad government rather than of anything else";[23] and that the aristocrats were justified in insisting on the necessity of institutional reforms.

[21] In general, see Guicciardini, *Storie Fiorentine*, pp. 212-214, then Landucci, *Diario Fiorentino*, ed. Jodoco del Badia, Firenze, 1883, p. 224, 228; Giovanni Cambi, "Istorie," ed. Fr. Ildefonso di San Luigi, *Delizie degli eruditi Toscani*, vol. XXI, Firenze, 1785, p. 163, writes: "Fu tenuto per il popolo tutto volgarmente, che detto Ducha vi fussi chiamato da' Ciptadini di Firenze potenti per rimutare lo stato. . . ."

[22] Guicciardini, *Storie Fiorentine*, p. 212; Parenti, *op. cit.*, II.II. 133, f. 311r (June 1502).

[23] "questo pare sia più presto proceduto per disordine et cattivo

Thus the mounting external and internal difficulties in the years 1501 and 1502 led to a number of attempts on the part of the Signoria to explore the possibilities of a constitutional reform which would be acceptable to all the citizens. These explorations were done by means of *pratiche*.[24]

Although the *pratiche* were not, during the republican period, a constitutionally established institution, they served the important purpose of giving the policy-making boards a means of testing the citizens' reactions to some of their proposals and of allowing the citizens to air their opinions. The *pratiche* were only advisory meetings; and their recommendations were not binding. If a recommendation of a *pratica* was to become law, the recommendation, like other proposed legislation, had to be approved by the Signoria and then submitted to the Great Council for its approval.

Usually the number of citizens invited to a *pratica* was small. Such *pratiche—pratiche strette*—were composed of the most prominent and wealthiest men of the city and therefore they were rightly considered to be a means by which the artistocrats could exert their influence on Florentine policy. But a *pratica* did not need to be limited in size. A much larger number of citizens might be called together to offer advice. These *pratiche—pratiche larghe* —could be convoked in the same way as a *pratica stretta;* but in a *pratica larga* an equal number of men from each quarter of the city had to be present. Sometimes a *pratica larga* was preceded by assemblies held in the single quarters of the city, and a number of citizens—the same num-

---

governo che per altre cagioni . . . ," Antonio Benivieni in Pratica of July 5, 1502, A.S.F., *Consulte e Pratiche,* vol. 67, f. 40v.

[24] See above, note 37 of Chapter I about the Pratiche.

ber from each quarter—were delegated to present the views of the quarter in the *pratiche larghe*. A *pratica larga* usually included men from the middle classes. But the most prominent aristocrats from each quarter were always present in a *pratica larga*. The average Florentine's feeling of awe and pride—and perhaps a little fear— of the aristocrats living nearby was expressed in his notion that the superior education and worldly knowledge of the aristocrats made them best suited to present the views of the quarter. And indeed, the self-assurance of the aristocrats, their convincing way of speaking and debating, and their familiarity with the larger issues of politics and economics led to the result that the aristocratic point of view, although sometimes modified, dominated even a *pratica larga*. In spite of the presence of men from the middle classes in a *pratica larga* it was by no means inevitable that its recommendations would reflect the middle class interests to such a degree that they would be approved by the Great Council.

None of the *pratiche*, which, between 1501 and 1502, were called together by the Signoria to discuss the problem of reform, had any practical result. Either the participants were unable to agree on the type of change which they considered necessary, or if they did agree, their recommendations were not submitted to the Great Council. But the protocols of these *pratiche* reveal the aims of the aristocrats and how, during these years, they were developing their program. The *pratiche* of these years show that the Florentines themselves were aware of the close connection between the city's pressing financial needs and the problem of institutional reform. Many speakers in these *pratiche* proposed methods which might facilitate the acceptance of new tax legislation; but other speakers expressed the opinion that Florence could not resolve its financial difficulties unless changes were made in its constitution. Gradually this latter view became dominant.

In January 1501, the Signoria called together a *pratica* consisting of thirty aristocrats, to discuss "what ought to be done about good government for the city."[25] Many speakers were of the opinion that the problems of the government were largely financial, and that a way must be found to guarantee the government sufficient tax income to meet its debts. Since additional taxes could be imposed only by the agreement of the Great Council, it was suggested that the majority required for the passage of tax legislation in the Great Council be lowered from two-thirds to one-half. Another proposal was put forth by twelve of the participants—Bernardo Rucellai, Piero Guicciardini, Alamanno Salviati, and Giovanni Batista

[25] The words of the Gonfaloniere addressing the Pratica were: "Domandò consiglio per parte della Signoria di quello si havessi ad fare per provedere al danaio bisogna di presente per dare la pagha a chi è a guardia in quello di Pisa et altro et circa a quello che occorressi per il buono governo della cittá, et etiam quello si ha ad fare per recuperare il credito et la fede che ha perduto la cittá." A.S.F., *Consulte e Pratiche*, vol. 66, f. 215r. This meeting took place on January 13, 1501, it is recorded *loc. cit.*, vol. 66, ff. 215r-222r. This is the only meeting in 1501, in which questions of domestic reform were discussed at length; meetings on January 9 (ff. 206v-209r) and on January 12 (ff. 210r-215r) were exclusively concerned with the financial aspects of the crisis. Guicciardini, *Storie Fiorentine*, pp. 207-209, gives some description of these meetings which, according to him, extended over several days. Parenti, *op. cit.*, II.IV.170, f. 159r-v, mentions that a plan by 12 leading aristocrats for constitutional reform was then presented to the Signoria; among them, according to Parenti, was Giovanni Batista Ridolfi, and the speech which Ridolfi made in the Pratica of January 13 and which is recorded in the protocols, fits well to Parenti's report. Thus my report about the meetings of January 1501 is based on the protocols of the pratica of January 13 and on Parenti.

Ridolfi among them. They presented a plan for the creation of a new deliberative council which should be composed of two hundred members belonging to the body for life. Eighty of the members would be elected by the Great Council, and ninety should come from the great Florentine families. In addition, all former *Gonfalonieri di Giustizia*, all former members of the Ten, and all former ambassadors should belong to this new council. The main duty of this proposed body would be to decide on financial legislation.

In some respects this proposal engendered the revival of an institution which had existed in Medicean times—namely, a council exclusively controlled by aristocrats. For despite the formal acknowledgment of the authority of the Great Council by granting it a right to elect eighty members to this council, the new body would have had a strictly aristocratic character. The financial function of this proposed council revealed the intent of the aristocrats to render the Great Council impotent by depriving it of its most powerful weapon.[26] One aspect of this proposed council involved an idea which transcended the traditional concepts of city-state government and even contained criticism of the assumption that every citizen had both the right and the capacity to govern. By including in this proposed council men who had formerly held high offices in the government, the aristocrats implied that political experience might be useful, and that an appropriate place in the government

[26] Again a return to ideas of the Medicean times when authority over financial measures was vested in the Council of the Hundred, see L. F. Marks, "The Financial Oligarchy in Florence under Lorenzo," *Italian Renaissance Studies*, ed. E. F. Jacob, London, 1960, p. 124. In the earlier part of the fifteenth century, the handling of financial legislation had sometimes been entrusted to special councils for a limited period.

68

should be given to the "political expert." The twelve aristocrats who proposed the new council in the *pratica stretta* of 1501 envisaged that such a council would form the "center of gravity and finally the government of the city."[27] However, their proposed council found no favor with the middle classes. The *pratiche strette* of 1501 ended without any positive result.

In January 1502, after the Great Council had again refused to pass needed tax legislation, the Signoria convoked new *pratiche*, this time *pratiche larghe*.[28] The speakers from three of the quarters put forth suggestions about how to facilitate the passage of tax legislation in the Great Council. Only one quarter, Santa Croce, had thought out a proposal for institutional reform. Its speaker, Francesco Pepi, said: "The illness of the city is so severe that we do not have much time to look for medicine."[29] As spokesman for Santa Croce, Pepi recommended the formation of a new council of three to four hundred members who were to be appointed by the Signoria and by the participants of these *pratiche*. This

---

[27] ". . . il pondo et governo finalmente della citta," Parenti, *op. cit.*, II.IV. 170, f. 159.

[28] Meetings took place on January 13, 14, 15, 1502. The meetings of January 13 and 14 (the one of January 13 with the wrong date "February 13") are recorded A.S.F., *Consulte e Pratiche*, vol. 66, ff. 384r-387r; the meeting of January 15 is recorded, out of order, on ff. 405r-408r, but these pages contain also some material which belongs to the previous meetings of January 13 and 14; the meeting of January 15 seems to have been mainly concerned with voting about the various proposals, and the protocol gives the results of these votes. These meetings are discussed by Parenti, *op. cit.*, II.IV.170, ff. 196r-197r, and by Cerretani, *Historia Fiorentina*, Ms. B.N.F., II.III.74, ff. 275v.-276r.

[29] "Iudicano che il male della citta sia tanto, che non aspecti tempo ad ricevere la medicina," A.S.F., *Consulte e Pratiche*, vol. 66, f. 408r. Pepi's speech indicated that he made his proposal for the majority of Santa Croce, but that the men of this quarter were not unanimous.

proposed council would relieve the Great Council of some of its functions. It would have power to appoint members to the Board of the Ten, as well as ambassadors and commissioners; and this new council was to pass, with a two-thirds majority, all financial legislation.

After three days of debate in these *pratiche*, a vote was taken and a great majority of the participants favored the proposal of Santa Croce over the less incisive ones of the other quarters. Evidently the feeling for the necessity of a constitutional reform had spread, and it was thought that the men of the middle classes found it preferable to accept some reforms, in which the Great Council had a voice, than to allow the crisis to grow to such an extent that they would be altogether powerless. This sort of consideration seems to be borne out by the report of one contemporary that the aristocrats were not unanimous in their support of this reform proposal because it did not go far enough in bringing the government under their control.[30] Not a few aristocrats calculated with cool cynicism that the political situation would soon deteriorate to such an extent that the middle classes would be forced to accept any type of reform which the aristocrats advanced. Thus the proposal of Santa Croce, which had embodied some reform—radical to the middle classes, not radical enough for the aristocrats—and which had been agreed to by the *pratiche larghe* of 1502, was not submitted to the Great Council. Again the *pratiche* which had been called together to discuss reform ended without result.

In the summer of the same year the revolt in Arezzo broke out and the existence of the Florentine republic was in jeopardy. Again the Signoria initiated *pratiche*

---

[30] Parenti, *op. cit.*, II.IV.170, ff. 196r-197r.

larghe which were to discuss how "to organize the city well and to introduce a good government."[31] The gravity with which the participants faced their task was indicated by the suggestion that the Signoria should seek God's help by forming a solemn procession of supplication and by more stringently enforcing the laws against luxury and gambling. If this were done then God might inspire the participants of this *pratica* to find a correct solution.

The speakers in these *pratiche* put forth a variety of proposals; some reiterated previous suggestions which were designed to ameliorate the city's financial problems, and others advanced extreme ideas such as the establishment of a temporary dictatorship in the manner of ancient Rome. But the majority of the participants had become aware that some institutional reforms were necessary. It was felt that this was not the time for daring innovations which might create violent opposition. Only if reforms were introduced "by regular methods and without scandal,"[32] could the aim of this *pratica* be realized—to arrive at conclusions acceptable to the Great Council.

The recommendations of the quarters were varied; but there was agreement on some essential points. All the recommendations complied with the demands of the aristocrats for a greater degree of continuity in the govern-

---

[31] "per ordinare bene la città et introducri un buono governo," Marcello Virgilio Adriani in introductory speech to a pratica on July 5, 1502, A.S.F., *Consulte e Pratiche*, vol. 67, f. 40r. Meetings took place on July 3, 5, 6, and the protocols of these meetings are in vol. 67, ff. 36r.-47r. For the developments leading to these meetings, see Parenti, *op. cit.*, II.IV.170, ff. 117v-120v; see also Cerretani, *op. cit.*, II.III.74, f. 493r.

[32] "per la via ordinaria et sanza scandolo," Niccolò Zati, speaking for the Ten, on July 5, A.S.F., *Consulte e Pratiche*, vol. 67, f. 41r.

ment and for the creation of a new council with exclusive control over financial affairs. It was hoped that the need for more continuity in the government would be satisfied by making the Board of the Ten, which previously had been appointed only in times of war, a permanent institution. Although the term of the individual members of this board would remain nine months, it was suggested that the election of the members was to be staggered in such a way that the term of only half of the members would end at the same time. The other recommendation of these *pratiche,* on which the delegates from three of the quarters (Santa Croce adhered to the proposal which it had made in the *pratiche* of the previous year) agreed, was that a council for the management of finances should be formed. In order to make these recommendations acceptable to the Great Council, it was decided that the members of the Board of the Ten as well as the members of the new council should be elected by the Great Council, and that the members of the new council should have a term, not for life—as many of the aristocrats had suggested—but for five years.[33]

These recommendations of the *pratiche* of 1502 were determined by the urgency of the situation. They also clearly constituted a compromise, and as it frequently

[33] It ought to be noted that, although the members of the new council would be selected by the Great Council, certain restrictions on the Great Council's freedom of choice were suggested; for instance one suggestion was that nominations of candidates were to be made by the Signoria and the Collegi; another was that the names of all former members of the Board of the Ten and the Board of the Eight were placed into bags from which the drawing for the new council would be made. Such measures would have guaranteed some aristocratic influence in this new council. The proposal of Santa Croce, providing for lifetime membership in the council and appointment of its members by the Signoria and the Collegi, was less "democratic."

happens in the case of a compromise, neither of the opposing groups seems to have been completely satisfied.
Because the proposed council was to be composed of men
elected by the Great Council, the aristocrats realized
that the new body would be dependent on the middle
classes. And the middle classes, in spite of the influence
which they could exert on the proposed council by electing its members, remained suspicious about the creation
of any new council because it would inevitably encroach
on the authority of the Great Council, and because it
might form the opening wedge for a return to oligarchic
rule.

It is not surprising then that the compromise recommendations of this *pratica* were shoved aside and that the
crisis of 1502 was resolved in an entirely different manner. The office of the *Gonfaloniere*—the titular head of
the republic and the presiding officer of the Signoria—
was transformed into a position to be held for life. Since
there are no records of deliberations preceding this development,[34] we can only speculate on the reasons for
this unexpected solution. The establishment of a *Gonfaloniere a vita* was also a compromise; but it was a far
more attractive compromise than had been the recommendations of the *pratiche larghe*. The *Gonfaloniere*
had no power independent from the other members of
of the Signoria, and therefore an extension of the term of
his office could not be considered as a change which
threatened the political influence of the middle classes.
Perhaps they were even favorably impressed by this proposal because a similar suggestion had been made by Savonarola, who had advocated the establishment of the

[34] Cerretani, *op. cit.*, II.III.74, f. 295r-v. remarked that "la Signoria
lo fe' sanza farne praticha."

Great Council which had brought the middle classes into the government.[35] Although the aristocrats could hardly be satisfied with such a change, most of them preferred some measure of reform to none at all. They hoped that if once the first step toward constitutional reform were taken, further progress along this road would be easier. The aristocrats might even have thought that from a purely tactical point of view there could be some advantage in beginning constitutional reforms with the creation of a *Gonfaloniere a vita;* with his help and authority resistance to further reforms might be squashed. To the aristocrats, the law of August 26, 1502, which established the *Gonfaloniere a vita,* appeared to be the beginning of a movement away from the *governo largo* of 1494.[36]

Yet under Piero Soderini, who was elected *Gonfaloniere a vita* by the Great Council in 1502, further constitutional changes were not undertaken. External threats, which had intensified the internal struggles, diminished. With the death of Pope Alexander VI in the summer of 1503, Cesare Borgia's power in central Italy collapsed, and soon afterwards the struggle between France and

[35] Savonarola mentioned his suggestion for introducing a "doge" in Florence in his confession, see Pasquale Villari, *La Storia di Girolamo Savonarola,* nuova edizione, Firenze, 1930, vol. II, p. CLV.

[36] The law of August 26, 1502, establishing the *Gonfaloniere a vita,* is in *Prov.,* vol. 193, f. 50r.-52r.; little attention seems to have been given to the last paragraph of this law which changes the election of the Council of Eighty in such a way that "per ciaschuno quartiere se ne imbcrsino solamente 28 di quelli che haranno vinto el partito et haranno più fave nere che gl'altri, cioè 21 per la maggiore et septe per la minore." The aristocrats could consider this as a step toward a council which they would dominate because the preference given to aristocrats in elections (see above, pp. 54 et seq.) would have produced chiefly aristocrats among those whose names were placed into the bags from which the members of the Council of Eighty were drawn.

Spain for hegemony over Italy found a respite; Spain ruled southern Italy and France controlled Milan. A temporary calm settled over Italy, giving Florence the opportunity to concentrate on the reconquest of Pisa which occurred in 1509. There was also an improvement in the financial situation of Florence both because external dangers subsided and because Soderini had a remarkable ability for handling fiscal affairs. The return of relative stability and safety to the Florentine republic eased the pressure on the middle classes to agree to further institutional reforms. Moreover, Soderini was not personally inclined to reform; he did not want to become the tool of the upper classes. Soderini believed he could maintain an independent position between, or even above, the opposing groups. Soderini's unwillingness to carry out the aristocratic program made him in the eyes of the patricians a traitor to the class from which he came. The aristocrats fought Soderini bitterly. Significantly, Alamanno Salviati, who had been an influential advocate of the law creating the *Gonfaloniere a vita*, became Soderini's sharpest, most intransigent adversary.

In 1508 the League of Cambrai was formed to halt the spread of Venetian power on the *terra-ferma*, and then Pope Julius II opened a campaign against the French; again Italy was a theatre of war. These events reawakened all the old tensions and conflicts and they became even more vehement. Soderini remained loyal to the French, and after their defeat in 1512 an isolated Florence faced the Spanish and Papal troops which threatened to restore the Medici. This crisis offered an opportunity for the aristocrats to get rid of Soderini, and under their pressure, the *Gonfaloniere*, who had become discouraged by the acrid criticism which he met on all sides, fled to exile in the autumn of 1512. To the aristocrats this appeared to be their chance to gain control of the government. In the two weeks which passed between the flight of Soderini and the restoration of the Medici by Spanish and Papal troops the aristocrats were in possession of the government. They forced the Great Council, which was demoralized by the collapse of Soderini's regime, to accept a law of constitutional reform which was an undiluted expression of the aristocrats' program.[37]

This law was built on the ideas which the aristocrats had voiced in the meetings of the *pratiche* around the turn of the century, although some of the stipulations of this law reflected the experiences of the aristocrats during the years of Soderini's rule. For instance, the aristocrats recognized the need for steadiness and continuity in the office of the *Gonfaloniere,* but they did not want to have another *Gonfaloniere a vita* because of their dissatisfaction with Soderini's refusals to accept their recommendations. Thus in the law which the aristocrats sponsored in 1512, it was specified that the term of the *Gonfaloniere* was to be limited to one year. Moreover this law contained a number of prohibitions in order to curtail his freedom of action. Following the example of Venice whose Doge was not permitted to open privately letters of state, the Florentine *Gonfaloniere* could perform this necessary function only in the presence of two other members of the Signoria.

The center of the constitutional reform of the aristocrats in 1512 was the creation of a Senate, organized in accordance with the suggestions made ten years earlier in the *pratiche.* The Great Council was to elect eighty

[37] Law of September 7, 1512, *Prov.,* vol. 65, ff. 388r.-390v. See also Anzilotti, *op. cit.,* pp. 52 et seq.

members of this Senate, and these eighty were to be joined by all persons who had been *Gonfalonieri* or ambassadors, or who had served on the Board of the Ten. These Senators would in turn elect fifty additional members to their body. The functions of this new Senate were such that there could be no doubt that it was meant to be the institution for the formulation of Florentine policy. Not only was this Senate given authority to approve with a two-thirds majority all fiscal legislation, but it had also the power to appoint the members of all the chief executive boards. Only the annual election of the *Gonfaloniere* was left to the Great Council. Under this constitution, no longer the Great Council, but the Senate was the "soul of the city."

A Florentine law was usually prefaced with a statement of justification. The first sentence of the law of September 7, 1512 is in accordance with the traditional concepts of government: "All ancient and modern republics which have had a long life and lived in peace and unity did so because dignities and benefices were fairly distributed among its citizens, because crimes were punished with justice, and merits liberally rewarded so that the citizens were content with their status, fearful to commit crimes, eager to do well, and willing not only to defend their republic in unity but also to increase its power." But the consequences which were drawn, in this law, from these presuppositions were novel: good government requires that "a republic possess the institution of a Senate." All the resentment and frustration which the patricians had harbored in the years since 1494 found expression in the succeeding phrase: "This had been considered and recommended by thoughtful citizens frequently in the past, but they were not believed till now when, with great losses for the city and danger to its freedom, experience has proved them to be right."[38]

• II •

The attempts of the Florentine aristocrats to bring about constitutional changes during the republican period are significant for the history of political thought because the aristocrats, in order to regain the power deprived them by the constitutional law of 1494, needed a theoretical justification for their political aims. In their search for an intellectual basis from which to advocate their claims, they would have to find new criteria for evaluating the soundness of a government.

Although practical considerations and examples, which governments like that of Venice had provided, influenced the constitutional arrangements of 1494, the fundamental presupposition underlying the law of December 22, 1494 was that political institutions were legitimate if they could be shown to have existed in the earliest times of the body politic. The correct procedure in politics, according to the prevailing mode of thinking, was to seek out the type of political institution which had existed in the historical—or mythical—past and to model new insti-

[38] "El governo delle antiche e moderne republiche le quali lungamente governarono e governano in pace et unione lo stato loro non da altra cagione essere derivato che dallo havere distribuiti gli onori et gl' utili convenientemente: et puniti gli errori con giustitia et premiati i meriti largamente accio chè gli uomini contenti de gradi loro et timidi dello errare et d'operare bene desiderosi la loro republica unitamente non solo mantenghino ma inchreschino. Et considerato come il aver delle sopradecte cose non puo essere dove non sia forma di senato el quale unito col capo publico possa et con maggiore forza et con miglior consiglio opporsi a pericoli che ogni di sopravino: Il che sendosi di molti prudenti cittadini per lo adrietro molte volte considerato e decto ne mai sendosi loro creduto se prima non e stato della esperientia con danno gravissimo della citta e pericolo della liberta dimostro."

tutions after the pattern of the old. A constitution was justified when it represented a restoration of the "old political order."[39]

When the aristocrats were driven into opposition to the dominance of the middle classes in the Great Council, they found themselves without an argument, without any justification for their position. The middle classes had pre-empted the traditional legitimation of political demands because the Great Council was considered to be a return to the old order. Moreover, in attempting to curtail the power of the Great Council, the aristocrats' proposals focussed on devising novel arrangements; the aristocrats wanted to divide power in such a way that they could regain a decisive voice in the government. In Medicean times the oligarchy ruled through the Council of the Seventy and the Council of the Hundred. Clearly this precedent influenced the proposals of the aristocrats. But after 1494 it was not possible simply to return to the old form of government. Thus the proposals of the aristocrats had to conform to a new situation, and they required a new justification.

The Florentine aristocrats were men from the wealthiest and most prestigious families; their influence penetrated almost every facet of life within the city, and reached beyond the walls of Florence. The aristocrats were also the cultural elite of the city. They were the patrons of the humanists, and the champions of a civilization in which the classical world was to be reborn. It is not surprising that the aristocrats would anchor their political claims to the concepts and teachings which the hu-

[39] For examples see *Prov.*, vol. 189, ff. 5v (April 20, 1498): "ridurre la nostra città al' ordine antico"; or *Balìe*, vol. 43, ff. 178r.-180r. (November 22, 1513): "modo et ordine dello antico stato et governo."

manists had derived from their study of the classical world. Although the events of 1494 brought about the end of one era of Florentine history and the beginning of a new era, many of the aristocrats who had been prominent during the Medici regime continued to play a part in the government of the city during the republican period. These aristocrats remained committed to the cultural aims and achievements of Medicean Florence, despite the political upheavals of the last years of the fifteenth century. One of the best known political and intellectual figures in the Florence of Lorenzo Magnifico was Bernardo Rucellai, whose late wife was a sister of Lorenzo. Nevertheless, Bernardo Rucellai became involved in a conflict with Lorenzo's son, Piero Medici, and even contributed actively to the overthrow of the Medici regime in 1494. Yet Rucellai carried on the intellectual tradition which had flourished under the Medici. In the spirit of the Medicean Platonic Academy, which had ceased to exist after the events of 1494, Bernardo Rucellai opened his large garden to his aristocratic friends, to humanists and scholars who met there to converse, to exchange reports of newly discovered manuscripts, and to listen to readings of literary compositions.[40]

Even though many of the same men who had enjoyed the stimulation of the Platonic Academy assembled in the Rucellai gardens, there was an important difference between the gatherings in the Medici villa on the slopes of Fiesole and those in the Rucellai gardens. In the times of the Medici the conversations in the Platonic Academy had centered on classical philosophy and literature, and

---

[40] See my article "Bernardo Rucellai and the Orti Oricellari: A Study on the Origin of Modern Political Thought," *Journal of the Warburg and Courtauld Institutes*, vol. XII (1949), pp. 101-131.

their meaning for the present. In the discussions in the Rucellai gardens, which took place in the first years of the sixteenth century when internal tension in Florence was approaching a climax, two topics aroused increasing attention: history and politics. Just how important these discussions in the Rucellai gardens were for the solidification and the fortification of the opposition to the republican regime is indicated by Francesco Guicciardini's later comment: "the Rucellai gardens sparked the flame which burnt the city."[41] These meetings of the aristocrats and humanists in the Rucellai gardens gave the aristocrats the possibility of considering their practical demands in a theoretical context. The fusion of practical political issues and theoretical reflections on government forms the distinguishing feature of a work written in the last year of the republic: the *Discorso di Logrogno* of Francesco Guicciardini.

• III •

While the storm clouds were gathering around the Florentine republic in the summer of 1512, Francesco Guicciardini, the Florentine ambassador to King Ferdinand of Aragon, accompanied the court to Logrogno.[42] There in the ample leisure which he enjoyed during his rather futile diplomatic mission, Guicciardini's thoughts turned to the perplexing and disturbing problems of his native city, and he set down his ideas on the Florentine constitution

---

[41] "Di quell' orto, come si dice del cavallo troiano, uscirono le congiure, uscinne la ritornata de' Medici, scinne la fiamma che abruciò questa citta," Francesco Guicciardini, "Oratio Accusatoria," *Scritti Autobiografici e Rari*, ed. R. Palmarocchi, Bari, 1936, p. 230, but see pp. 229-231 for Guicciardini's evaluation of the political significance of the meetings in the Rucellai-Gardens.

[42] Concerning Guicciardini's life and career, and for literature about him, see the appendix.

in a long memorandum which, deriving its title from the place where it was written, is called the *Discorso di Logrogno*.[43]

Francesco Guicciardini was exceptionally suited to be a theoretician of Florentine aristocratic policy. Scion of a well-known aristocratic family, Guicciardini was familiar with the leading Florentine politicians; despite his youth—he was only twenty-nine years old when he wrote the *Discorso di Logrogno*—he had been initiated in the arcana of government. The literary work on which Guicciardini had been engaged before leaving for Spain—a history of Florence from the times of the rise of the Medici to his own days—is full of details about the political events in the times of Savonarola and Soderini, and his account corresponds so well to the documentary records that he must have received his information from the main participants.[44] It seems a sound assumption that he relied particularly for his information on his father-in-law, Alamanno Salviati, for whom he expressed deep admiration. Salviati had been instrumental in formulating the law which created the *Gonfaloniere a vita,* but then he had become a leader of the opposition against Piero Soderini who was elected *Gonfaloniere a vita.* Salviati's role in Florentine politics was carefully delineated in Guicciardini's *Florentine History*, which echoed the complaints of Salviati and his group that, to the detriment of Florence, Soderini disregarded the advice of the "wise citizens."[45]

Guicciardini's *Florentine History* clearly shows a bias

[43] Printed in Guicciardini, *Dialogo e Discorsi del Reggimento di Firenze,* ed. R. Palmarocchi, Bari, 1932, pp. 218-259.

[44] For a study of Guicciardini's "sources," see Nicolai Rubinstein, "The 'Storie Fiorentine' and the 'Memorie di Famiglia' by Francesco Guicciardini," *Rinascimento,* vol. IV (1953), pp. 171-225.

[45] For Guicciardini's views on Alamanno Salviati see Guicciardini, *Scritti Autobiografici e Rari,* pp. 66-68.

in favor of the aristocrats and demonstrates that Guicciardini fully shared their politcial views and aims. Another influence which Guicciardini frequently acknowledged was that of his father, Piero Guicciardini. He also was a prominent politician and he had been entrusted with important offices and diplomatic missions under the Medici as well as during the times of the republic. Piero was a cautious man and not always in agreement with the more partisan views of his son.[46] Piero belonged to the literary group around Lorenzo Magnifico and he was a friend of Marsilio Ficino, whom he chose to be Francesco's godfather. Piero saw to it that his son had a humanist education which was more thorough than that of the average young Florentine patrician. Francesco learned Latin and Greek. He heard the lectures of the well-known humanist Marcello Virgilio Adriani. He studied law in Florence, Ferrara, and Padua when humanist methods began to influence legal studies. In Padua Francesco lived in the house of Filippo Decio, one of the most incisive minds among the legal scholars of the time.[47] Thus the man who wrote the *Discorso di Logrogno* was a convinced adherent of aristocratic policy, and he was also a man conversant with the methods and ideals of humanism.

Ever since the manuscript of the *Discorso di Logrogno* was discovered among Guicciardini's papers in the last century, its importance for Guicciardini's political thought has been recognized. It was the first of Guicci-

[46] See Guicciardini, *Scritti Autobiografici e Rari,* pp. 57-58, 71-72, 280.

[47] On Guicciardini's legal education, see Paolo Rossi, *Guicciardini Criminalista,* Milano, 1943, pp. 19-30; and on Decio and his influence see Myron P. Gilmore, "The Lawyers and the Church in the Italian Renaissance," *Humanists and Jurists,* Cambridge, 1963, pp. 61-86, particularly p. 83.

ardini's many treatises on Florentine constitutional problems, and it was the one in which he stated his thoughts
most clearly and succinctly. Although some of his later
writings on this subject were more elaborate, he never
deviated in essentials from the ideas which were contained in the *Discorso di Logrogno*. However, the close
connection between the *Discorso di Logrogno* and contemporary Florentine politics has been generally overlooked. The *Discorso di Logrogno* was a reflection of the
debates and discussions which were going on in Florence
in the times of Soderini; it was a summary of the aristocratic demands for reform at that time. This is shown by
the general constitutional scheme which Guicciardini
proposed, as well as by his emphasis on particular issues
which had been objects of dispute in Florence in the preceding years.

Since the Great Council and the *Gonfaloniere a vita*
were the two constitutional innovations of the republican
era, Guicciardini treated them prominently and thoroughly. But instead of presenting a systematic explanation of the nature and value of these institutions, he
wrote about the practical effects which they had on Florentine politics.

Guicciardini's discussion of the Great Council focussed on the crucial role which it had in the filling of
executive offices. His aristocratic proclivity is reflected
in his condemnation of the "ambition which had come
over everyone to want to have a part in all dignities."[48]
Political administration, he felt, required special talent
and knowledge which not everyone possessed. Moreover,

[48] "Una ambizione universale in ognuno a tutti li onori, ed una
presunzione di volersi ingerire in tutte le cose publiche di
qualunque importanzia," Guicciardini, *Dialogo e Discorsi del Reggimento di Firenze*, p. 219.

quick rotation of offices was incompatible with the continuity and steadiness required for the conduct of political affairs. Nevertheless, he was aware that, when the Great Council had filled offices by the electoral procedure, the outcome had usually been favorable to the aristocrats. Thus Guicciardini believed that although the *governo largo* could err in affairs which demanded discrimination and experience, the choices of the Great Council in electing officials were "not without reason."[49] Therefore, he favored leaving to the Great Council the right of filling the executive boards if this function were exercised by election. Guicciardini even recommended a further enlargement of the Great Council. Such a measure, instead of increasing the importance of membership in the Great Council, would actually diminish it; for obviously if the Great Council was enlarged, not everyone who was a member could possibly expect to enjoy the benefit of office.

Guicciardini's views on the establishment of the *Gonfaloniere a vita* also show his engrossment in the conflicts which were going on in Florence at the time of his departure from the city early in 1512. The law of 1502, which created the *Gonfaloniere a vita*, appeared to him to be fundamentally justified because life-long tenure of the office contributed to constancy in government. But like most of the aristocrats, Guicciardini disapproved of the independent position which Soderini had taken after he had been elected *Gonfaloniere a vita*. Thus, although Guicciardini favored the lifetime *Gonfalonierate*, he wanted to introduce some safeguards which would prevent the *Gonfaloniere* from achieving an independent

[49] "non sono fuora di ragione," Guicciardini, *Dialogo e Discorsi del Reggimento di Firenze*, p. 224.

85

position. In Guicciardini's opinion, the main source of Soderini's power was his complete domination over the Signoria whose quickly rotating members bowed to the experience of the *Gonfaloniere,* the one permanent official. Thus Guicciardini wanted to weaken the influence of the *Gonfaloniere* by blunting the instrument so useful to his ambition. The Signoria, according to Guicciardini's plans, should be denied the right of judging and punishing crimes against the state and it should be deprived of the functions of sending out diplomatic missions and of employing chancellery officials for such purposes—a barbed reference to the manner in which Soderini had used Machiavelli's talents in order to free himself from dependence upon the diplomatic reports of his aristocratic adversaries. Furthermore, Guicciardini recommended a change in the procedure of initiating legislation. The customary method was that proposed legislation was submitted to the Great Council only after it had been agreed to by the Signoria—including the *Gonfaloniere.* The latter's presence at these deliberations made him a decisive factor in stimulating or repressing legislative proposals. In order to break this stranglehold of the *Gonfaloniere* over proposed legislation, Guicciardini suggested that not only the Signoria as a whole, but also its individual members, should have the right to present legislation for the approval of the Great Council. Thus even laws to which the *Gonfaloniere* was opposed could come up for a vote.

Guicciardini's general approach to the constitutional issues in Florence—as his views on the Great Council and the *Gonfalonierate* show—was similar to that of most aristocrats: to shun radical changes, such as the elimination of the Great Council; but to reform existing institutions so as to make them more accessible to aristocratic control. That Guicciardini shared the views of the majority of aristocrats about how to remedy the constitutional problems in Florence is evident from his plan for a new institution which would take over the functions which he wanted removed from the Signoria, the Great Council, and the *Gonfaloniere*. He placed the greatest emphasis on the need for such an addition to the machinery of government: "Certainly one of the most important things in order to maintain true and full freedom is the existence of a middle link which keeps the ignorance of the masses in check and bridles the ambition of the *Gonfaloniere*."[50]

Guicciardini's "middle link" is almost identical with the council which the aristocrats had been advocating since the turn of the century and which finally they forced through the Great Council in the autumn of 1512 He called this "middle link" a senate—the same term used by the aristocrats to describe the new council which they advocated. The size, composition, and functions of the senate, which Guicciardini outlined, corresponded to those which the aristocrats had proposed. His senate was to have about 200 members. After considering carefully whether a one year term or a lifetime membership was preferable, he decided that senators should have tenure for life. In addition to 80 members elected by the Great Council, the senate should be composed of all former *Gonfalonieri* (that is, those men who had held this office prior to the introduction of the *Gonfaloniere a vita* in 1502—a group which therefore would slowly die out), all

---

[50] "È certo delle più importante cose a mantenere la libertá vera ed intera è questa che sia uno mezzo che regoli la ignoranzia della multitudine e ponga freno alla ambizione di uno gonfaloniere . . . ," Guicciardini, *Dialogo e Discorsi del Reggimento di Firenze*, p. 227.

former members of the Board of the Ten, and all former ambassadors and commissioners. Since some important and influential citizens might not be included in these categories, 30 additional senators should be elected by the Signoria, the Sixteen *Gonfalonieri*, and the Board of the Twelve Good Men. Guicciardini expected this senate to become "the steering-wheel of the city and the arbiter of everything."[51] It was to control foreign policy by means of its function of appointing all ambassadors and military commissioners. The members of the Board of the Ten, although elected to that office by the Great Council, should be senators. The senate was to debate and to pass all legislative proposals before they could be submitted to the Great Council; and the senate was to have full and exclusive control over fiscal legislation.

Gonfaloniere a vita, Senate, Great Council—these were the three essential parts of Guicciardini's concept of an ideal constitution for Florence. Yet it is not by chance that his constitutional scheme combines monarchial, aristocratic, and democratic elements, realizing, therefore, the idea of mixed government. By adapting his constitutional scheme to this classical idea, Guicciardini indicated that he was aware that single, practical reforms ought to be conceived as integral parts of a comprehensive organization which had a sound theoretical basis and corresponded to the best rules of politics. If the world of Florentine aristocratic politics, into which Guicciardini had been born and in which he had grown up, was one influence in the *Discorso di Logrogno*, the world of humanist thought, in which he had been educated, was the other.

Allusions to a classical concept, however, do not make

[51] "el timone della città e moderatore di ogni cosa," Guicciardini, *Dialogo e Discorsi del Reggimento di Firenze*, p. 240.

a treatise a humanist product and, indeed, the *Discorso di Logrogno* is very different from the usual political treatises written by humanists. The influence of humanism on the *Discorso di Logrogno* lies in the basic assumptions which stood behind the author's constitutional scheme. This can be elucidated only by a brief analysis of the nature of humanist political writings.

The primary concern of the humanists was the revival of rhetorics—a discipline which had flourished in antiquity. Since the ultimate purpose of rhetorics had been to show how ethical norms could be applied to human behavior, the humanists tried to present the doctrines of great philosophers and writers in a comprehensible way so that men would be inspired to live and act in accordance with them. The works of the humanists were, therefore, of an imitative nature; it was not their intention to propound a new philosophy or to reveal new wisdom. In form and content the humanists borrowed freely from the ancients. Their political writings, which were designed to demonstrate the necessity of following ethical rules in practical politics, were essentially restatements of classical ideas clothed in modern dress.

Three themes appear most prominently in the humanist writings on politics. The concern with ethical norms for social behavior is clearly expressed in treatises which, in character, resemble the medieval "Mirror of Princes," but which, in content, reflect the humanists' propensity for incorporating classical ethical values into the traditional Christian scheme, as well as their awareness of the diffusion of public responsibility in the Italian city-state.[52] Thus the humanists wrote not only about "the

---

[52] See my article "The Humanist Concept of the Prince and 'The Prince' of Machiavelli," *Journal of Modern History*, vol. XI

good prince," but also on "the good citizen" and "true nobility."[53] The example of Petrarch, who wrote on the "ideal prince," was followed by most of the well-known humanists—Poggio, Pontano, Ficino. In their treatment of this theme, they used a somewhat standard method which consisted of enumerating the cardinal virtues and of demonstrating the advantages which would accrue to everyone if rulers and citizens possessed these virtues and acted according to them.

Another type of humanist political literature owed its origin to the imitation of classical utopias, such as those of Plato and Cicero. The humanists wrote books on "the ideal government,"[54] or, more specifically, on the "best monarchy" or the "best republic"; or sometimes they made a "comparison between republic and monarchy."[55] Because in their political writings the humanists placed a particular cause—monarchy or republic—in relation to the general good which was undisputed and permanent, they seldom came into contact with issues that required expression of a personal choice or conviction. Patricius, for example, could write about the "best republic" as well as about the "best monarchy."[56]

(1939), pp. 449-483; the references to literature, given in this article, make extensive bibliographical data here unnecessary.

[53] For the themes treated in humanist political writings the old work by Cavalli, "La scienza politica in Italia," *Memorie dell'-Istituto Veneto*, vol. XI (1862), pp. 405-433, XII (1864), pp. 127-143, 289-314, 481-504; XIII (1866), pp. 5-26, 233-272, 333-367 provides a useful survey.

[54] For instance, Filippus Beroaldus, "De optimo statu libellus," *Varia Opuscula*, Basilea, 1515, pp. 123-133.

[55] Lippus Brandolinus, "De comparatione Rei publicae et Regni," published in *Irodalomtörténeti Emlékek*, vol. II, Budapest, 1890.

[56] Francesco Patricius, *De institutione Rei Publicae* and *De regno et regis institutione;* Platina wrote a treatise on *De Principe* (dedicated to Federigo Gonzaga) and *De optimo Cive* (dedicated to

Still another type of humanist political writing was the panegyric, adopted from the classical pattern. The humanists wrote about single city-states, describing their constitutions and their political achievements. In the times of the conflict between Florence and Milan at the beginning of the fifteenth century, two famous treatises of this kind were written by Loschi and Salutati, the former praising Milan, the latter extolling the pre-eminence of Florence.[57] These treatises frequently served the purpose of propaganda; often they were commissioned, or sometimes they were written in the hope of gaining the favor of a ruler or a government.

In contrast to the view of earlier scholars, who regarded these treatises of the humanists as purely rhetorical exercises, recent scholars stress the close connection of the humanist political literature with the political problems of the times in which they were written.[58] The space

---

Lorenzo de' Medici), the two works being of partly identical contents, see Giacento Gaida's introduction to "Platynae Historici liber de vita Christi ac omnium pontificum" in Muratori, *Rerum Italicarum Scriptores,* nuova edizione, vol. III, part I, p. XXIX.

[57] See Hans Baron, *Humanistic and Political Literature in Florence and Venice,* Cambridge, 1955, particularly chapter II. A later praise of Milan is that of Pier Candido Decembrio, "De Laudibus Mediolanensium urbis panegyricus," *Archivio Storico Lombardo,* serie Quarta, vol. VIII (1907), pp. 27-45; but almost every city had a humanistic laudatio: for instance Padua by Michele Savonarola, Bologna by Garzoni (both printed by Muratori, *Rerum Italicarum Scriptores,* nuova edizione, vol. XXIV, Parte XV and vol. XXI (1733), pp. 1143-1168). Contarini's *De magistratibus et Republica Venetorum* is, in certain respects, a continuation of this genre although the character has changed because of his adoption of a much more concrete and practical political approach. Among the many 15th century praises of Venice, Francisci Nigri *De aristocratia,* Ms. Bibl. Marc., Cl. VI, No. 6, 2753, represents an interesting combination of laudatio and political theory

[58] I refer particularly to the works of Hans Baron and E. Garin.

which Patricius gave to a careful discussion of the advantages and disadvantages of the alternative methods of filling offices by election or by lot was certainly inspired by the role of this issue in his own time.[59] Lippus Brandolini showed remarkable insight in the peculiar nature of the Italian city-state when he rejected the traditional classical notion of the inferior social position of the business man; Brandolini emphasized the necessity of giving the merchant a leading role in politics and praised his ability in the handling of political affairs.[60] The mention which many humanists made of the valor of the citizen army of the ancient world is a pointed comment on the defects of the system, customary in their own times, of hiring a condottiere and mercenaries.[61]

Despite references to the existing political problems, the humanists did not advocate, in their writings, measures which might reform the political situation. The panegyrics of the individual city-states were typical of this limitation. The humanists did not analyze the institutions of the city which they praised; instead the humanists just listed them and labelled them with classical terms. For instance, Leonardo Bruni Aretino, whose treatise praising Florence is one of the least rhetorical panegyrics, ascribed to the captains of the *Parte Guelfa* the same function as had the *Areopagoi* in Athens or the

---

[59] Franciscus Patricius, *De institutione Rei Publicae*, Argentinae, 1594, p. 123.

[60] Lippus Brandolinus, *op. cit.*, p. 163: "Si nostrarum civitatum senatus videres, aliter profecto sentires. Tanta enim est in viris illis gravitas, tanta prudentia, tantus usus, tanta facundia, tanta etiam doctrina ut cum in senatu sunt mercaturae nunquam operam dedisse viderentur, sed Romanam illam in dicendis sententiis et copiam et gravitatem referunt."

[61] See now C. C. Bayley, *War and Society in Renaissance Florence,* Toronto, 1961, particularly pp. 219-240.

Ephori in Sparta;[62] if this characterization of the captains of the *Parte Guelfa* was meant to be more than flattery, it would show a singular lack of understanding for the role of the *Parte Guelfa*. The humanists were content to write about human society as it ought to be; they never made a systematic attempt to show how the real world could be transformed into the ideal world which they described. Palmieri illustrated the method the humanists used in their search for a perfect society by referring to the story of Zeuxis' procedure for choosing a suitable model for his portrait of Helen of Troy. The Greek painter assembled the five most beautiful women of his time and selecting from each of them her most perfect feature, he fashioned a portrait of composite beauty.[63] The humanists selected from countries and cities, all over the globe past and present, the customs, institutions, and offices which they regarded as most nearly perfect and worthy of imitation. Combining these diverse and varied customs and institutions, they constructed what they believed to be an ideal government.[64] Naturally this ideal government could never become a reality because it was a composite of incompatibilities. In the writings of the humanists on politics the world of political practice and the world of political theory remained far apart.

Nevertheless, humanist thinking on politics implied

[62] "Quod igitur Romae censores, Athenis areopagitae, Lacedaemoniae ephori, hoc sunt in Florentina civitate Guelforum duces," Bruni, "Laudatio Florentinae Urbis," *Beiträge zur Geschichte und Literatur der Italienischen Gelehrtenrenaissance*, ed. Th. Klette, vol. II, Greifswald, 1889, p. 102. On Bruni's "Laudatio," its text and its relation to works of the same genre, see Hans Baron, *The Crisis of the Early Italian Renaissance*, Princeton, 1955, particularly Chapters IX and X.

[63] Matteo Palmieri, *Libro della Vita Civile*, edition of 1529, p. 57.

[64] The above-mentioned writings of Patricius provide typical examples of this method of procedure.

the use of concepts and methods which could be shaped into instruments for the development of a more realistic political theory. As Palmieri's reference to Zeuxis shows, the humanists pointed to the need for a comprehensive knowledge of different political organizations which had existed in other times and at other places. In modern terminology, the humanists suggested a comparative method, and their writings, presenting the political facts which were contained in classical writings, provided the material on which such a method could be based.

Moreover, although political utopias might be impossible to realize, the concepts which underlie utopian political thinking have their practical value. Since a political utopia outlines a political order in its totality, the mind is forced to see beyond single issues and institutions and to view the organization of government as a coherent whole.

Finally, in accordance with the general principles of humanist philosophy, the humanist political writings emphasized the influence of man's power in forming political institutions. The humanists stressed the importance of the role of state-founders and law-givers—Lycurgus, Solon, Minos, Rhadamantes.[65] Because to us these figures are purely mythical or enveloped in shades of uncertainty, we are inclined to regard references to them as rhetorical flourishes. But to the men of the early sixteenth century these state-founders were historical figures who bore the same reality as Scipio, Brutus, or Florence's Messer Buondelmonte, and they were counted among the heroes in history because they demonstrated man's control over his social institutions. The state-founders and law-givers offered concrete proofs of man's creative ability in the world of politics.

[65] For instance, Patricius, *De institutione Rei Publicae*, p. 9.

The suppositions of the utopian and rhetorical humanist treatises on politics—the relevance of classical political
experiences to sixteenth-century politics, the conviction
of the man-made nature of political institutions, the conception of political order as a unit comprising the totality of society—were also those of Guicciardini's *Discorso
di Logrogno:* theoretical validity was given to the aristocrats' political program. In the *Discorso di Logrogno,*
he placed his suggestions for reforms in the framework
of a systematic and comprehensive examination of the
laws and institutions of Florence. Rather than merely rec-
ommending the introduction of a few laws which would
eliminate the most obvious weaknesses of the prevailing
government, he proceeded more radically. "To put
everything together in one heap and to give form to this
mass and to reshape it and dissect it in the way a baker
treats flour."[66] Thus Guicciardini believed that man could
fashion, according to his will, the society in which he
lived. His references to the great law-givers of antiquity indicate that, like the humanists, he regarded these
ancient heroes as historical figures. Like the humanists,
too, Guicciardini considered that the exercise of man's
creative powers in politics required a knowledge of how
other governments functioned. For the *Discorso di Logrogno* Guicciardini drew from the rich materials of ancient history, from the political experiences of Athens,
Sparta, Rome, and Carthage.[67]

The important difference, however, between the usual

---

[66] "fare uno cumulo di ogni cosa e ridurre tutta questa massa in
una materia, e di poi riformarla e ridistinguerla tutta a uso di chi fa
cose da mangiare di pasta," Guicciardini, *Dialogo e Discorsi del
Reggimento di Firenze*, p. 219.

[67] For instance, Guicciardini, *Dialogo e Discorsi del Reggimento
di Firenze*, pp. 221 et seq.

humanist political treatises and the *Discorso di Logrogno* was that Guicciardini always kept firmly in his mind the actual conditions which existed in Florence. For instance, he was aware that the situation in Florence determined the types of reforms which were possible or necessary. Florence was not an island, but rather was surrounded by states competing for power. "If force could destroy her [the city], it would not be enough that it was well organized in the interior and lived according to reason."[68] Guicciardini considered a military organization which would enable the city to defend itself as a prerequisite to any reform.

Moreover, Guicciardini was conscious that if reforms were to have practical value, the nature of the human beings who belonged to this body politic had to be taken into account. In contrast to the humanists' conviction of the ideality of classical antiquity, Guicciardini assumed that the men and institutions of the past had not been—any more than those of his own time—perfect. Critically examining the nature and function of classical institutions, he was selective in the choice of those he found worth imitating. The existence of particular laws or institutions in classical times was not in itself a proof of their exemplary value; the question which concerned Guicciardini was how they had functioned and what effects they had had. The standard according to which political institutions were to be gauged was that of rational efficiency.

This criterion runs through the entire *Discorso di Logrogno;* it can be characterized as an examination of

---

[68] "non basterebbe che la fussi ordinata bene drento e vivessi con la ragione, se la forza la potessi soprafare," Guicciardini, *Dialogo e Discorsi del Reggimento di Firenze,* p. 220.

the existing Florentine political institutions from the point of view of how and to what extent they corresponded to the purposes for which they had been established. Guicciardini wanted to eliminate, because it was "a useless thing,"[69] the customary method of having on each executive board, an equal number of members from each quarter of the city. He reasoned that by following this traditional method of proportioning offices a less able man might hold office only because a more suitable candidate came from a quarter whose quota was already filled. This method diminished efficiency.

Even Guicciardini's fundamental concern—the re-establishment of aristocratic control in the government—was presented as a demand of rational efficiency. In outlining the manner in which his proposed senate should be formed, he explained that a good government depended on utilizing the experience and knowledge of former high officials. Since most of these former office holders were aristocrats, the partisan political aim of joining them in a senate was evident, but this suggestion was enveloped in the general principle of rational efficiency.[70] When Guicciardini discussed the role which the aristocrats ought to have in the affairs of government he referred not to inherited rights or status but to the special contribution which they could make to the society. The aristocrats were men of ambition, and unlike most of his contemporaries, Guicciardini counted ambition as a virtue. Thus the aristocrats added to political life a psychological qual-

---

[69] "cosa inetta," Guicciardini, *Dialogo e Discorsi del Reggimento di Firenze*, p. 247; see also p. 120.

[70] "Acciò che le resoluzione importanti si faccino per mano di chi sappi ed intenda," Guicciardini, *Dialogo e Discorsi del Reggimento di Firenze*, p. 241, but see in general pp. 240-243.

ity which, as Guicciardini believed, the other groups of society lacked.[71]

At the beginning of the sixteenth century Florentine politicians, as we have seen, argued about politics in two different ways. The one way was to "go back to the principles" and to justify political demands by stating that their fulfillment would restore the political order which had existed at the time of the foundation of the city-state and corresponded, therefore, to God's will. This argumentation from tradition prevailed in discussions on politics. However, another method of reasoning about politics could also be noticed; and it was employed with increasing frequency. A government ought to be organized on the basis of practical experience, historical knowledge, and human wisdom. This second way of reasoning about politics was used consistently—almost exclusively—by Guicciardini in his *Discorso di Logrogno*.

However, traces of argumentation from tradition can be found in the *Discorso di Logrogno*. Guicciardini acknowledged that freedom was the soul of the Florentine city-state and that the all-embracing purpose of government was the maintenance of justice. However, in the context of the *Discorso di Logrogno*, this recognition of traditional values carried little weight. Guicciardini indicated that he believed that freedom was attained when the citizens lived in security under laws, and he regarded justice not as an all-inclusive task, but as one among the many functions of government. Although he intended to preserve a republican form of government in Florence, he implied that he did not consider this form of government to be sacred. Rather he argued that it would be dif-

[71] See note 35 of Chapter I, but also Guicciardini, *Dialogo e Discorsi del Reggimento di Firenze*, pp. 227, 250, 251.

ficult to introduce any other type of government because the citizens had become accustomed to a republic.[72] Moreover, only a republic provided the opportunity for the development of the particular talents of the aristocrats —talents needed by a well-organized government.[73] In defending the republican form of government, Guicciardini used a rational justification based on practical requirements demanded by the special situation of Florence.

The *Discorso di Logrogno* is significant as one of the earliest, if not the first comprehensive literary work, in which reasoning about politics is systematically based on the criterion of rational efficiency. The extent to which such political argumentation gained acceptance is shown by its use in a number of memoranda that were written by Florentine aristocrats shortly after Guicciardini wrote the *Discorso di Logrogno*. Indeed the use of the criterion of rational efficiency by these authors—Lodovico Alamanni, Niccolò Guicciardini, Alessandro Pazzi—indicates the hold which this method of argumentation had, because the authors were concerned with political problems far different from those which had occupied Francesco Guicciardini. The political situation in Florence had changed completely. When these memoranda were written, the Medici once again ruled the city.

---

[72] "Né accade disputare quale sia migliore amministrazione o di uno o di pochi o di molti, perché la libertá è propria e naturale della cittá nostra. In quella sono vivuti e'passati nostri, in quella siamo nutriti noi . . . ," Guicciardini, *Dialogo e Discorsi del Reggimento di Firenze*, p. 223.

[73] "E adunche bene per eccitare questa onesta ambizione nelli spiriti grandi e dare loro occasione di operare cose gloriose, mostrare questo luogo e questa commoditá di potere venire a uno grado che non può essere maggiore in una cittá libera; gli altri meno generosi e di minore ingegno o sufficienza assai si riscalderanno colla speranza delli altri magistrati e degnità, . . . ," Guicciardini, *Dialogo e Discorsi del Reggimento di Firenze*, p. 239.

In November 1512 the Medici returned to power to Florence, abolished the Great Council, and restored the system of government which had existed in the times of Lorenzo Magnifico. The aristocrats were in a squeeze; the great mass of the citizens held them responsible for the overthrow of Soderini and the fall of the republic, and the Medici did not fully trust them either. Thus they shared the Medicean unpopularity, but they lacked the possibility of being able to exert influence on Florentine politics. In this predicament the aristocrats disagreed among themselves. Some of them felt that the time had passed when an independent aristocratic policy could be successfully pursued, but other aristocrats kept to their old goal: to be the "steering wheel" of Florentine politics. But whereas in the republican period the aristocrats had viewed the extensive functions of the Great Council as the main obstacle to their ambitions, they now saw that the unlimited powers of the Medici stood in the way of achieving their aims.[74]

Thus some of the aristocrats tried to persuade the Medici that in the interests of a stable government, their regime should be broadened; in particular, these aristocrats advocated the reopening of the Great Council. If this were done the aristocrats hoped that they could gain a commanding position by acting as mediators between the Medici and the bulk of the citizens. It is interesting and characteristic that although their recommendations were

[74] For details about the Medici restoration see the following chapter pp. 131 et seq. The changed situation in Florence is reflected in minor modifications which Guicciardini made in his plans for a constitutional reform of Florence. Whereas in his earlier *Discorso di Logrogno* the Great Council was to have no part in tax legislation, in his later *Dialogo del Reggimento di Firenze* the Great Council was to have a very limited part in determining tax legislation, see pp. 231-232, and p. 129.

changed to fit the altered situation, the advice which these aristocrats—for instance, Niccolò Guicciardini, and Alessandro Pazzi—tendered the Medici was again presented as corresponding to the requirements of a well-organized government. Also, in their efforts to give their suggestions theoretical validity they employed the same methods of argumentation which Francesco Guicciardini had used in the *Discorso di Logrogno*.

These aristocratic writers rejected the notion that there existed one perfect political order which fitted every society throughout all the ages.[75] The form of government which had been established in Florence at the time of its foundation, these writers held, did not have to be maintained as God-given and immutable. In Florentine history different periods could be distinguished in which different forms of government had existed. At times there had been a popular regime; at other times, an oligarchy. Therefore, these writers believed that one ought to examine all forms of government to discover which form had been most successful; thus one could organize the government of the present time according to this standard. Models for good government should be sought after not only in the past history of Florence; the experiences of antiquity should be studied as well. Yet these writers realized that "the ancient times of the Ro-

[75] "Discorso di Lodovico Alamanni sopra il fermare lo stato di Firenze nella devozione de' Medici," November 25, 1516, printed in Rudolf von Albertini, *Das Florentinische Staatsbewusstsein im Uebergang von der Republik zum Prinzipat*, Bern, 1955, pp. 362-371, particularly p. 368; then Alessandro de' Pazzi's "Discorso al Cardinale Giulio de' Medici 1522," printed in *Archivio Storico Italiano*, vol. I (1842), pp. 420-432; then Francesco Guicciardini, "Del Governo di Firenze dopo la restaurazione de' Medici," *Dialogo e Discorsi del Reggimento di Firenze*, pp. 260-266; then Niccolò Guicciardini, "Discursus de Florentinae Rei publicae ordinibus," printed in Albertini, *op. cit.*, pp. 377-394.

mans and the Greeks are no longer."[76] Thus classical patterns were to be used only with discrimination. They suggested that the events which preceded the end of the Roman republic might be more relevant, and therefore more instructive, to their own times than the achievements which had brought the Roman republic to the pinnacle of its greatness.

These writers discussed all the principal institutions of Florence. They felt such a comprehensive examination was needed because laws and institutions of a state formed an interconnected whole.[77] A city was a unit and they gauged the stability and strength of a government

[76] "Non sono più e' tempi antichi de' romani e de' greci," Guicciardini, "Del modo . . . ," *Dialogo e Discorsi del Reggimento di Firenze,* p. 274. See also Alamanni in Albertini, *op. cit.,* p. 366.

[77] Although an organic concept of political society was hardly new, such a procedure in describing the working of a government was regarded as novel, see the discussion on method by Donato Giannotti in his "Della Repubblica de' Veneziani Dialogo" completed in November 1526 (see Roberto Ridolfi, "Sommario della Vita di Donato Giannotti," *Opuscoli,* Firenze, 1942, p. 68). In Giannotti's dialogue one of the speakers says that Sabellicus' work on the Venetian magistrates "non è di molta utilità. Perciocchè ancora che egli racconti in esso tutti i vostri Magistrati, nondimeno egli non dipinge dinanzi agli occhi de' lettori la forma, la composizione, il temperamento di questa Repubblica." He receives the answer: "Voi non siete dal vero punto lontano. Perciocchè ciascuna Repubblica è simile ad un corpo naturale, anzi per meglio dire, è un corpo dalla natura principalmente prodotto, dopo questo dall' arte limato. Perciocchè quando la natura fece l'uomo, ella intese fare una università, una comunione. Essendo adunque ciascuna Repubblica, come un'altro corpo naturale, deve ancora i suoi membri avere. E perchè tra loro è sempre certa proporzione, e convenienza, siccome tra i membri di ciascuno altro corpo, chi non conosce questa proporzione, e convenienza, che è tra l'un membro e l'altro, non può come fatto sia quel corpo comprendere. Ora questo è quello dove manca il Sabellico. Perciocchè, avvenga che egli racconti tutti i Magistrati, nondimeno egli non dichiara come l'uno sia collegato con l'altro, che dependenza abbia questo da quello, tal che perfettamente la composizione della Repubblica raccoglier se ne possa." (Giannotti, *Opere,* vol. I, Pisa, 1819, pp. 20-21).

according to its capacity to harness all the available forces within it. Some of the writers elaborated here on the idea which Guicciardini had adumbrated when he had emphasized that the state ought to utilize the peculiar psychological quality which the aristocrats possessed—ambition. It was realized that the degree of concern for political problems varied according to the economic status and interests of the different groups of the population. Under a well organized and stable government, the psychological needs of each group of society would have to be satisfied.[78]

The idea around which most of the Florentine aristocratic writers of the early sixteenth century constructed their constitutional schemes was that of mixed government. In the history of European political thought from the sixteenth to the eighteenth centuries, the concept of mixed government had an illustrious career; it formed the basic pattern in every aristocratic political theory. But later political writers referred not to Florence—which had become the capital of a grand duchy under the Medici—as the embodiment of this idea of mixed government, but rather to Venice as proving the excellence of this kind of government.

The importance of the discussions and writings which we have just analyzed went beyond the interest which attaches to them in the history of the idea of mixed government. They reveal the emergence of a method of procedure which began to dominate the development of political thought. It was assumed that the institutions of society, as creations of man, ought to be subjected to

---

[78] See Alamanni, "Discorso," in Albertini, *op. cit.*, p. 369 on "satisfare . . . a tre sorte de homini . . ."; this idea was then later fully developed by Giannotti, etc.

rational criteria of efficiency and usefulness. It was no accident that this mode of political thinking was advanced by men who advocated the return to aristocratic political control in the Florentine city-state. Aristocratic government, by requiring a division and limitation of power, demands a greater degree of rationalization and cries out more urgently for theoretical justification than monarchy and democracy which, in keeping power unified in one place, appear to be more "natural" forms of government.

Chapter 3 THE CRISIS IN THE ASSUMPTIONS ABOUT POLITICAL THINKING

Man's approach to the issues of practical politics is dependent on his *a priori* assumptions about two questions: what man is able to do in politics and what he ought to do. The development which we have just analyzed—the gradual application of new criteria to the evaluation of the forms of political organization—was only one aspect of the far-reaching repercussions which the political struggle in Florence had on political thought. Another consequence is perhaps even more important: the change in man's basic assumptions about the nature of politics. It can be observed that men began to alter their views about the forces working in political life and to adumbrate new ideas about the aims of political society.

• I •

In analyzing the question whether men were changing their views about the forces which they saw working in politics, we might ask what they considered to constitute the presuppositions of political success.

Whom did the Florentines regard as great statesmen? What were the qualities which had enabled them to achieve their successes? An investigation centering on the opinions held about individual leaders reveals more specifically and concretely the changing views about the forces determining the course of politics than would a discussion of theoretical writings which, if they touched on the subject of political leadership at all, treated of it according to traditional literary patterns. The political personality who held the greatest fascination for Florentines of the early sixteenth century was Lorenzo Magnifico de'Medici. The return of the Medici to Florence in 1512, after eighteen years of exile, posed the question: was it possible to restore the system of government by which Florence had been ruled in the previous century? The motives and the actions of Lorenzo Magnifico, under whom the Medicean system of government had been at its zenith, became a topic of intense debate.

In the various political memoranda on the constitutional problems of Florence which were written between 1512 and 1522,[1] the evaluation of Lorenzo Magnifico and of his system of government was a principal issue. Lorenzo was depicted as the prototype of a successful statesman, and he provided an example which his descendants ought to imitate. In Lorenzo's case, as the writers of these political memoranda agreed, the question regularly put in

---

[1] The most important are the memoranda by Paolo Vettori, Niccolò Guicciardini, Lodovico Alamanni published by Rudolf von Albertini, *Das Florentinische Staatsbewusstsein im Uebergang von der Republik zum Prinzipat*, Bern, 1955, pp. 345-377; Francesco Guicciardini's, "Del Governo di Firenze dopo la Restaurazione de' Medici," "Del modo di assicurare lo stato alla casa de' Medici," "Dialogo del Reggimento di Firenze," all published in Guicciardini, *Dialogo e Discorsi del Reggimento di Firenze*, ed. R. Palmarocchi, Bari, 1932; Alessandro de' Pazzi's "Discorso al Cardinale Giulio de' Medici," *Archivio Storico Italiano*, vol. I (1842), pp. 420-432; Machiavelli's "Discorso delle cose Fiorentine dopo la morte di Lorenzo." Niccolò Valori's "Vita di Lorenzo," printed in Philippi Villani, *Liber de civitatis Florentiae Famosis Civibus*, ed. G. C. Galletti, Firenze, 1847, pp. 164-182 also has political purposes although it is a eulogy rather than a political memorandum.

classical literature—whether a man owed his successes to personal virtue or to *Fortuna*—had to be answered that although *Fortuna* had smiled on Lorenzo, his personal qualities had been decisive. Success had come to him because he had pursued a wise and conscious policy.[2] These writers praised Lorenzo for the untiring energy with which he had devoted himself to his political tasks; but they did not ignore the dark sides of his regime. They mentioned that Lorenzo had used public money for personal purposes, but they excused him by explaining that the precarious political situation had absorbed him to such an extent that he could not give sufficient attention to business affairs.[3] These writers emphasized Lorenzo's "simple manners";[4] he had acted not like a prince, but rather he had exerted power within the existing institutional framework. Lorenzo's habit was "to deal with politics in the government palace, to come into the public places every day and to give a friendly hearing to all who came to him, to be an easy companion of the citizens, who saw him as a brother rather than a superior."[5] These writers represented Lorenzo as a leader who kept all groups of the population contented. "He tried to honor and please all citizens: to those who were well-born and

[2] See particularly Pazzi, *loc. cit.*, p. 423 on the part of virtú and Fortuna in Lorenzo's achievement.

[3] Pazzi, *loc. cit.*, p. 422.

[4] " . . . Laurentius semper intererat tam comis, et humanus, ut popularius nihil excogitari possit," Valori, *loc. cit.*, p. 177. On Lorenzo's "vita civile," see also Machiavelli's comparison of the older and younger Lorenzo in his letter to Francesco Vettori, February/March 1514 (*Opere* [Biblioteca di Classici Italiani-Feltrinelli Editore], vol. VI, p. 331).

[5] " . . . il tenere lo stato in palazzo, il venire in piazza ogni dì et dare facile audientia et grata a chi la voleva, l'esser familiare co' cittadini, faceva che a' cittadini pareva havere un fratello et non uno superiore et per questo più lo amavano . . . ," Alamanni in Albertini, *op. cit.*, p. 369.

powerful, he gave influence and recognition as far as possible."[6]

As these passages show, these writers were most interested in Lorenzo's domestic policy, and they were particularly concerned with the aspects of it which were relevant to the political situation after 1512. Their presentation of Lorenzo Magnifico's concern to maintain republican forms of life was meant to convey a warning to his descendants that they ought not to use their position to establish a tyranny. By describing Lorenzo as a *primus inter pares*, these writers expressed their disapproval of the behavior of the younger Lorenzo, Piero Medici's son and the Magnifico's grandson, who appeared in public accompanied by an armed guard, who conducted state affairs in the Medici palace arrogating the functions of the magistrates, and who made political decisions in consultation with only a small number of close friends.[7] The description of the rule of their great ancestor was intended to turn the younger generation of Medici away from the course towards absolutism.

The portrait of Lorenzo Magnifico delineated in these writings was a purposeful construction rather than the result of a search for historical truth. But it cannot be called an invention because it was the continuation and elaboration of a distortion which had begun much earlier. There is a long and tortuous story behind this glorification of the Magnifico. The view of Lorenzo's contemporaries about him had been very different, almost opposite to that of the aristocrats writing in the second dec-

---

[6] "Et tutti li ciptadini honorava et carezava, et a quelli che erono nobili et potenti dava authorità et riputatione quanto ragionevole era," Niccolò Guicciardini in Albertini, *op. cit.*, p. 354.

[7] For details about the policy of the Medici after their restoration, see below, pp. 131 et seq.

ade of the sixteenth century. Of course the humanists, poets, and scholars whom Lorenzo had befriended and patronized showered him with praise and adulation, but the Florentine politicians who had felt constrained by Lorenzo's political eminence judged him with marked reserve. They noted with approval the reputation which Lorenzo enjoyed among the rulers of Italy and the princes of Europe; it was a cause of Florentine pride to have one of their citizens called the "arbiter of Italy."[8] But even in the field of foreign policy, where Lorenzo's successes were most willingly acknowledged, they were ascribed to lucky circumstances—to *Fortuna*—rather than to virtue.[9]

Concerning Lorenzo's domestic policy, the judgment of his contemporaries was much more skeptical, if not entirely negative. Criticism of Lorenzo came not only from the disgruntled politicians who had been slighted by the Magnifico—from men like Rinuccini who called Lorenzo "a most pernicious and cruel tyrant."[10] Even men who lacked political ambitions complained in their diaries that Lorenzo acted like a "prince," and they applied to him the word "tyrant."[11]

[8] "Ogniuno lo predicava che governava l'Italia," Landucci, *Diario Fiorentino*, ed. Jodoco del Badia, Firenze, 1883, p. 65; Lorenzo's dominating role in Italy was emphasized also by writers who were critical of him, like Parenti, *Storia Fiorentia*, Ms. B.N.F. II.IV.169, f. 128r, or Giovanni Cambi, "Istorie," ed. Fr. Ildefonso di San Luigi, *Delizie degli Eruditi Toscani*, Firenze, 1785, vol. XXI, p. 67: "dava dipoi trachello alla bilancia."

[9] "Nell' altre imprese di fuori l'aiutò molte volte la fortuna. . ," Parenti, *op. cit.*, Ms. B.N.F. II.IV.169, f. 127r.

[10] "perniciosissimo e crudelissimo tiranno," *Ricordi Storici di Filippo di Cino Rinuccini colla continuazione di Alamanno e Neri suoi figli*, ed. G. Aiazzi, Firenze, 1840, p. CXLVI.

[11] As an example may serve Cambi, "Istorie," *loc. cit.*, p. 65: "perchè detto Lorenzo di Piero di Coximo de' Medici s'era fatto chapo di detta Ciptà, et Tiranno. . ," but also at many other places;

A Florentine aristocrat, Piero Parenti, who was no opponent of the Medici, has left a comprehensive and revealing description of the sentiments of the Florentines towards the Magnifico at the time of his death. Parenti did not deny Lorenzo's sensitivity to explosive domestic issues or his cleverness in handling them. But although these talents kept Lorenzo securely in power, they were not sufficient to make his regime popular. According to Parenti, the news of Lorenzo's death was received in Florence with mixed feelings. The great mass of the people were relieved because they had been heavily taxed by Lorenzo. For the same reason the middle classes were not inclined to mourn him. Among the great families, those who had been close to Lorenzo were apprehensive that they might have "to step down and perhaps lose their power"; the others, however, were optimistic because they expected that "the republic would again enjoy liberty and they would get out of serfdom." Thus, "actually the news was secretly welcomed by the citizenry although nobody dared to show it."[12]

When the arrogance and recklessness of Lorenzo's son Piero had brought about the fall of the Medici family, the regime was officially condemned as a despotism; because the time of Lorenzo's supremacy had always been regarded as the climax of the Medicean era, his reputa-

---

Landucci, *op. cit.*, p. 59, indicates that he regarded Lorenzo's building activities as "princely." The views of contemporaries about the tyrannical character of Lorenzo's rule are discussed by Joseph Schnitzer, *Savonarola, ein Kulturbild aus der Zeit der Renaissance*, vol. I, Muenchen, 1924, pp. 50 et seq.

[12] "E principali divisi infra di loro si vedevano: chi molto era intrinseco a Lorenzo e seco il ghoverno havea nelle mani, forte se n'attristò, riputando doverne abassare e forse perderne lo stato; chi non così era intinto e del carico del ghoverno netto, più presto se ne rallegrò stimando la republica doverne rihavere la libertà e loro uscire di servitù," Parenti, *op. cit.*, Ms. B.N.F. II.IV.169, f. 128r.

tion was altered to correspond to that of a typical tyrant. When Savonarola preached his famous sermon on the evils of tyranny, he described a tyrant as a person who rushed his country into war to maintain himself in power, who distracted the masses by festivals and spectacles, who built palaces for himself with the money of the city, and who corrupted the youth and had spies in the magistrates. If personally the tyrant appeared friendly and mild mannered, this, Savonarola said, was only a sign of his devilish cleverness; "he transforms himself into an angel of light to wreak greater damage."[13] The political practices which Savonarola described as characteristic of tyranny had been those of the Magnifico. Although Savonarola may have magnified Lorenzo's weaknesses, all Florence was well aware that fundamentally his picture was taken from life.

The denunciation of Lorenzo around the time of his death, and his glorification which was developed in the second decade of the sixteenth century, form sharp contrasts. This reversal of opinion was not sudden; the process of idealizing Lorenzo had set in around the turn of the century and had gradually gained momentum. From 1501 on, there are indications that the Florentines began to look back longingly to the period of Lorenzo Magnifico. Torn by inner dissensions and tumbling from one crisis into another, the Florentines began to see the preceding era in a rosier light. In September 1501 Parenti noted in his diary that disorder and tension in Florence led men "to praise the times of Lorenzo de'Medici; and

[13] "E però quanto il tiranno di fuori si dimonstra più costumato, tanto è più astuto e più cattivo e ammaestrato da maggiore e più sagace diavolo, il quale si transfigura nell' Angelo della luce per dare maggiore colpo," Savonarola, *Trattato circa il Reggimento e Governo della Città di Firenze*, Libro II, chapter 2.

many began to advocate a form of government similar to that of the Magnifico, and indicting the present they spread information among the masses about the pleasures of the past."[14] Parenti rightly suspected ulterior motives behind the insistence that the times of Lorenzo Magnifico had been a Golden Age of Florence. When Parenti was making these observations the demands of the aristocrats for reform of the republican regime had become intense, and the crisis had not yet been alleviated by the acceptance of the law creating the *Gonfaloniere a vita*. The aristocrats hoped to strengthen their demands for greater influence in the government by pointing out the beneficient effects of a government in which the majority of the people had had no power.

This new image of Lorenzo Magnifico and his rule dominated the discussions in the Rucellai gardens.[15] Humanists who frequented these gatherings wrote wistfully about the era in which they had enjoyed the protection and the favors of the Medici; they depicted it as a peaceful, orderly, and prosperous period in which art and scholarship had flourished. From this circle came also the first literary re-evaluation of Lorenzo Magnifico. The host of the group which assembled in the Rucellai gardens—Bernardo Rucellai—composed during the first six years of the sixteenth century a history of the French in-

[14] "Questo disordine faceva comendare e tempi di Lorenzo de Medici, et molti appitivano si tornassi a simile stato et seminavano per il vulgo la buona stagione preterita, biasimando la presente," Parenti, *op. cit.*, Ms. B.N.F., II.IV.170, f. 190v.

[15] See my article "Bernardo Rucellai and the Orti Oricellari. A Study on the Origin of Modern Political Thought," *Journal of the Warburg and Courtauld Institutes,* vol. XII (1949), pp. 101-131. On the political significance of the meetings in the Rucellai gardens, see also above, pp. 80 et seq., and on Rucellai's historical work see also below, pp. 258 et seq.

vasion. In the introduction to his work Rucellai dealt with the topic of Lorenzo's foreign policy, and his remarks, although brief, elevated Lorenzo to the rank of a great statesman. Rucellai tried to show that Lorenzo's successes had been due not to *Fortuna;* rather Lorenzo's foreign policy had emanated from a supremely intelligent, rational mind. His policy had been based on a proper understanding and a correct estimate of the working of historical forces. Moreover, his policy was determined by the pursuit of a constant principle: the idea of balance of power.

Rucellai's description of Lorenzo as the first great proponent of a balance-of-power policy and as the keeper of the peace in Italy made a deep impression, and soon it was taken up by others writers. However, as long as the republic lasted the evaluation of the personality and policy of the Magnifico remained a disputed issue. For instance, Bartolomeo Cerretani, a Florentine aristocrat somewhat younger than Rucellai, was completely convinced of Lorenzo's greatness. In his history of Florence, Cerretani elaborated on Rucellai's views, but he was aware that, in lauding Lorenzo, he might be accused of partiality. He wrote that he had felt bound to express his admiration for Lorenzo because "truth is the highest value in history."[16]

Thus when the Medici returned in 1512, the process of idealizing Lorenzo was well under way; the foundations had been laid for the writers of the second decade of the sixteenth century. But whereas Rucellai and others had

---

[16] "Saranno forsse alcuni che di partialità mi noteranno i' lodare . . . a' quali solo una parola vo' responbere, che la verità nella historia precede tutto," Cerretani, *Istoria Fiorentina*, Ms. B.N.F., II. III.74, f. 166r.

been primarily concerned with Lorenzo's foreign policy, the interest of those writing in the second decade of the sixteenth century was in Lorenzo's domestic policy. By the end of this decade all the components had been brought together for the construction of an integral picture of Lorenzo as a ruler who kept order in Florence and preserved the peace in Italy. Such a full-length portrait was executed by a Florentine aristocrat, Niccolò Valori.[17] A relative of the Medici, who, however, had lost their favor by his pro-republican attitude, Valori was anxious to return to their graces. Valori's treatise on Lorenzo took the form of an eulogium in which Lorenzo's virtues were exemplified by his life. Valori's account of Lorenzo's education and intellectual interests gave occasion to praise his piety and prudence; Lorenzo's attention to scholars and poets showed his desire for true fame; his behavior towards the Pazzi and his other enemies among the Florentines proved his magnanimity; in his negotiations with other princes, particularly with King Ferdinand on his trip to Naples, and in his relationships to others, Lorenzo displayed gravity and urbanity; his collections, his building activities, and the conduct of his household demonstrated his magnificence. According to Valori, Lorenzo's actions were not determined by personal whims, but in all affairs—foreign as well as domestic —he had shown himself to be guided by firm principles, a man of reason and moderation. Lorenzo had preserved the peace in Italy and he had fended off the possibility of foreign invasions by adhering to the idea that— and here Valori used Rucellai's words—"things must be

---

[17] On the probable date of Valori's piece—between 1517 and 1519—see my article "Guicciardini, Machiavelli, Valori on Lorenzo Magnifico," *Renaissance News*, vol. XI (1958), pp. 107-114.

kept in equal balance." In Valori's opinion Lorenzo had maintained political stability in Florence because he had exercised his power through the existing republican institutions, thus pleasing the people, and because he had allowed the aristocrats to share in the conduct of government. Valori's portrait combined the concept of Lorenzo as the advocate of the principle of balance of power, with which his idealization had begun in the republican period, and the concept of Lorenzo as *primus inter pares* which the aristocrats had developed after 1512. Valori had been a favorite pupil of Marsilio Ficino, and the Platonic image of the philosopher-king can be seen behind this picture of the Magnifico.[18]

Valori's synthesis of the previous evaluations of Lorenzo Magnifico was not the end, however; the climax was reached more than twenty years later with the characterization of Lorenzo in Guicciardini's *History of Italy*. This picture of the Magnifico—more than all others— has influenced the judgments on Lorenzo in the following centuries. Because of the importance of this presentation of Lorenzo, the process by which Guicciardini arrived at his evaluation must be described in detail. The gradual changes and developments in the views of the Florentines, which we have just analyzed, are mirrored in the successive writings of Guicciardini.

[18] See Alison M. Brown, "The Humanist Portrait of Cosimo de' Medici, Pater Patriae," *Journal of the Warburg and Courtauld Institutes*, vol. XXIV (1961), pp. 186-221 for the manner in which Lorenzo's grandfather Cosimo was eulogized. The fundamental features of these eulogies—patriotism, patron of arts and literature, philosopher-king—are the same, and also the method of tying the praise to the scheme of virtues is traditional, but for this reason the emphasis which in the eulogies of Lorenzo was placed on his role as balance-of-power statesman in foreign policy, and as primus inter aristocratic pares in domestic policy is significant.

Guicciardini faced the problem of estimating the political importance of Lorenzo Magnifico for the first time when, around 1508 or 1509, he composed a *Florentine History*. He devoted a long section to a characterization of Lorenzo;[19] it shows clearly the ambivalent attitude of the men of this period towards the Magnifico. Although Guicciardini recognized greatness in Lorenzo, he was critical, almost hostile. The characterization was constructed around two themes. The one was the problem of the nature of Lorenzo's rule. Guicciardini accepted the view which had prevailed since Savonarola's time that Lorenzo had been a tyrant, but Guiccardini added immediately that it would have been impossible to find "a better and more pleasant tyrant."[20] Guicciardini tried to substantiate this somewhat equivocal statement by examining Lorenzo's personal character. To what extent had he measured up to the recognized scheme of princely virtues and vices? Again the result was ambiguous. Lorenzo had been in possession of such virtues as prudence, liberality, magnificence; but they had been balanced by the vices of arrogance, cruelty, vindictiveness, and most of all, suspiciousness. Nor had Lorenzo avoided entirely the dangers inherent in the virtues he possessed. Lorenzo's liberality led him to take money from the city

[19] Francesco Guicciardini, *Storie Fiorentine*, ed. Roberto Palmarocchi, Bari, 1931, Chapter 9, pp. 72-82. Special attention to Guicciardini's representation of Lorenzo Magnifico is given in Vittorio de Caprariis, *Francesco Guicciardini dalla Politica alla Storia*, Bari, 1950; there on pp. 33-48 is an analysis of the Lorenzo portrait in the *Storie Fiorentine*. De Caprariis agrees that the Lorenzo-Portrait of the *Storie Fiorentine* is somewhat undecisive, although he attributes this to Guicciardini's literary immaturity and his polemical tendency rather than to the political situation at the time when Guicciardini was composing this work.

[20] "Un tiranno migliore e piú piacevole," Guicciardini, *Storie Fiorentine*, p. 80.

and to use it for his private purposes; his prudence bred such over-confidence that he embarked on the unnecessarily daring trip to Naples in order to reconcile King Ferdinand. Guicciardini recognized, however, Lorenzo's unusual intelligence. Evidently Guicciardini's aim was to present an independent judgment. He neither wanted to subscribe to the official view of Lorenzo as the embodiment of the evils of tyranny, nor did he want to idealize Lorenzo at the expense of the popular regime as did the more discontented aristocrats. But the result of Guicciardini's efforts to avoid the pitfalls of political prejudices was a compromise, not a new and original synthesis.

Perhaps because he felt dissatisfied with this evaluation of Lorenzo, Guicciardini remained fascinated by the man and seemed never to tire of discussing his personality and actions. In his *Dialogo del Reggimento di Firenze*, written in the 1520's, a principal topic was an examination of Lorenzo's system of government.[21] The dialogue is divided into two parts. In the second part, Guicciardini outlined what he considered to be the most suitable constitution for Florence. He presented here in a more elaborate form the ideas which he had developed in the *Discorso di Logrogno*. However the ease with which, after 1512, the Medici had discarded the influence of the aristocrats, had impressed Guicciardini and led him to suggest a slight strengthening of the power of the Great Council as a counterweight against the danger of absolutist rule.[22] In this discussion, he focussed on the particu-

[21] Francesco Guicciardini, "Dialogo del Reggimento di Firenze," *Dialogo e Discorsi del Reggimento di Firenze, pp.* 3-172; for the date of its composition—1521-1522—see Roberto Ridolfi, *Vita di Francesco Guicciardini,* Rome, 1960, p. 538; see also de Caprariis, *op. cit.,* pp. 69-85 for a penetrating analysis of the Dialogo.

[22] See above, note 74 on p. 100.

lar problems of Florence; he believed that it was fruitless to speculate abstractedly about perfect forms of government, and he drew a sharp line between what might seem just and right in theory and what was possible in practice.[23]

This outline of a plan for a good government in Florence is preceded by a long comparison of the Medicean system of government of the fifteenth century and the popular government of 1494. The second part of the dialogue—the presentation of a good government—was necessary because the comparison of the governments existing before and after 1494 illustrated that both had great weaknesses. The first part containing the comparison of the Medici regime and the government established in 1494 is certainly the most interesting[24] because it shows Guicciardini's attempt to shun preconceived ideas and traditional notions. According to Guicciardini, no government can exist without the use of force,[25] and therefore

[23] "Ma come si avessi a ordinare e fondare bene uno governo populare, non sarebbe forse difficile el trovare, perché ne sono pieni e' libri antichi di uomini eccellenti che si sono affaticati a scrivere de' governi, e ci è la notizia degli ordini e delle leggi che hanno avuto molte republiche, tra le quali tutte o si potrebbe imitare el migliore, o di ciascuno quelle parte che fussino piú notabili e piú belle. . . . Ma io non so se a noi è a proposito el procedere cosí, perchè non parliamo per ostentazione e vanamente, ma con speranza che el parlare nostro possa ancora essere di qualche frutto, . . . non abbiamo a cercare di uno governo immaginato e che sia piú facile a apparire in su' libri che in pratica, come fu forse la republica di Platone . . ," Guicciardini, *Dialogo e Discorsi del Reggimento di Firenze*, p. 99.

[24] This is also the opinion of de Caprariis, *op. cit.*, p. 81.

[25] ". . . tutti gli stati, chi bene considera la loro origine, sono violenti, e dalle republiche in fuora, nella loro patria e non piú oltre, non ci è potestà alcuna che sia legitima. . . ," Guicciardini, *Dialogo e Discorsi del Reggimento di Firenze*, p. 163; but see also the more famous formulation of this idea in the "Discorso di Logrogno," *ibid.*, p. 222: "Non è altro lo stato e lo imperio che

a discussion of whether or not a state is tyrannical is irrelevant. The only criterion which has to be applied is that of the effects which a government will have on the well-being of the community.[26] The efficiency of any form of government depends on the special circumstances which exist in each society; thus a discussion of the working of the government machinery in a particular political society is necessary. The criterion of rational efficiency which Guicciardini applied in the *Discorso di Logrogno* is in the *Dialogo del Reggimento di Firenze* explicitly stated and justified as the only valid method which might lead to practical political results.

By applying this method to an analysis of the merits and faults of the systems of government existing before and after 1494 in Florence Guicciardini concluded that the Medicean system of government was superior to the popular government. Therefore in his *Dialogo del Reggimento di Firenze* Guicciardini presented Lorenzo in a much more favorable light than he had in his *Florentine History*. He no longer held against Lorenzo the tyrannical character of his regime,[27] nor was he interested in Lorenzo's personal qualities—his virtues and vices. Lorenzo had taken great care to have justice fairly admin-

---

una violenzia sopra e' sudditi, palliata in alcuni con qualche titulo di onestá." For the meaning of stato in this period, see below, p. 177.

[26] "E però sempre è piú approvato e chiamato migliore governo quello che partorisce migliori effetti. Ed infine, discorrete quanto volete, bisogna, se io non mi inganno, ritornare a quello mio primo fondamento: che gli effetti de' governi sono quegli che danno la sentenzia," Guicciardini, *ibid.*, p. 41; but also p. 15: "a volere fare giudizio tra governo e governo, non debbiamo considerare tanto di che spezie siano, quanto gli effetti loro. . . ."

[27] See Guicciardini, *ibid.*, p. 25, where it is admitted that the Medici regime was a "stato tirannico" or also pp. 77-78, but the context makes clear that such a statement is rather inconsequential.

istered,[28] he had shown great intelligence and foresight in the conduct of foreign policy,[29] he had sought the co-operation of the aristocrats, he had left all others in peace, and he had tried to keep all groups of society contented.[30] Moreover, Lorenzo had been fully aware that his position, and that of his family, was tied up with the power and prosperity of Florence.[31] Expressing great admiration for Lorenzo, Guicciardini emphasized that he had never used his power for personal purposes—for the increase of his wealth or for the gratification of caprice and passion—but that he had followed a purely rational course, making his decisions according to what appeared to him best for the good of the city. Guicciardini had confidence in man's capacity "to eliminate, to a certain degree, the power of chance and fortune."[32] Thus, in order to make of Lorenzo an example which everyone ought to study, Guicciardini did not transform Lorenzo into a crypto-republican as had those who wrote about him in the second decade of the sixteenth century; Guicciardini adopted their positive view of the Magnifico, but in a new, purely political frame of reference. In evaluating a political personality, Guicciardini did not form his opinion according to religious and ethical values which could be applied to all fields of human activity. The measure of worth of a political figure was formed by his capacity to use the possibilities inherent in the political situation; politics had its own criteria to be derived from the existing political opportunities. Such views im-

[28] Guicciardini, *ibid.*, p. 56 et seq.
[29] Guicciardini, *ibid.*, pp. 60 et seq.
[30] Guicciardini, *ibid.*, p. 77.
[31] Guicciardini, *ibid.*, p. 73.
[32] "escludere quanto si può la potestá del caso e della fortuna," Guicciardini, *ibid.*, p. 61.

ply a growing realization of the autonomy of politics.

Guicciardini's final characterization of Lorenzo Magnifico in the *History of Italy* was determined solely by criteria based on political considerations. This portrait of Lorenzo has been called a "transfiguration,"[33] for here Lorenzo assumed almost superhuman proportions. This enlargement of the figure of the Magnifico resulted from the perspective into which he was placed. The stage on which he had acted was no longer Florence, but the whole of Italy. The function which he had successfully fulfilled was no longer that of governing a city-state, but of maintaining peace in Italy. Lorenzo's perception and insight had enabled him to understand that there could be peace in Italy only when "the affairs of Italy were balanced in such a way that no part had too much weight"; and Lorenzo had devoted himself "with the greatest diligence" to this aim.[34]

Guicciardini opened his *History of Italy* with this famous description of Lorenzo as the arbiter of Italy, and he returned briefly to the subject of Lorenzo in the fifteenth chapter of the same first book. There he wrote that the great esteem in which Lorenzo had been held during his lifetime "had been transformed into radiant fame, because with his death, the harmony and happiness seemed

---

[33] De Caprariis, *op. cit.*, p. 117: ". . . la trasfigurazione di Lorenzo il Magnifico, il quale, nel vestibolo della grande opera storica, si leva, dignitoso e solenne, a costruttore della pace d'Italia, interprete vivente di essa."

[34] "E conoscendo che alla republica fiorentina e a sé proprio sarebbe molto pericoloso se alcuno de' maggiori potentati ampliasse più la sua potenza, procurava con ogni studio che le cose d'Italia in modo bilanciate si mantenessino che più in una che in un' altra parte non pendessino: il che, senza la conservazione della pace e senza vegghiare con somma diligenza ogni accidente benchè minimo, succedere non poteva," Guicciardini, *Storia d'Italia*, book I, chapter 1 (vol. I, p. 3, in the edition of C. Panigada, Bari, 1929).

to have gone out of Italy."[35] The nostalgic tone of this passage seems to indicate Guicciardini's feeling that the period in which Lorenzo had lived was a thing of the past, never to return. The image of Lorenzo as it finally appeared here reflected the history of the early sixteenth century: it was shaped by the eagerness of the aristocrats first to discredit the popular regime, and then to constrain the absolutist tendencies of the Medici, as well as by the realization of the need for a joint Italian effort against the foreigners. The key to Lorenzo's successes in both domestic and foreign affairs, Guicciardini felt, lay in his mastery of rational political calculations; he was depicted as the representative of a policy based on reason.

But when one reads Guicciardini's wistful remark about the Golden Age which had existed under Lorenzo, it might be questioned whether the men of Guicciardini's time were completely convinced that a policy of rational calculations, in which Lorenzo had excelled, was at all applicable to their own time of rapid, unexpected, almost miraculous changes in the political scene. They had witnessed the sudden fall of Lodovico Moro, who had claimed to be able to move the European rulers like pieces on a chessboard, the brief and meteoric career of Cesare Borgia, the collapse of the Venetian domination over the *terra-ferma*, the *"Papa terrible,"* Julius II, who stubbornly pursued his aims against overwhelming odds and disasters, and the struggle between France and the Empire for hegemony over Italy, in which the pendulum swayed wildly from one side to the other. Political suc-

---

[35] ". . . dopo la morte si convertì in memoria molto chiara, parendo che insieme con la sua vita la concordia e la felicità d'Italia fussino mancate," Guicciardini, *Storia d'Italia*, book I, chapter 15 (vol. I, p. 88 in Panigada edition).

cess in the early sixteenth century appeared to have little connection with rational calculations. Thus the interest in Lorenzo, though originally inspired by a desire to find an example to follow, served now to bring into sharper focus the changed situation of the early sixteenth century, and to throw light on the qualities of leadership required by these new times.

The Florentines were deeply puzzled by the emergence of political personalities and leaders whose conduct did not correspond to their ideas of a policy based on rational calculation. The Florentines tried to penetrate the secret which could explain the success of actions which ought to have led to ruin. Their concern with this problem is evident in the reports with which the Florentine ambassadors followed the career of the *"Papa terrible."* Julius II was one of the demonic personalities of his age, who, because of the long duration of his political influence and activities, astonished his contemporaries more than Cesare Borgia or any other of the "dark heroes" of the time. A phrase which indicates the bewilderment aroused by the personality and actions of Julius II is to be found in a report of the Florentine ambassador, Giovanni Acciaiuoli, written in October 1504; he stated that in the Rome of Julius II things proceed "outside of all reason."[36] Because of the great value which Florentines placed on making political decisions according to reason, this statement was an expression of sharp disapproval. When Acciaiuoli made this remark Julius II had just succeeded in regaining for the Church State the territories of the Romagna which, when he had ascended the Papal throne, had been in the control of Cesare Borgia. The

[36] ". . . fuora di ogni ragione . . . ," A.S.F., *X di Balìa, Carteggio, Responsive,* vol. 80, c. 1.

impetuosity with which Julius had embarked on this enterprise and the obstinacy with which he had carried through this task had filled the Florentines with grave doubts about Julius' political abilities. They saw him falling into traps set up by his enemies, and Acciaiuoli had reported that the notion was widespread in Rome that Julius "had been a more successful cardinal than he would be a successful Pope."[37] The view of the Florentines was not essentially changed by Julius' success in rendering helpless and impotent within one year the feared Cesare Borgia. The Florentines remained skeptical about the political talents of the Pope; they saw his triumph over Cesare Borgia as the work of fortune, "outside of all reason."

Nevertheless, Julius' handling of the first great crisis of his Pontificate revealed to the ambassadors the exceptional situation in Rome under this Pope. The usual diplomatic methods of observation and analysis had to be modified and adjusted to the peculiarities of Julius. The Pope "determines everything and makes decisions without consulting anyone";[38] "by his nature he throws himself precipitately into decisions."[39] Consequently his future moves could not be deduced from a cool and rational weighing of the forces and interests involved; nor were the usual sources of information—the opinions of favorites, the talks with highly placed officials—of much assist-

[37] ". . . che Sua Santità in minoribus fussi stato più sufficiente Cardinale, che per molti rispetti non riuscirebbe papa," *ibid.*, vol. 78, c. 201 (May 24, 1504).

[38] "Sua Santità determina e fa le sue resolutioni sanza conferirle con altri," *ibid.*, vol. 85, c. 101 (January 30, 1507, from Francesco Pepi).

[39] "Dubita non si getti per la natura sua ad qualche precipitosa deliberatione," *ibid.*, vol. 85, c. 370r. (April 19, 1506, from Alessandro Nasi).

ance. In their reports the Florentine diplomats hardly speculated about possible divisions and distributions of interests. All the efforts of the Florentine ambassadors were directed toward providing a clear picture of the personality of the Pope. They have left a close-up of Julius II conducting diplomatic negotiations. When Julius encounters resistance, he changes his voice, looks grim and breaks off the conversation.[40] He immediately interrupts speakers who make statements with which he disagrees, if necessary with a little bell which he keeps on a table next to him.[41] Once the Pope has made up his mind about an issue, there is no use returning to it even if new arguments can be profferred.[42]

To the Florentine ambassadors, the personal inclinations and the passionate nature of the Pope were the only key to his actions. When negotiations with the French were in progress about the formation of the league against Venice, the outcome, according to the Florentine ambassadors, depended exclusively on the question whether the Pope's hatred for the Venetians would prove greater than his jealousy of the leading French minister, Cardinal d'Amboise.[43] Naturally the series of successes which Julius obtained—first against Cesare Borgia, then against

[40] "Volli replicare, non mi lasciò ma dixe: 'Andatevi con Dio' con tanta alteratione quanto dire si può. Andai subito. . . ," *ibid.*, vol. 106, c. 77 (September 19, 1511, from Pierfrancesco Tosinghi), but there are many similar statements, particularly in the reports of the Florentine ambassadors from the year 1511.

[41] "Interropto con la voce et col campanuzzo," A.S.F., *Signori. Carteggio, Responsive. Originali,* vol. 28, c. 121 (June 11, 1505, from Giovanni Acciaiuoli).

[42] "Sua Santità è di natura che malvolentieri se li può replicare, et ancora quando ha facto una conclusione si può con difficultà farlo ridire," A.S.F., *X di Balía, Carteggio. Responsive,* vol. 108, c. 81v. (January 23, 1513, from Jacopo Salviati e Matteo Strozzi).

[43] *Ibid.,* vol. 92, c. 63 (May 6, 1508, from Roberto Acciaiuoli).

the Baglioni in Perugia and the Bentivogli in Bologna, and finally in the League of Cambrai against Venice—began to influence the Florentine views about the Pope. The ambassadors felt there might be a connection between the single-mindedness and passionate energy which the Pope put into his political actions, and their successful outcome. But the view in which the Florentines had grown up—that cool reasoning alone should determine the actions of statesmen—had too strong a hold over them to overcome entirely the feeling that the Pope's apparent disregard for the prerequisites of a sane policy would once catch up with him and lead him into defeat.

The kaleidoscopic events of the last two years of Julius' rule stimulated a renewed examination of the problems raised by the Pope's conduct. When the French, Julius' former allies against whom he had suddenly turned, won the battle of Ravenna, Julius appeared to be powerless. All the doubts of the Florentines about the wisdom of the Pope's conduct of policy seemed to have been completely justified. The time for an abandonment of his willful enterprises and for the adoption of a sound rational policy seemed to have come. The Florentines, who were allied with the French, began negotiations to reconcile Julius with the French King. At first the Pope seemed to admit that he needed peace, although Antonio Strozzi, the Florentine ambassador, never felt sure that the Pope "said what he really meant";[44] he "is inclined towards peace not by his will, but only by force of necessity."[45] Upon the first slight indication that the French

---

[44] "e benchè me lo dicesse molto efficacemente, pure non se ne sta con l'animo sicuro se dice da vero . . . ," *ibid.*, vol. 109, c. 316v. (April 16, 1512, from Antonio Strozzi).

[45] "N.S. è inclinato alla pace più o meno secondo che la neces-

triumph was less complete than it had appeared, the hopes of the Pope revived; he began to use delaying tactics. To the Florentine ambassadors this was renewed confirmation of the Pope's obstinacy and of his lack of understanding of how politics ought to be managed. Julius was unable "to hear the truth and lets himself be easily persuaded that what he wishes is true."[46]

It was a great shock to the Florentines when again the Pope escaped paying the debts of his political sins. The French losses at Ravenna had been so severe that they had to withdraw from northern Italy; the control over the Apennine peninsula reverted to Julius and his allies. Now fear and awe filled the Florentine reports from Rome. The Florentine ambassadors began to dread negotiations with the Pope, who was again dominating Italian politics. The Florentines avoided approaching the Pope when he was rumored to be in a bad mood. They hesitated to make demands of which he might disapprove. They broke off the conversation as quickly as possible when the Pope got heated and excited. In order to explain their failure to advance the Florentine interests, the ambassadors gave detailed descriptions of the sudden bursts of anger into which the Pope exploded whenever he was contradicted.[47] The Florentine ambassadors had reason to treat the Pope gingerly. The whole of Julius' ire was now directed against the Florentines because

---

sità lo strigne più tosto che la volontà . . . ," *ibid.*, vol. 110, c. 65v. (May 10, 1512, from Antonio Strozzi).

[46] "Il che nasce per non intendere la verità et volentieri persuadersi quello che desidera esser vero," *ibid.*, vol. 110, c. 243r (June 3, 1512, from Antonio Strozzi).

[47] See the reports from January and September 1512, frequently discussing the "mala dispositione" of the Pope, *ibid.*, vols. 108 and 111.

they were the chief supporters of the detested French.

Yet the Florentine ambassadors were deeply impressed by the Pope's recent triumphs. Although the source from which his successes sprang remained incomprehensible to the Florentine ambassadors, they began to realize that his passionate pursuit of the objects of his desire and his reckless disregard for dangers and obstacles was a cause of his success rather than a liability. The Florentine ambassadors felt as if they were confronted by a volcano of great and hidden force, incalculable in its destructiveness. Thus the final word of the Florentine ambassadors was one of admiration. When Julius II lay on his deathbed the Florentine ambassadors reported that the Pope, in full knowledge of his approaching end, gave his last orders "with the same vigour as in the times of his health. He understands all issues and decides about them as if he were not ill at all."[48]

The change in the attitude of the Florentine ambassadors to Julius II—from arrogant disdain to reluctant admiration—reveals the uncertainties which the Florentines felt about their trust in reason, as well as their growing realization that other qualities were required of a successful statesman.

• II •

In these years, as men were altering their opinions about the qualities needed by a successful leader, there

---

[48] "Con quel medesimo vigore che è suto da sano. Intende, ode vede e giudica non altrimenti che se non havessi mal veruno," *ibid.*, vol. 108, c. 294v (February 20, 1513, from Jacopo Salviati and Matteo Strozzi); this report was written, when, after the restoration of the Medici, the relations between Florence and Julius II had improved.

was also a change in the views about the means by which man could control the course of events. Force, which previously had been thought to be just one of the several factors which determined politics, now came to be regarded as the decisive factor. To be sure, Florentine politicians had never been such visionaries that the importance of force in the political world could have entirely escaped them; but they had considered other factors, such as law and diplomacy, to be equally effective.

This notion—that politics was ruled primarily by force—emerged fully in the second decade of the sixteenth century. Whereas most of the aristocrats stuck to the idea that by acting as mediators between the Medici and the people they could become the "steering wheel" of the government, a certain number of aristocrats believed that all of the aristocrats ought to accept, without reservations, the leadership and the control of the Medici. The former group of aristocrats were mostly older men who had entered politics under Lorenzo Magnifico. The latter group of aristocrats, who favored submission to Medicean domination, were younger men, frequently the sons of the political leaders in the time of Lorenzo and the republic. Although certainly not all of the younger men abandoned the aristocratic camp for that of the Medici, all those who did were young; the split among the aristocrats corresponded to a difference of generations.

The younger men were the prophets of force. Their evaluation of its importance in politics was rooted in the events which took place in the years preceding the return of the Medici. Italian helplessness in the face of foreign invasion since 1494 had been an impressive demonstration of the decisive role of force in politics. The consequence of the Italian defeat was a mounting criticism of the reliance on condottieri and mercenaries. In their writings the humanists had kept alive the idea of a citizen army—because that was the method which Rome had followed.[49] An attempt was made to infuse greater strength into the Florentine military organization by putting into practice the idea of a citizen army. Machiavelli, then a chancellery official, drafted the law by which the population of the rural areas under Florentine rule was conscripted for military service. There was widespread recognition of the desirability and usefulness of such a measure. Guicciardini approved of it in his *Discorso di Logrogno*. Lodovico Alamanni ascribed, exactly as Machiavelli, "the present shame and serfdom of Italy" to the "habit of using mercenary soldiers"; "the Italians have forgotten how to carry arms themselves."[50]

Military strength became the chief criterion for judging the importance of another power. Machiavelli, reporting from Rome about the first months of the pontificate of Julius II, emphasized the Pope's political impotence because he had neither money nor soldiers.[51] But of the two elements which, according to the frequently used classical adage, a Prince must have—"iron and gold"—the gold became negligible; iron alone determined success.

The significant development which took place after

---

[49] See C. C. Bayley, *War and Society in Renaissance Florence*, University of Toronto Press, 1961, chapter 5.

[50] "Poco obligo habbiamo veramente co'nostri antichi, e quali, deviando Italia da' suoi buoni ordini, la ridussono ad governo di preti et di mercanti, et mettendo in uso la militia mercenaria, l'hanno condotta alla presente ignominia et servitu," Alamanni in Albertini, *op. cit.*, p. 372.

[51] November 11, 1503: "Non aver ancora nè genti nè denari conviene di necessità che giocoli di mezzo in fine," Machiavelli, *Opere*, Milano, 1805, vol. V, p. 52; the entire report on pp. 49-53.

the return of the Medici was that the notion of military force as the exclusive determinant in politics was extended from foreign policy to domestic affairs. Paolo Vettori, a young aristocrat, addressed to Cardinal Giovanni Medici, later Pope Leo X, a memorandum in which he wrote that, while before 1494 "your forefathers, in maintaining their rule, employed skill rather than force; you must use force rather than skill."[52]

The choice between two different modes of ruling, to which Vettori here alluded, had faced the Medici immediately upon their return to Florence, and it remained a lively issue in the discussions on, and the divisions within Florentine politics during the entire second decade of the sixteenth century. In September 1512, after Soderini had been sent into exile, the Florentine aristocrats took control of the government and tried to persuade the Medici to return to Florence as private citizens. The aristocrats hoped that the Medici would be content to live under the constitution which had been revised in accordance with the aristocratic interests. The youngest son of the Magnifico, the politically inexperienced and easily compliant Giuliano de' Medici, seems to have consented to this plan of the aristocrats, but the head of the family was his older brother, Cardinal Giovanni, and the final decision lay with him. Paolo Vettori and Giovanni Rucellai, both aristocrats of the young generation, rushed to Campi, a few miles outside Florence, where Cardinal Giovanni was staying, in order to convince him that the position of the Medici and of their adherents would not be secure under a constitution which, although it increased

---

[52] "Li antecessori vostri . . . usorno in tenere questo Stato piu industria che forza. A voi è necessario usare più forza che industria . . . ," Paolo Vettori in Albertini, *op. cit.,* p. 345.

the aristocratic influence, kept the Great Council alive. Cardinal Giovanni was advised that he should make use of the presence of the Spanish troops to make a radical change in the government of Florence. After the young aristocrats had presented their arguments, Cardinal Giovanni postponed a final decision until he had come to Florence, where he would be able to examine the situation more closely. There, the acknowledged leaders of the aristocratic faction, men of the older generation—Jacopo Salviati, Lanfredino Lanfredini, and Piero Alamanni—explained their views to Cardinal Giovanni; they told him that the Florentine people, after having tasted the pleasures of power, would never be satisfied without the Great Council. Thus the Medici would be secure only if they left intact the existing constitutional arrangements. In all probability these older aristocrats were sincerely convinced of the validity of their arguments, but their views were not unbiased. If their advice had been followed, the aristocrats, not the Medici, would have controlled Florentine politics.

However, the young diehards again exerted their influence—in the opposite direction. After deliberations which went on through day and night, the younger aristocrats won out. Bells called all the males of Florence to a meeting in the Piazza della Signoria; by order of the Medici, Spanish troops were stationed at the entrances of the Piazza. There, under the pressure of these armed forces, the people approved the decrees read to them: the Great Council was closed and the government of Florence was entrusted to a commission with extraordinary powers (*Balìa*) of forty citizens. The justification for these measures was stated in an official resolution: it was not possible "to preserve freedom and to remove all

obstacles to it without full, free, total and absolute authority and power."[53]

The division among the aristocrats, which had come out in the weeks after the overthrow of the republican regime, continued throughout the following ten years. The older generation of aristocrats never abandoned their hopes that they would be able to regain political control; and their hopes were never entirely quashed by the actions of the Medici. Although the manner in which the Medici had seized the government in 1512 showed their disdain for constitutional bodies, and although the Medici continued to rely on force, they did not establish an overtly absolutist regime. They exerted their power behind a republican façade, controlling the offices and councils in much the same manner as had Cosimo and Lorenzo. But the Medici of the sixteenth century did little to conceal the fact that distribution of honors and offices depended on their will. In October of 1512, the *Balìa* elected twenty *Accoppiatori*, mainly the heads of pro-Medici families.[54] Their chief task was to nominate the *Gon-*

[53] "Libertatem conservare et cuncta illi contraria amovere" is not possible "sine plenaria, libera, totali et absoluta potestate, auctoritate et balia," A.S.F., *Balìe*, vol. 43, f. 30r., September 16, 1512. I have given the account of the events, accompanying the return of the Medici to Florence, mainly on the basis of Cerretani, *Storia in dialogo della mutatione di Firenze*, Ms. B.N.F., II.I.106, ff. 148v.-154r. Cerretani is the best narrative source for the period of the Medici restoration, diarists like Cambi and Landucci give some interesting details; also Parenti, although, for this period, Parenti is less full than for the period before 1512. Nardi, *Istorie della Città di Firenze*, and Nerli, *Commentarii de' fatti civili occorsi nella città di Firenze dal 1215 al 1537*, were written two decades after the events, but contain information which cannot be found at other places. Of modern scholarly works, discussing the events of the Medici restoration, I refer to Anzilotti, *op. cit.*, Albertini, *op. cit.*, and to the Machiavelli biographies mentioned in the appendix.

[54] A.S.F., *Balìe*, vol. 43, f. 59r. (October 19, 1512).

faloniere and the other members of the Signoria. From the lists of candidates for offices, the names of all those who might be unfriendly to the new regime were removed. In the summer of the next year the basis of the government was broadened by the establishment of deliberative bodies: a Council of the Seventy and a Council of the Hundred, both revivals of councils which had existed in the times of Lorenzo Magnifico. The members of these councils were appointed by the Signoria, but since the Signoria, in turn, was appointed by the pro-Medici *Accoppiatori,* it did nothing but ratify a list of names of prospective council members which Leo X had prepared in Rome and had then transmitted to his nephew, Lorenzo, in Florence for further scrutiny.

Although the traditional executive boards continued to function, the members of these boards had been so carefully sifted that it did not make any difference whether the Medici made use of this machinery, or whether they commanded directly what they wanted to be done. The Florentines were not unaware that the magistrates and councils existed only to preserve the formal aspect of a republic. Niccolò Guicciardini wrote that "although the Medici did not abolish the Signoria and the other offices, all things which were of some importance were carried out according to the will of the Medici rulers."[55] People complained that all important business was transacted in the Medici palace and that the Palazzo della Signoria stood empty. Many of the aristocrats resented being used. "What value has it for a citizen," wrote

[55] "Et benchè el supremo magistrato et gli altri non levassino, pure tutti questi le cose che erano di qualche importanza facevano secondo la volontà de' Signori Medici," Niccolò Guicciardini in Albertini, *op. cit.,* p. 355.

Francesco Guicciardini, "to be nominally an *Accoppia-tore* if the whole office had not enough strength to appoint one single member to the Signoria of its own volition"?[56]

These aristocratic critics wanted the Medici to make concessions which would allow the aristocrats more influence in the government. But the Medici paid little heed to these warnings. The Medici had listened to those of the aristocrats who regarded force as the only guarantee of a stable government. Soldiers remained in the city and guards were placed at the entrances of the public buildings. Giuliano de'Medici had, upon his return to the city, shorn his beard, a sign of princely distinction, and mingled freely with the citizens; but Pope Leo X soon removed him from Florence and replaced him with his much more autocratically inclined nephew Lorenzo whose close friends came from the younger generation of aristocrats. Lorenzo wore Spanish dress and he kept his Spanish beard to emphasize his superior rank.[57] He was difficult to approach; people addressed him only with

[56] "Che conto ha a fare uno cittadino di essere verbigrazia accoppiatore, se in tutto quello magistrato non ará tanto caldo che possi fare uno de' signori?", Guicciardini, "Del modo di assicurare lo stato ai Medici," *Dialogo e Discorsi del Reggimento di Firenze,* p. 272.
[57] May 1515 "tornò da Roma in Firenze il Magnifico Lorenzo . . . venne colla barba lunga al viso," Parenti, *Storia Fiorentina,* Ms. B.N.F., II.IV.171, f. 115r. "Quando e' ciptadini andorono a far motto a Lorenzo a chasa, tutti gli facievano un poco di cienno di chapuccio, e dirivava da cierti sateliti, et adulatori, che gli mostravano reverentia: e tal cosa non fu mai fatta affirenze da ciptadino privato . . . ," Cambi, "Istorie," *loc. cit.,* Firenze, 1786, vol. XXII, pp. 49-50, there on p. 154: "tutti e' ciptadini dal maggiore al minore cominciorono a vestire nero . . ." Cerretani, *Storia in dialogo,* Ms. B.N.F. II.I.106, f. 170r.: "parve che [Lorenzo] fussi fatto signore al tutto e ciascuno dice: 'Signor sì' et 'signor, no,' traendosi ogni spetie d'huomo la berretta e'l cappuccio . . ."

their hats in their hands. There was no doubt that Lorenzo occupied a much more powerful position than any
previous member of his family. He combined the civil-
ian role of chief representative of the Medici family in
Florence with the military position of commander of the
Florentine troops. In order to prevent dissatisfaction with
the Medici regime from growing into an open revolt, the
Medici kept troops in the surrounding areas; military
strength remained their main support. Every set-back
which the Medici suffered—the French victory over the
Pope's allies at Marignano, the wounding of Lorenzo in
the war of Urbino—revealed the unpopularity of the regime in Florence: the frightened citizens closed their
shops, and the city was filled with rumors about revolution, but the military forces at the disposal of the Medici
were enough to keep order.

The procedures which the Medici used for ruling Florence strengthened the awareness of the differences between form and fact, between appearance and reality
in politics. Some of Lorenzo's friends among the younger
aristocrats began to regard discussions and speculations
about constitutional arrangements as little more than time-
wasting intellectual exercises. Lodovico Alamanni told the
Medici that they need not take the constitutional projects
and ideas of the older generation seriously: "They are
'wise citizens' and one does not have to bother much
about them, because wise men make no revolutions."[58]
The reasoning of the older aristocrats—that a broadening
of the government and respect for constitutional forms
was necessary because of the dissatisfaction of the masses
—Alamanni thought silly: "One needs to fear their votes

---

[58] ". . . e' sono savii et de' savi non si de' temere, perchè non
fanno mai novitá," Alamanni in Albertini, *op. cit.,* p. 370.

and not their arms; they put their main trust in miracles."[59] In the joy of having discovered in force the real key to the understanding of politics, traditional concepts were arrogantly shoved aside and the picture of politics became simplified to the extreme. It was a sign of the atmosphere which had been created in this time of sham constitutionalism that even an aristocrat who was opposed to Medicean absolutism, Francesco Guicciardini could write: "Every government is nothing but violence over subjects, sometimes moderated by a form of honesty."[60] The distinction between monarchy and tyranny seemed to him meaningless because force is an integral element of all political regimes.

A further logical step would have been to recommend to Lorenzo that he abandon all pretense of maintaining constitutional forms of government and base his regime exclusively on force: that he should become an absolute ruler. Guicciardini reported that "people have not been lacking who have believed and have tried to persuade Lorenzo that it would be safer for him and his adherents to take over absolute rulership in the city, in fact and in title, than to hold the government under some veil of republicanism and freedom." But Guicciardini shrugged off this idea with a brief remark: "Such a procedure would, in the course of time, emerge as being full of difficulties, of suspicion, and finally of cruelty."[61] Alamanni

[59] ". . . et sono da temere le loro fave et non le loro arme, et la loro confidentia è più ne' miraculi che in altro," Alamanni in Albertini, *op. cit.*, p. 366.

[60] See above, note 25 on p. 118.

[61] "Non voglio omettere di dire che non è mancato e non manca chi ha avuto opinione ed ha, e forse ha fatto opera di persuaderlo, che sarebbe più sicurtá di costoro pigliare assolutamente el dominio della cittá in fatti ed in titolo, che tenere el governo sotto questa ombra di civilitá e di libertá; cosa che io non intendo disputare

indicated as a possible course of action open to the Medici "to kill all those who might be able and willing to deprive them of their power." But Alamanni rejected such a brutal use of force out of moral considerations as well as out of concern for Lorenzo's reputation: "Killing citizens without reason and dipping one's hands into blood, I am sure, can never find the approval of Your Excellency as a courageous and magnanimous person. . . . You prefer to compete with Caesar and Camillus than with the godless Agathocles, the cruel Sulla and the vicious Liverotto da Fermo."[62] Alamanni's statements show that the enthusiasm for advancing extreme views in theory is frequently not matched by eagerness for seeing them realized. Moreover, in this period men had become conscious that traditional views about politics were deficient, and that a new basis for politics had to be found; but this was all. Men were still groping for a clear and definite formulation of their new insights.

At the end of the fifteenth century, the contrast between *ragione* and *Fortuna* had created different attitudes to politics. *Fortuna,* as the emissary of God, had

---

ora, ma io per me giudico che non potrebbono pigliare partito piú pernizioso e per loro e per noi, e che questo maneggio riuscirebbe nel processo del tempo pieno di difficultá, di sospetti ed a ultimo di crudeltá.," Guicciardini, "Del modo di assicurare lo stato ai Medici," *Dialogo e Discorsi del Reggimento di Firenze,* p. 281. It was widely said in Florence that Filippo Strozzi and Francesco Vettori, close friends and advisors of Lorenzo Medici, were pushing him towards an absolutist course; see Francesco Vettori's letter to his brother Paolo in Oreste Tommasini, *La vita e gli scritti di Niccolò Machiavelli,* vol. II, Roma, 1911, pp. 1066-68.

[62] "Il secondo modo dell'uccidere senza cagione e cittadini et l'insanguinarsi nella sua patria le mani, so che Sua Ex. tia come valorosa et magnanima non approverrà mai . . . vorrà più presto gioastrare con Cesare et Camillo che con lo impio Agathocle, col crudelissimo Sylla et con scelerato Liverocto da Fermo," Alamanni in Albertini, *op. cit.,* p. 367.

strengthened the feeling that man was in the hands of un-controllable forces; man's conduct of affairs ought to re-main within the God-given traditional framework. The opposing point of view was that man's reason gave him the power to shape the course of politics; by making use of experience he could impress efficiency and perfection upon the political order. But this latter view had hardly come into its own when political events seemed to dem-onstrate that reason was only one, and perhaps not even a very effective, instrument in the political struggles. This was the confusing and perturbing situation in which Florentines who thought about politics found themselves in the second decade of the sixteenth century.

• III •

The extent of the crisis in political thinking can be gauged from the deepening of the problem. The fore-most issue was, and remained, the form which the Flor-entine constitution ought to have, but men became aware that this was more than a technical question; it involved the problem of the intrinsic nature of a good society.

The person who was least worried about this problem was Pope Leo X, the real ruler of Florence from 1512 to 1521. Indeed, if the question of a good society occurred to him at all, he was satisfied with a clear and simple an-swer: he was convinced that the times of his father, Lo-renzo Magnifico, had been a Golden Age. Leo X was shrewd enough to realize that the rulers of Florence af-ter the republican interregnum would have to use more rigorous means to dominate the city than Lorenzo had employed. But fundamentally Leo X remained wedded to the political methods of the fifteenth century. This was reflected in his foreign policy, where he relied chiefly on rational diplomatic calculations and the balance-of-power game. Leo X recognized the need for force in securing the Medici rule over Florence, though he was not in accord with his nephew Lorenzo's ambition to become the absolute ruler of the city. Such a striking break with tradition did not appeal to Pope Leo. He considered the regime which he had established in Florence in 1512 as a restoration. An essential part of this policy was to recreate the style of life and the splendour which, it was believed, had flourished in Florence under the Magnifico.

With Leo's stimulus, patronage of literature, art, and scholarship again became fashionable among the great families. Such activities were considered a sure way of gaining Leo's favor. Some of the aristocrats, following the example of Lorenzo Magnifico and his friends, turned to the writing of verse, and to the composing of plays, which they had produced in their palaces or gardens. The meetings in the Rucellai gardens, now with a grandson of Bernardo Rucellai as host, had a new flowering and the visit of every prominent foreigner became an occasion for festivities and discussions.[63] As youths, Lorenzo Mag-

[63] The meetings of this period in the Rucellai gardens are usually treated in connection with the origin of Machiavelli's Discourses; see for literature the bibliographical appendix on Machiavelli. For a recent general treatment of the political significance of the Rucellai gardens, see Albertini, *op. cit.*, pp. 74-90, although, in my opinion, the relation of the meetings in the Rucellai gardens to Machiavelli and to the anti-Medicean conspiracy of 1522 has frequently led to an overemphasis on the political nature of these meetings and to a neglect of their literary character; moreover, it ought to be kept in mind, that only a particular group of "young men" was actively anti-Medicean and "democratic." Giovanni Rucellai, son of Bernardo Rucellai and friend Trissino's, wrote his tragedy *Rosmunda* in 1515/6. Lorenzo Strozzi, son-in-law of Bernardo Rucellai (on Lorenzo Strozzi see Francesco Zeffi, "Di Lorenzo Strozzi autore di queste vite," *Le Vite degli Uomini*

nifico and his brother Giuliano had dominated the social life of Florence by forming two companies of young aristocrats whose aim was to surpass the other in tournaments, processions, and festivals. Just as these rival companies of youthful aristocrats in the fifteenth century had expended their wealth, their wit, and their prowess in civic spectacles, so also the young aristocrats of the sixteenth century were organized in two competing companies, the one under the leadership of the younger Giuliano, the other under the younger Lorenzo. The ablest Florentine painters and sculptors participated in the arrangement of these civic displays, the most spectacular of which was the week-long festival in 1515 by which the Florentines celebrated the first visit of Giovanni Medici as Pope Leo X to his native city.[64]

It has been said that just as Lorenzo Magnifico had tried to seduce the masses by festivals and entertainments, so also his successors used the same means to console the

---

Illustri della Casa Strozzi, Firenze, 1892, particularly pp. XI-XIV, and Pio Ferrieri, *Studi di Storia e di Critica Letteraria*, Milano, 1892, pp. 221-332), wrote comedies which were produced before Lorenzo de' Medici, Duke of Urbino, and he was responsible for the famous 'carro di morte,' described by Vasari. Alessandro de' Pazzi, like Giovanni Rucellai a nephew of Lorenzo Magnifico, wrote tragedies (for literature on him see Albertini, *op. cit.*, p. 85). Luigi Alamanni (on him, see Henri Hauvette, *Un exilé florentin à la cour de France au XVI siècle: Luigi Alamanni (1495-1556)*, Paris, 1903) was a well-known poet whose first literary works were composed and read in the years of the Medici restoration. Jacopo Nardi (on him and on literature about him, see Albertini, *op. cit.*, pp. 306 et seq.) dedicated his comedy *I due felici rivali* to Lorenzo de' Medici, Duke of Urbino.

[64] The propagandistic impact of the spectacles connected with this visit is reflected in the long and detailed accounts which diarists from the middle classes provide, see Cambi, "Istorie," *loc. cit.*, vol. XXII, pp. 81-91; Landucci, *Diario*, pp. 352-359; Bartolomeo Masi, *Ricordanze*, ed. by Gius. Odoardo Corazzini, Firenze, 1906, pp. 162-176. In general, see the literature mentioned above, note 53.

citizens over their loss of participation in the government. It is certainly true that these shows served as propaganda, for they were the media through which the ideas of the ruling group were communicated to the masses. But these festivals were more than a means to an end; they were visible proof that the Golden Age of the Magnifico had returned to Florence. The Medicean idea of a secular paradise was a government in which the wise combination of reason and force would guarantee peace and order—requisites for the development of all human talents.

The spirit of this restoration found expression in the most brilliant of the processions arranged by the younger Medici; it had as its theme the triumph of the Golden Age. The song accompanying the procession alluded to recent events in Florentine politics, and while it sounded the famous motif of the power of gold and iron over human life, it suggested that the time of force in politics had passed like a bad dream:

"From iron was born a golden age . . . "

The procession was meant to convey the idea that the attributes of an ideal society had returned to Florence; in the procession were figures which symbolized peace and justice, religion and wisdom, strength and beauty. The first figures were Saturn and Janus, the rulers of the original Golden Age, with Fury tamed under their feet. Then came Numa Pompilius, the founder of religion and laws, and Titus Manlius Torquatus, Roman Consul at the time when Rome was at the peak of her power and virtue. Then came Caesar and Augustus, surrounded by the poets and writers who had given eternal fame to their reigns; and they were followed by Trajan as the embodiment of a just ruler. At the end of the procession, rising out of the back of a slain soldier, there appeared the Golden Age itself, personified by a young boy whose entire body had been gilded.

The procession was not exclusively tuned on a happy and optimistic note. Some lines of the accompanying song seemed to sound a warning:

"One age follows another in this world
And changes good in bad and bad in good."

Certainly the melancholic emphasis on the transitoriness of youth and life, and on the impermanence of all things human, was fashionable. But the gesture of tiredness which in the confident Florentine world of the fifteenth century was hardly more than a charming pose must have touched a deeper, more responsive chord in the sixteenth century. At least it was carefully noted that the boy who had represented the Golden Age died a few days later: the gilt which had been applied to his body destroyed his skin.[65]

To many Florentines these brilliantly colored and glit-

[65] The details about this "trionfo" can be found in Vasari's "Life of Pontormo" in Vasari, *Le vite de' più eccellenti Pittori Scultori ed Architettori* (*Opere*, ed. G. Milanesi, vol. VI, Firenze, 1881, pp. 252 et seq.). Jacopo Nardi is reported to have composed the poem:

"Couli, che dà le leggi alla Natura,
E i varj stati e secoli dispone,
D'ogni bene è cagione,
E il mal, quanto permette, al mondo dura:
Onde, questo figura
Contemplando, si vede,
Come con certo piede
L'un secol dopo l'altro al mondo viene,
E muta il bene in male, e'l male in bene."

and later: "Così nasce dal ferro un secol d'oro." For another version of Nardi's poem see *Canti Carnascialeschi*, ed. O. Guerini, Milano, 1893, pp. 89 et seq. See also Jacopo Nardi, *Historie della Citta di Fiorenza*, edition of 1582, p. 158v: ". . . furon fatte in Fiorenza molte feste, & spettacoli per dilettare, & recreare il popolo, & massimamente nel prossimo sequente carnouale, che furono fatte grandi, & belle mascherate con trionfo del secolo d'oro, come per buono augurio della felicità de futuri tempi."

tering processions of gods, heroes, and virtues seemed pale and shadowy. The Medici had returned to Florence with the outlook of exiles: for the Medici the world had ended in 1494 and it began again only when they came back to Florence in 1512; for them the intervening period did not exist. But those who had lived in Florence throughout the eighteen years of the republic had a different perspective. They had seen the sudden collapse of Medici rule in 1494 and then they had witnessed the overthrow of another political regime. Many of them must have felt that the restored regime could not last, and that the causes of instability and its cure must be more fundamental.

It seemed to many that Savonarola, who had admonished the Florentines that political stability and well-being depended on moral reform, came nearer to the truth than all the others with their clever political plans. The persistence of Savonarola's ideas emerged clearly in 1527, when, thirty years after the Frate's death, in a final short-lived attempt to regain freedom, the Florentines threw off the Medici yoke and proclaimed Florence to be a "city of Christ." The process of the survival of Savonarola's ideas throughout the period of the Medici restoration is difficult to trace.[66] The existence of Savonarolians, or of a Savonarolian sect was frequently mentioned, but the expression was used loosely and sometimes it was

[66] An interesting document proving the strength of Savonarola's ideas, is the "Recitazione del caso di Pietro Paolo Boscoli," printed *Archivio Storico Italiano*, vol. I (1842), pp. 283-309, see particularly p. 296; see also the letter from Ulisse da Fano to Lorenzo Strozzi (without date, 1519?), A.S.F., *Carte Strozziane, 3ª Serie*, vol. 220, c. 163, where Savonarola, in a somewhat ironic way, is called "el gran propheta," and Lorenzo Strozzi is characterized as "uno, e non de' mediocri suoi seguaci." See then, most of all, Cerretani, *Storia in Dialogo*.

simply meant to designate all those who wanted to re-establish the Great Council. But there is ample proof that there were many in Florence who adhered to the ideas of the Frate in their entirety, and believed in the interdependence of Christian reform and a stable social order. At the time when the Medici and their followers were parading through the streets of the city in the costumes of pagan antiquity, Florentines crowded the churches whenever a preacher appeared in the pulpit who spoke in the Savonarolian vein, prophesying the end of the world if people did not desist from their sinful life, and promising that if they changed their ways, Florence and Tuscany would become the center of the political and moral renewal of the world. After 1512, hardly a year passed without the appearance in Florence of another preacher of doom and salvation. Some of these preachers were false prophets who used their hold over the people to extort money or to seduce women; but despite these disillusionments, people flocked again and again to the churches in order to hear a new preacher of the Savonarolian stamp raise his voice.[67]

Some of these preachers revived the spirit of Savonarola in all its seriousness and rigidity. The most influential of these was the Franciscan Francesco da Montepulciano.[68] When he preached the coming end of the world

[67] The most famous of the "false prophets" was the so-called Don Teodoro, see Landucci, *Diario*, p. 349, and Cambi, "Istorie," *loc. cit.*, vol. XXII, pp. 59 et seq. and also, Parenti, *Istoria Fiorentina*, Ms. B.N.F. II.IV.171, f. 112 about Don Teodoro: "ripigl[i]eva certe propositioni di Frate Jeronimo." Parenti gives much material about the religious excitement in Florence, and in Schnitzer's excerpts from Parenti's work (*Quellen und Forschungen zur Geschichte Savonarolas*, ed. J. Schnitzer, vol. IV: *Piero Parenti*) these notices have been published rather extensively.

[68] On Francesco da Montepulciano, see Cambi, "Istorie," *loc. cit.*, vol. XXII, pp. 37-39; Landucci, *Diario*, pp. 343-344; Cerretani,

"in words as terrifying as can be imagined" the whole
city seemed to be cloaked in gloom, and when he died,
"the whole population came to kiss his hands and feet; it
was astounding to see the crowd, especially the number
of women who were convinced he was a saint and wanted
to touch him."[69]

The government of the Medici was suspicious of these
preachers and whenever possible tried to prohibit their
appearance. The interest which their sermons aroused
seemed to be an expression of political dissatisfaction.
However the measures of the government against the cult
of Savonarola were not effective. "In fact, one could not
eradicate," wrote Parenti, "here in Florence the view of
Savonarola's saintliness; he had a very great number of
adherents for religious as well as for political reasons."[70]
This somewhat naive statement is significant because it
shows that the impact of these preachers extended beyond
the poorer and ignorant parts of the population which,
at that time, as in any city of Europe, were susceptible to
the violent words of itinerant preachers. These sermons
made an impression also on wealthier and better educated
people in Florence. Full of resentment over the depri-
vation of their political influence, these people were fascinated by the relevance of Savonarolian ideas to the uncertain situation which existed in the city.

Storia in Dialogo, Ms. B.N.F. II.I.106, ff. 166r-166v; Parenti, in
Schnitzer, *Quellen,* vol. IV, p. 302 et seq.

[69] "Concorsevi tutto el popolo a baciarli le mani et piedi; cosa
maravigliosa fu'l vedere la moltitudine maxime delle donne, le quali
sancto el predicavano et toccare lo volevano," *ibid.,* p. 303.

[70] "In effecto non si poteva spegnere qui in Firenze la openione
della sanctita di frate Jeronimo, el quale ci haveva moltissimi parti-
giani si per religione et si per rispecto dello stato, le quali chose
non venendo a proposito del nuovo reggimento, erano aspramente,
come s'e decto, prohibite," *ibid.,* p. 307.

An aristocratic champion of Savonarola's ideas was Bartolomeo Cerretani; his *Storia in dialogo della mutatione di Firenze*[71] is a revealing study in the thinking of those who were called the Savonarolians. The dialogue is Cerretani's second work. His first was a history of Florence, which terminated with the fall of the republic in 1512. The second work was written at the beginning of the 1520's and contained the history of the events between 1512 and 1520. The dialogue of Cerretani's invention took place in 1520 in Modena between four young Florentine noblemen; two of these aristocrats had left Florence in 1512, and after having travelled through Europe, they met up with two of their compatriots who had remained in Florence during these years. The two travellers tell about what they have seen and heard in Europe and the two others report about what has happened in Florence. Cerretani's choice of the form of a dialogue may owe something to the author's striving for literary originality, but it was also appropriate because the author was interested not so much in the actual events as in their bearing on a question which puzzled him: have the events which have happened during the twenty years after Savonarola's execution justified his prophecies? Was he a true prophet?

To Cerretani, two of Savonarola's prophecies seemed of principal importance. Savonarola had predicted a reform of the Church, and he had stated that the popular regime, introduced in Florence in 1494, would never perish. Cerretani's purpose was to show that the intervening events had justified the Frate. The travellers reported

---

[71] Ms. B.N.F. II.I.106; some excerpts were published *Quellen und Forschungen zur Geschichte Savonarolas*, ed. J. Schnitzer, vol. III: *Bartolomeo Cerretani*, Munich, 1904.

about visits to Reuchlin and Erasmus, and about the sensation caused by Luther's writings. They had returned to Italy convinced that, all over Europe, the corruption of the Church was deeply resented and a thorough reform was regarded as an absolute necessity. The two who told about the events in Florence emphasized that the Medici had committed numerous mistakes and that the regime they had established was unstable. The recent deaths of both Giuliano and Lorenzo de' Medici, neither of whom left legitimate sons, necessitated a change in the government, and would, the speakers believed, result in a return to the popular regime.

However, even this confirmation of Savonarola's predictions did not resolve all of Cerretani's doubts; he found it necessary to raise again the question: had Savonarola been inspired by God? Was he a saintly figure? One of the speakers in Cerretani's dialogue reiterated the objection frequently voiced in the Frate's lifetime, that Savonarola had not been exclusively concerned with saving souls; rather he had intervened in political affairs and had taken an active part in them. He was said to have "wanted to make himself head of our city, both its spiritual and its secular head."[72] Those who refuted these accusations argued that it had been Savonarola's duty to concern himself with the establishment of good laws because religion can flourish only in a well-organized society. "If Savonarola founded a popular regime, if he created laws against vice and against the luxurious dresses of women and youths, if he taught us to live in a republican spirit and required priests, monks, and nuns to conduct themselves like the pious men of olden times, was this an error

---

[72] "e' mostrò in molti modi di volersi far capo nella citta nostra, non solo del temporale, ma dello spirituale," Cerretani, *Storia in Dialogo*, II.I.106, f. 142r. (in *Quellen*, ed. Schnitzer, vol. III, p. 100).

or did he do right"?[73] Cerretani reinforced this argument by citing the famous proverb that a government cannot be maintained by paternosters. Although Cerretani agreed that this was true for the world as it was constituted, he drew from this proverb the unique conclusion that the political order ought to be changed in such a way that it *could* be ruled by paternosters. Cerretani believed in Savonarola's recommendation that all groups of the population should participate in the government so that one group would not rule over the other. Then the government belonged to everyone, and force would not be needed to maintain it. With the elimination of force, social surroundings would be conducive to the flowering of true religion; there would be a restoration of the society at the time of the foundation of the Christian Church. "To renew the Church means to reintroduce the spiritual and secular regime which existed in the times of the first Christians."[74]

The Savonarolians held to the traditional belief that the only means to political success was obedience to the commandments of God. If the popular regime, which Savonarola had advocated and helped to found, had collapsed —at least temporarily—the reason was that the people had failed God by refusing to give up their sinful ways. If the popular regime was to be restored the people had to change their lives and become true Christians. The

[73] "Se lui fece et fondò un vivere publico, se creò legge circa l'honestà et vestire di donne, et giovani e fanciulle, se lui c'insegnò vivere a uso di republica civilmente et con quella religione, che ne richiede al secolo et a' sacerdoti e monache, la vita di quelli antichi religiosi, o puossi dire, che costui habbi errato o fatto bene?", Cerretani, *Storia in Dialogo*, II.I.106, f. 144v (in *Quellen*, ed. Schnitzer, vol. III, p. 101).

[74] "Il rinuovare la Chiesa è rintrodurre el vivere spirituale, temporale come fu al principio di que' primi christiani," Cerretani, *Storia in Dialogo*, II.I.106, f. 155v.

spread of the idea of the need for Church reform indicated that these hopes for a good society were not unfounded. However, the central point of the Savonarolians was that political reform—the re-establishment of a popular regime—depended on the moral conversion of man, on the birth of a new spirit among the citizens. The Savonarolians thought little of worldly-wise men who believed that by their own intelligence they could control the course of events; the belief in politics based on reason was anathema to the Savonarolians. Thus a strange link connects the Savonarolians who believed that the world should be ruled by paternosters and those who were advocates of a policy based on force.

These prophets of force were also skeptical about the influence which reason and intelligence could exert on politics; they also believed that the prerequisite for successful political action was a spiritual regeneration of the citizens. Force was viewed, by its advocates, as having a two-fold role in politics: force gave security and stability to those who governed; and force also provided greater coherence and strength for the entire state. The prophets of force recommended the creation of a citizen army not only because of the obvious practical advantage of being less expensive, but also because it was expected these armies would be animated by a new spirit. Citizens defending their homes would fight with greater heroism and develop a greater willingness to undergo sacrifices. The secret of the success of the Romans was, as Alamanni said, their discipline. "What else made the Roman soldiers so perfect but the strictness of their leaders and particularly of Torquato"?[75] The advocates of force wondered,

---

[75] "Che altro fe' sì perfetta la militia de' Romani che la severità de' lor capi et maxime di Torquato?", Alamanni in Albertini, *op. cit.*, p. 374.

however, whether it was possible to introduce in Florence the radical changes—such as a citizen army—which they believed necessary for the political regeneration of the citizens. Egoism seemed to have become all-pervasive; "one's own interest is master and leads all men." The danger was that men had become too soft for strenuous effort; "they are effeminate and nerveless and inclined to a protected and, considering our resources, a luxurious life; they possess little love for fame or true honour, but much for wealth and money."[76] However these required virtues of discipline and abnegation seemed incompatible with the emphasis on the acquisition of wealth which dominated a commercial city.

In contrast to some of the humanists of the fifteenth century who had recognized business as a useful training for the conduct of affairs of state, the pursuit of commercial interests came to be considered as making man unfit for government and politics.[77] Antonio Brucioli's dialogue *Della Republica* provides the most striking expression of this view held by the advocates of force. Brucioli's work was published in 1526, but its conception had taken place a few years earlier when he had been in Florence and had frequented the meetings in the Rucellai gardens.[78] At the outset of this dialogue one of the

[76] ". . . gli animi degli uomini effeminati ed enervati e vòlti a uno vivere delicato e, rispetto alle facultá nostre, suntuoso; poco amore della gloria ed onore vero, assai alle ricchezze e danari," Guicciardini, "Del modo di ordinare il governo popolare" *Dialogo e Discorsi del Reggimento di Firenze*, p. 219.

[77] Guicciardini, *ibid.*, pp. 257 et seq.

[78] On Brucioli's relation to the Rucellai gardens, see Delio Cantimori, "Rhetoric and Politics in Italian Humanism," *Journal of the Warburg and Courtauld Institutes*, vol. I (1937/8), pp. 83-102 and Albertini, *op. cit.*, pp. 79-83. Brucioli and Lodovico Alamanni were friends of Machiavelli, but although some of their ideas might have been influenced by Machiavelli, their writings show that they had their own views and convictions.

speakers presented the accepted view that trade is the mainstay of a republic and that the merchant class is the most important part of a society, but at the end of the discussion he had become convinced that this view was false and that among the professions, trade is "the last, the vilest, and the least necessary."[79] Whereas the speaker had at first spoken of the military profession with contempt, he later recognized that it deserved the first, the most honored place in society. Brucioli was clear-sighted enough to realize that the acceptance of such a new scheme of values required a thorough change in the social order. In an ideal republic great differences of wealth ought not to be allowed. The middle classes ought to predominate as they had predominated in the past. To us it seems illusionary to expect that such a change could ever take place. But to Brucioli and to some of his contemporaries such an ideal republic was not a figment but the restoration of a society that had existed in republican Rome.

If the Medici attempted to legitimate their rule by dangling before the eyes of the Florentines the picture of a past—half recent, half classical—in which peace, wealth, and happiness had existed side by side, if the Savonarolians wanted to return to the times of early Christianity when social conditions had permitted man to live for spiritual ends, even the advocates of force found the justification for their harsh new doctrine in an ideal past: their Golden Age was the Iron Age of Rome.

[79] ". . . dell'ultime, e più vile et di minima necessità . . ," Antonio Brucioli, "Della Republica," *Dialogi*, Venezia, 1526, p. XVIIIv.

Chapter 4 MACHIAVELLI

The most famous victim of the restoration of the Medici rule in 1512 was Niccolò Machiavelli.[1] He was dismissed from his office in the chancellery and exiled to
his small estate near Florence in Sant'Andrea da Percus-
sina; for a short time he was imprisoned.

It may be questioned whether "victim" is the appropriate word to use here. Machiavelli himself regarded the
loss of his job in the chancellery as the greatest misfortune of his life, but it was the requisite of his fame. In
the enforced leisure of the last fifteen years of his life,
which coincided with the years of the rule of the Medici
before their second expulsion from Florence, Machiavelli wrote the literary works which have kept his name
alive: the *Prince,* the *Discourses, Mandragola, Clizia, The
Art of War,* and the *Florentine History.*

Machiavelli's comedies, his history, and his book on
warfare would hardly attract as much attention as still
they do today, if the author of these works had not been
the author of the *Prince* and the *Discourses.* These two
treatises signify the beginning of a new stage—one might
say, of the modern stage—in the development of political
thought.

Machiavelli wrote the *Prince* and the *Discourses* in the

---

[1] On Machiavelli, see the bibliographical essay in the appendix,
where I explain and justify my views on particular facts of
Machiavelli's career and on debated problems of his concepts and
thinking. The annotations of this chapter will be chiefly limited
to documenting textual statements by references to Machiavelli's
works.

years immediately following his removal from office. As he declared in the dedication of the *Prince*, he wanted to impart to others the knowledge which he had "acquired through a long experience of modern events and a constant study of the past."[2] One might say that the *Prince* and the *Discourses* are the works of a defeated politician who reflects on the mistakes which brought about the failure of his cause. The dominating idea in these two works is an appeal to recognize the crucial importance of force in politics.[3] Like his contemporaries, Machiavelli had learned about the role of force in the preceding twenty years, when foreign rulers and armies had appeared in Italy. The circumstances surrounding the return of the Medici to Florence—the dependence of Italy on the outcome of the struggle between France and Spain and the aid of Spanish soldiers in the overthrow of the republic—confirmed Machiavelli's views on the role of force. In a practical way Machiavelli expressed these views by insisting on the formation of a people's army to replace the practice of using mercenaries. This military reform, which had found an increasing number of advocates in the second part of the fifteenth century,[4]

[2] ". . . imparata con una lunga esperienza delle cose moderne et una continua lezione delle antique. . . ," *Il Principe*, dedicatio (Niccolò Machiavelli, *Opere* [*Biblioteca di Classici Italiani*, Feltrinelli editore], vol. I, Milano, 1960, p. 13).

[3] The most famous statements are those from *Il Principe*, in chapt. 6 about the "profeti armati" (*Opere*, vol. I, p. 32) and in chapt. 18 (*Opere*, vol. I, p. 72): "Dovete adunque sapere come sono dua generazione di combattere: l'uno con le leggi, l'altro, con la forza: quel primo è proprio dello uomo, quel secondo delle bestie: ma perché el primo molte volte non basta, conviene ricorrere al secondo." About force as a necessary "last recourse," see *Discorsi* II, chapt. 21 (*Opere*, vol. I, p. 342): "Non é per questo che io giudichi che non si abbia adoperare l'armi e le forze; ma si debbono riservare in ultimo luogo, dove e quando gli altri modi non bastino."

[4] See C. C. Bayley, *War and Society in Renaissance Florence*,

had been Machiavelli's greatest concern when he was in the chancellery; in the *Prince* and in the *Discourses* he stressed the importance of such a measure at every possible occasion.

The *Prince* and the *Discourses* are tied to issues of political immediacy, to questions that were being discussed when Machiavelli was writing. When Machiavelli wrote the *Prince* a topic of speculation was how Pope Leo X would provide for his brother and his nephew; for it was generally assumed that, like previous popes, he wanted to establish them on a throne. In a letter to Francesco Vettori, Machiavelli remarked that a treatise on princeships which he was writing "ought to be welcome to a prince and especially to a new prince. Therefore I am dedicating it to his Magnificence Giuliano."[5] The theme of the *Discourses* is the prerequisites for the establishment of a good republic. Again this was a question of immediate political significance. In the first years after the return of the Medici it was by no means clear that they would settle in Florence as permanent rulers. Both Giuliano and Lorenzo seemed inclined to prefer ruling a less troublesome state. Thus the form which a republican government ought to take remained a much debated issue in Florence. Although in the *Discourses* Machiavelli wrote about republics in general terms, he took up specific issues which mirrored the political experiences of the Florentines during the republic. For instance, Machiavelli discussed the age qualifications for the holding of

---

Toronto, 1961, chapter V: "The Survival of the Military Tradition from Bruni to Machiavelli."

[5] ". . . et a un principe, et maxime a un principe nuovo, doverrebbe essere accetto; però io lo indrizzo alla M. tia di Giuliano," December 10, 1513 (*Opere*, vol. VI, p. 304).

offices[6] and the appropriate length of office terms;[7] he made suggestions for avoiding boycotts of public services by prominent citizens[8] as had happened in 1502. He criticized the Florentines for their unwillingness to permit their military commanders to take initiative.[9]

Moreover, in the *Discourses* Machiavelli took a stand on the decisive issue of the republican period: whether a *governo largo* or a *governo stretto* was preferable.[10] He showed his preference for a *governo largo* by discussing issues relevant to the question of the influence which the people should have in a republic: whether the people elect the right political leaders,[11] whether they are more grateful than a prince to those who serve them,[12] whether they maintain treaties better than a prince.[13] The *Discourses* were written—and must be read—in the light of the problems which disturbed and eventually destroyed the republican regime.

Machiavelli's theoretical assumptions about the forces determining success in politics belong to the intellectual climate of the time. His basic approach is rationalistic. He regarded all men as equal factors; all are evil in the

[6] *Discorsi* I, chapt. 60.
[7] *Discorsi* I, chapt. 35 and III, chapt. 24.
[8] *Discorsi* I, chapt. 50.
[9] *Discorsi* II, chapt. 33 and III, chapt. 15 (*Opere*, vol. I, pp. 378, 434-435).
[10] See *Discorsi* I, chapt. 5, but also many other passages, for instance: ". . . sono migliori governi quegli de' popoli che quegli de' principi," *Discorsi* I, chapt. 58 (*Opere*, vol. I, p. 265). In general, in the *Discorsi*, Machiavelli compares rule by princes with rule by people, but what he says about republics makes evident that he envisages a "governo largo." This preference is most clearly expressed in his "Discorso delle cose fiorentine dopo la morte di Lorenzo" (printed in *Opere*, vol. II, pp. 261-277).
[11] *Discorsi* I, chapts. 47 and 58 (*Opere*, vol. I, p. 264) and III, chapt. 34.
[12] *Discorsi* I, chapt. 29.
[13] *Discorsi* I, chapt. 59.

sense that all pursue only their own egoistic interests.[14] On this assumption their actions become calculable. In the *Prince* as well as in the *Discourses* Machiavelli outlined forms of government which used these egoistic drives of men in such a way that they would not endanger the government but would even increase the strength of the political body. Machiavelli's chapter on conspiracies in the *Discourses*[15] is a striking example of his rationalistic approach. By minimizing the idealism of motives for attempting the assassination of a tyrant, he arrived at the conclusion that conspiracies have no chance of succeeding because every man, thinking first of his own safety and interests when the inevitable dangers of conspiracy arise, will save himself at the expense of others.

But Machiavelli was aware that conducting politics according to pure reason had limits. He was extremely critical of irresoluteness and delay. Determination and will power were the qualities which might prevail against all reason. His description of Cesare Borgia[16] underlined his belief that purposeful decision is inherently superior to hesitation that comes from weighing all possible odds. The precipitateness of Julius II gave him an advantage because it kept his enemies unbalanced.[17] Action and initiative were preconditions for success in politics; neutrality and the middle-way were fatal.[18]

[14] Among the many expressions of this thought, the strongest is in *Principe*, chapt. 17.

[15] *Discorsi* III, chapt. 6.

[16] In the famous chapter 7 of *Il Principe*.

[17] See *Principe*, chapt. 25 (*Opere*, vol. I, pp. 100-101), or *Discorsi* III, chapt. 64 (*Opere*, vol. I, p. 499).

[18] *Discorsi*, II, chapt. 23 with the title "Quanto i Romani nel giudicare i sudditi per alcuno accidente che necessitasse tale giudizio fuggivano la via del mezzo," but also *Discorsi* I, chapt. 26, II, chapt. 15 or III, chapt. 40 (*Opere*, vol. I, pp. 194, 315 and 494).

Both the terminology and the methods of argumentation which Machiavelli used were those of his time. Experience and authority were the two sources from which he drew material to demonstrate his political views. And authority was to him, as it was to most of his contemporaries, the knowledge of the ancient world which could be found in classical writers. Like the humanists, Machiavelli's aim was to present classical wisdom so that it could be applied to the problems of his own time. He did not scruple to insert in the second chapter of the *Discourses* a passage from Polybius, and to adjust Polybius' words to his own purposes.

That Machiavelli worked within the intellectual framework of his time rather than formulating a new method seems to contradict his statement in the first book of the *Discourses* that he was opening "a new route which had not yet been followed by anyone."[19] In view of the role which his chief political works have played in the development of political thought this might be taken as a true, almost final evaluation of his work. However, if this statement is read in its context, it has a more precise even a more modest meaning than we, aware of the impact of Machiavelli's writings and thought, might attribute to it. Machiavelli intended to do for politics what others had been doing for art, jurisprudence, and medicine: to clarify and to codify the principles which the ancients had

---

[19] ". . . ho deliberato entrare per una via, la quale, non essendo suta ancora de alcuno trita . . . ," *Discorsi* I, proemio (*Opere*, I, p. 123). This sentence has been frequently commented upon, and some writers have even seen an allusion to Columbus in this phrase. Actually, it is a classical topos; see the section "Exordialtopik" in E. R. Curtius, *Europaeische Literatur und Lateinisches Mittelalter*, Bern, 1948, pp. 95 et seq., and see, for one classical form of this topos, Lucretius, *De Rerum Natura*, I, 926: "Avia Pieridum peragro loca nullius ante trita solo."

followed. Machiavelli only wanted to state that he was applying to politics those methods which had been successful in other areas.

We have described the institutional and political life of Florence, as well as the issues which disrupted the republic, and the changes in political assumptions and ideas which occurred in this period; and now we have indicated the connection between Machiavelli's political writings and these issues and ideas. Nevertheless, none will deny the originality and novelty of Machiavelli's writings. But if Machiavelli's works are considered in the political and intellectual framework of his time, it becomes apparent that his originality did not consist—or did not primarily consist—in the ideas which he proffered; his contribution was to weave them together in such a way that a new vision of politics emerged.

The problem which every student of Machiavelli faces is why was it he who constructed out of the ideas and the trends of political thought in his time a synthesis of permanent value. Every intellectual activity is individual. It has been said that Machiavelli possessed the gift of creative imagination. In more concrete terms one might say that the author of the *Prince* and the *Discourses* was also a writer of comedies and poems. Both an artist and theoretician, he was uniquely equipped to give literary expression to his insights on politics.

When Machiavelli discussed the prerequisites of achievement he said that there had to be not only a situation which permitted action and a man capable of action, but also there had to be a favorable occasion.[20] This

[20] For instance, see on the importance of "occasione," *Principe*, chapt. XXVI, the "Exhortatio," or *Discorsi* II, chapt. 29, particularly: "Fa bene la fortuna questo, che la elegge uno uomo,

insight can be applied to his own work. He had grown up, lived, and worked in a world in which political issues and ideas could no longer be comprehended in the traditional intellectual framework. Machiavelli's creative powers led him to a new synthesis; but it should be added that he had a particular stimulus: the position from which he looked upon the political world was different from that of his contemporaries who wrote on politics. His position was identical neither with that of the humanists nor with that of the Florentine aristocrats. Machiavelli differed from the humanists about the purposes of political literature, and he looked upon the Florentine political scene from an angle opposite to that of the aristocrats. This difference may be the point of departure for an analysis of Machiavelli's thought. Although he used the same methods, worked with the same concepts, and discussed the same issues as others had, he modified them and widened their meaning, so that politics was seen in a new light.

The circumstances of Machiavelli's life were drastically altered after the return of the Medici to Florence. Indeed, the year 1512 is generally considered to have been the turning point in his life: from a *vita activa* of practical politics he turned to a *vita contemplativa* of writing. However, this view is misleading, for it suggests a transformation of his personality and interests which never occurred. Throughout his entire life he was concerned with both political action and writing. An indefatigable secretary in the chancellery, he wrote letters

---

quando la voglia condurre cose grandi, che sia di tanto spirito e di tanta virtù che ei conosca quelle occasioni che la gli porge" (*Opere*, vol. I, p. 366).

and reports, he composed memoranda and drafted legislation; and in addition to his official tasks, he sometimes
set down his ideas and observations in short treatises, and
he wrote poems. Whether he was on a diplomatic mission
or in Florence, he must have spent several hours every
day at a writing table. When he was dismissed from his
job and barred from politics he continued to write, and,
as that was his only outlet, his interest in literary activity increased.

Nonetheless, his passion for politics never diminished.
Every bit of information about politics which he could
gather from letters or conversations set him to speculat-
ing about the plans and intentions of the Great. He looked
back with longing to the years when he had negotiated
with rulers and politicians, and he never doubted that
this was his true vocation. After 1512 his constant aim
was to regain a position which would enable him to have
a part in determining the course of events. Almost everything that he wrote after 1512 was produced for the single purpose of gaining the support of those who could
help him to resume his career in active politics. The ambitions of the younger Medici, first Giuliano and then Lorenzo, for founding a dynasty stimulated him to prepare
a treatise on the policy to be followed by a "new prince."
The favors which playwrights enjoyed at the court of
Pope Leo X induced him to turn his attention to the writing of comedies. In the dedication to the *Discourses* he
confessed that he would never have written this work
had not two of his patrons, Zanobi Buondelmonti and Cosimo Rucellai, exerted pressure on him to do it. His last
extended literary work, the *Florentine History*, was commissioned by the Florentine Studio, more particularly,
by the head of the Studio, Cardinal Giulio Medici. Machi-

avelli accepted this commission because he rightly regarded it as a first step on the way back into the graces of
the Medici. Later when the Medici began to give him
some minor official jobs, he threw himself into these
tasks, relegating to a second place the continuation of the
Florentine History. To Machiavelli, writing was a weak
substitute for political action; writing—even about politics—was a means to that end.

Yet, had Machiavelli lacked his passion for political action, he would have been destined for a life of literature.[21] His natural gifts—an imaginative and penetrating
mind, an acute sense for language and style—as well as his
education and training pointed him towards a literary
career. He had grown up in circles which admired the
humanist literati and saw in them the prophets of a new
civilization. His father Bernardo, a lawyer, was a friend
of Bartolomeo Scala, First Chancellor of Florence from
1464 to 1497, and one of the best known Florentine humanists of the second part of the fifteenth century. Bernardo had taken care that his sons were educated to ap-
preciate the wisdom of the ancients. When Niccolò
Machiavelli was elected to a post in the chancellery he became a member of an elite which took very seriously its
reputation for guarding and transmitting the humanist
tradition; since the times of Salutati and Bruni the Florentine chancellery had been a center of humanist
studies.[22] Machiavelli's chief in the chancellery, Marcello

[21] On Machiavelli's education, see Appendix.
[22] See E. Garin, "I Cancellieri Umanisti della Repubblica Fiorentina da Coluccio Salutati a Bartolomeo Scala," *Rivista Storica
Italiana*, vol. LXXI (1959), pp 185-208; Garin shows that the tradition of employing humanists in the Chancellery was maintained
throughout the fifteenth century, although the close connection
between political and humanist ideas which had existed in Salutati's
times had disappeared.

Virgilio Adriani, or colleagues like Gaddi and Verino, who served in the chancellery as secretaries or notaries, were all outstanding humanists. They regarded their government employment as necessary and welcome because of the financial security and status it provided, but their main interest was literary and scholarly work. In the literary spirit prevailing in the chancellery, Machiavelli wrote a poem, the *Decennale;* he was proud of his verses and he openly regretted that Ariosto, who, in "Orlando Furioso" had recorded the names of so many poets, had omitted the name of Machiavelli.[23]

When Machiavelli took up writing as a means of getting himself back into politics, he was conscious of the literary tradition and he was fully aware of what his readers expected. He realized the advantage in conforming to accepted standards, and therefore he presented his ideas in a conventional way. In the *Prince* he used as his pattern the treatises on ideal rulers, a common literary form since the Middle Ages. Like the usual treatise of this sort, the *Prince* begins with a definition of the various forms of government. Then Machiavelli departed from the traditional pattern and discussed the problems of a "new prince" and the evils resulting from the use of mercenaries. Finally he returned to those topics customarily found in books on rulers: the qualities which a prince ought to possess. And the work ends in traditional style with a peroration. The *Discourses* were also cast in the form of a popular literary genre: commentary on a classical author. The conventional aspect of the *Discourses* is

---

[23] "Io ho letto a questi dí *Orlando Furioso* dello Ariosto. . . . Se si truova costí, raccomandatemi a lui, et ditegli che io mi dolgo solo che, havendo ricordato tanti poeti, che m'habbi lasciato indietro come un cazzo . . . ," Niccolò Machiavelli a Lodovico Alamanni, 17 dicembre 1517 (*Opere*, vol. VI, p. 383).

somewhat disguised because Machiavelli's comments do not always follow successively the text of Livy. Machiavelli divided the *Discourses* into three books, each with a different theme, each containing his observations on all those chapters of Livy relevant to the three themes. But this systematic arrangement is not fully developed; great parts of the *Discourses* are simply straight comments on succeeding chapters of Livy. In his other works he pursued traditional patterns still more slavishly. His comedies are either translations of classical plays or else they were composed in strict adherence to classical examples. In his *Art of War* he adopted the classical pattern of a dialogue and inserted lengthy passages translated from Vegetius. In his *Florentine History* he followed the prescriptions for writing history which had been set by humanists.[24]

Conformity to traditional patterns also strengthened his message: Machiavelli was conscious that his unconventional suggestions would appear even more striking if they were presented in a conventional manner. This technique served well his aim to jolt his readers, but it was also in harmony with the paradoxical bent of his mind. To a contemporary, he was a man who loved to assume the role of an *advocatus diaboli*. Several years after Machiavelli's death, Luigi Guicciardini, the elder brother of the historian Francesco and a friend of Machiavelli in their younger years, wrote a dialogue in which Machiavelli was one of the speakers. Luigi Guicciardini let this figure contradict what the others were saying, and in a letter to

[24] On Machiavelli's methods in the *Istorie Fiorentine* see below, pp. 236 et seq. I have discussed the relation of Machiavelli's writings to humanist patterns in various articles; they have now been collected and published in Italian translation, in my book *Niccolò Machiavelli e la vita culturale del suo tempo*, Bologna, 1964.

his brother Francesco, he stated directly that he had made Machiavelli a participant of this dialogue because he needed a speaker who, with difficulty, believed what ought to be believed.[25] One has sometimes the feeling that whenever Machiavelli read the statement of another writer or heard about a generally accepted view, his first reaction was to doubt these notions and to try to discover what would happen if the opposite was maintained. Whether one reads the *Prince* with its corroding analysis of the common assumption that a prince ought to be liberal, magnanimous, loyal and beloved,[26] or whether one reads in the *Discourses* his attack against the accepted views about military affairs in his time—that artillery was decisive,[27] that fortresses were important,[28] and that success in war depended on money[29]—one finds always the proposition of a view directly the reverse of common opinion. Machiavelli seemed to have delighted in "defending a cause which had been rejected by all writers."[30]

If Machiavelli freely indulged in his penchant for paradox it was because he was anxious to attract attention: he wanted his writings to have a practical effect. His aim was to instruct those in power in what he had learned

[25] ". . . per dipignere uno che con difficultà credessi le cose da credere, non che quelle da ridersene . . . ," see my article "Machiavelli in an unknown contemporary Dialogue," *Journal of the Warburg Institute*, vol. I (1937/38), pp. 163-166, and also Luigi di Piero Guicciardini, *Del Savonarola*, ed. Bono Simonetta, Firenze, 1959 [*Biblioteca dell' Archivo Storico Italiano*, vol. VIII], pp. 39-40.

[26] *Il Principe*, chapts. XV-XIX.

[27] *Discorsi* II, chapt. 17.

[28] *Discorsi* II, chapt. 24.

[29] *Discorsi* II, chapt. 10.

[30] ". . . volendo difendere una cosa, la quale, come ho detto, da tutti gli scrittori è accusata. . . ," *Discorsi* I, chapt. 58 (*Opere*, vol. I, p. 262); see also *Il Principe*, chapt. 15.

about the nature and functioning of politics, and to urge them to act according to his knowledge. Because he was wholly committed to the world of practical politics—and not to the realms in which abstract truths were precisely and finely elucidated—he frequently couched his insights in extreme and shocking statements. In spite of his talents and his training, in spite of his familiarity with literary forms and methods, he always felt superior to those who preferred a quiet life of scholarship to the rigours of political action. In his *Florentine History* he once remarked that when poets and philosophers begin to play a role in a society that society is entering its decline.[31] This comment is a reference to the relation, which he saw, between the diminution of Florentine political power and the reputation which men of letters enjoyed in Florence; but it also indicated that he looked with disdain upon those for whom literary work was an end in itself. Even when writing became the only vent for his intellect it was not his primary intention to produce a work of literature; rather he was anxious that his writings have an impact.

In the light of Machiavelli's uncertain attitude to literary work—the pride which he took in his knowledge of the literary craft combined with the much greater satisfaction which he felt in being not merely a man of letters but a practical politician—it is hardly surprising that he was less concerned with the explanation of facts than

---

[31] "Onde si è dai prudenti osservato come le lettere vengono drieto alle armi, e che nelle provincie e nelle città prima i capitani e che i filosofi nascono. . . ," *Istorie Fiorentine*, libro V, chapt. I (*Opere*, vol. VII, Milano, 1962, p. 325). Machiavelli places literary fame below political and military fame also in *Discorsi* I, chapt. 10 (*Opere*, vol. I, p. 156, but see also p. 157, where Machiavelli criticizes writers who were corrupted by princely patronage).

with making an impressive argument. This led him to inconsistencies within his works. For example, he represented the King of France as being both all-powerful and limited by law.[32] In one instance in the *Discourses* he stated that the people of the Roman republic had been poor, and in another place he declared that they had been wealthy.[33] He could justify with many examples drawn from ancient and modern history that the people elected the right men for the right jobs,[34] yet later he asserted that the Florentines had elected the wrong men to be military commissioners.[35] He could also use the same example, in different chapters, for entirely different purposes.[36] However, these inconsistencies appear only in his subsidiary argumentations; unity is provided by his general vision of politics. He was eager to state as forcefully as possible the ideas which he thought important and necessary to impress upon his readers. But he was not a man who builds a system in which every detail has an appointed spot and forms part of a whole.

In arguing a view and in proving a point Machiavelli followed the same methods which were regularly used in his time. Like the humanists, he believed that actions and

[32] For statements on France, see *Il Principe*, chapts. 4 and 19, and *Discorsi* I, chapts. 16 and 55, III, chapt. 1 (*Opere*, vol. I, pp. 26, 77-78, 176, 255, 383); the position of the French King, the role and influence of Parliament, the relation of the nobles to the people, are always somewhat differently characterized, according to the point which Machiavelli wanted to prove.

[33] For poverty in Rome, see below, note 50, but in *Discorsi* II, chapt. 6, Machiavelli emphasizes that the Roman conduct of war made state and people rich.

[34] *Discorsi* I, chapt. 47 and III, chapt. 34.

[35] *Discorsi* III, chapt. 16 (*Opere*, vol. I, pp. 437-438).

[36] For instance see the divergent reasons given for Giacomini's loss of favor in *Discorsi* I, chapt. 53 and *Discorsi* III, chapt. 16 (*Opere*, vol. I, pp. 252 and 438).

events of the ancient world had a general significance beyond the particular context within which they stood.
The purpose of literary work was to extricate the meaning from the fact. This method of allegorical interpretation had been used in the Middle Ages for revealing
God's plans for men. Machiavelli used this method in a
purely secular way, deducing from singular historical situations general rules of political behavior. In the *Prince*
the close connection between Machiavelli's interpretative
procedure and the allegorical methods used by theolo-
gians and humanists is strikingly demonstrated; Machiavelli referred to the Bible story of David and Goliath in
order to prove his thesis that a prince ought not to rely
on mercenaries, but ought to have his own army."When
David offered Saul to fight Goliath, Saul armed him with
his own weapons; but when David was clad in them, he
rejected them because he could not show his own value
in them; he wanted to confront the enemy with his own
sling and knife."[37] There is a slightly dubious air about
references to the Bible in Machiavelli's works, and he
might have held his tongue in cheek when he inserted in
his recommendations for a citizen army a Bible story interpreted along allegorical lines. However, such irony
would have been more clumsy than subtle if he had suddenly employed a method of interpretation at variance
with the rest of his book. Actually he quite frequently
used the method of allegorical interpretation in his presentation of the events of Roman history. When he

[37] "Offerendosi David a Saul di andare a combattere con Golia,
provocatore filisteo, Saul, per darli animo, l'armò dell' arme sua:
le quali, come David ebbe indosso, recusò, dicendo con quelle non
si potere bene valere di se stesso, e però voleva trovare el nimico
con la sua fromba e con il suo coltello," *Il Principe*, chapt. 13
(*Opere*, vol. I, p. 60).

pointed out that the execution of the sons of Brutus showed that the heirs of liberators from tyranny are threats to the maintenance of freedom,[38] or that the duel between the three Horatii and the three Curatii proved the necessity of employing all one's forces at once,[39] he ascribed to these events a meaning hardly conveyed by the facts themselves.

But this method of deducing a general meaning from single facts was not entirely adequate for Machiavelli's aim. To goad politicians into taking action in accordance with his insights and convictions, Machiavelli took recourse to the technique of designing examples to fit his purposes. In the thirty-ninth chapter of the first book of the *Discourses* he ascribed the abolition of the Office of the Ten to the distrust of the people for the aristocrats, and according to Machiavelli's account, the Ten were reestablished only after the revolts in Arezzo and in the Valdichiana had made the Florentines realize what a mistake it had been to eliminate this office. Machiavelli, as secretary to the Ten, must have known better than anyone else that the Office of the Ten had been reinstated before the outbreak of the revolt in Arezzo.[40] A most arresting instance of Machiavelli's construction of examples appears in his discussion of Cesare Borgia in the *Prince*. As emissary of the Florentine government, Machiavelli had stayed with Cesare Borgia in the days of Sinigaglia and again in the weeks of Cesare's negotiations with Julius II after the death of Alexander VI. Neither the facts which Machiavelli then reported to the Florentine

[38] *Discorsi* III, chapt. 3, also I, chapt. 16.
[39] *Discorsi* I, chapts. 22, 23 (*Opere*, vol. I, p. 188).
[40] See above, p. 61; but see also *Discorsi*, I, chapt. 38 (*Opere*, vol. I, p. 221) which shows that Machiavelli placed the revolt of Arezzo correctly in the year 1502.

government about Cesare's proceedings at Sinigaglia, nor the picture which Machiavelli gave of Cesare, anxiously grasping for straws after the loss of papal support, corresponds to the outline given in the *Prince* of a Cesare Borgia whose moves were part of a well-conceived plan which was carried out with single-minded ruthlessness, and who fell only because of an illness inflicted by *Fortuna*. It is evident that by shaping historical events Machiavelli made Cesare Borgia more serviceable as an example of a "new prince."

Machiavelli's treatment of Cesare Borgia in the *Prince* is famous; it is considered to be the most impressive formulation of the spirit of Renaissance politics. But this chapter of the *Prince* deserves attention also because it shows most vividly the distinctive features of Machiavelli's approach and methods. Like his contemporaries, Machiavelli tried to formulate rules of behavior, and, again like his contemporaries, he deduced these rules from experience. But Machiavelli used the material which experience offered in an almost arbitrary manner, and he transformed and stylized facts and events with freedom and ease. Moreover, he was not interested in producing rules which were of general value and applicable to the behavior of every individual. His books were addressed only to those who acted in the political world: to rulers and to politicians. But in concentrating exclusively on the interaction between political behavior and political events, his main theme became the necessary connections which exist in the world of politics. The *Prince* and the *Discourses* were intended to reveal the laws which govern the world of politics.[41]

[41] Machiavelli aimed at the "regola generale," *Discorsi* I, chapt. 9 (*Opere*, vol. I, p. 153) or *Il Principe*, chapt. 3 (*Opere*, vol. I, p. 25). Politics was to be a science like medicine; for references to

Because Machiavelli approached literary work with the interest and aims of a practical politician, his writings differ from those of his humanist contemporaries. Yet his writings are by no means similar to the usual works on practical politics of the time, the expressions of aristocratic interest and policy. As we have seen, some of the Florentine aristocrats set down statements of their program and their aims and in doing so, they began to adopt new methods: they came to evaluate the nature of a political organization by using the criteria of rational efficiency; and they began to realize the necessity of judging political institutions not in isolation, but as parts of the entire social and political structure. Machiavelli recognized these principles and his writings show that he absorbed them, but he inserted into his discussions notions which had not appeared in the context of political thinking, and he attached new or wider meanings to those which had. A reason that his writings differ from those of his aristocratic contemporaries who wrote on practical politics is that Machiavelli viewed the political scene from one pole, the aristocrats from the other. What Machiavelli saw in the political situation was not what the aristocrats saw; what he believed to be a remedy for Florence's political ills was not a part of the program of the aristocrats. Machiavelli was in an uncommon—and unenviable—position: he was a writer with practical political aims and he was not a member of the Florentine ruling group. Not only was he not a member of this group; he opposed it.

Machiavelli's opposition to the aristocrats was rooted in personal circumstances and was strengthened by the

---

medicine see *Il Principe*, chapt. 3, *Discorsi*, proemio, or III, chapt. 1.

obstructionist policy of the aristocrats during the republican regime. The Machiavelli were one of the patrician families of Florence, but Niccolò belonged to an impoverished branch, the decline of which he had experienced in his own lifetime. That he was excluded from the ruling group was the result, it seemed to him, of not having sufficient wealth. His impecuniosity was more than a private worry; it appeared to limit the ways in which he could exercise his passion for political action, and it was a source of humiliation. Whereas for some a job in the chancellery was a stepping-stone to social prominence, and for others it was a pleasant sinecure, for Machiavelli it was a diminution of status. But he welcomed this employment and he was eager to do well, for this provided him with an opening into the world of politics.

The opportunity for his rise to considerable influence in the republican regime came about largely as a result of the struggle between Soderini and his aristocratic opponents. Soderini had noticed Machiavelli's unusual intelligence and had come to rely on him when, as *Gonfaloniere*, Soderini needed assistants who were not tied to the aristocratic group. Thus a bond was formed between the *Gonfaloniere* and Machiavelli. Niccolò felt so obligated to Soderini that in the years of the Medici restoration, he hesitated to go to Rome, where Soderini was living, because he thought that while a visit to Soderini would damage his chances with the Medici, he could not go to Rome without calling on his former chief. Machiavelli had to be reminded by Francesco Vettori that, in any case, Machiavelli had been elected to his post in the chancellery three years before Soderini had become *Gonfaloniere*.[42] Al-

[42] Machiavelli to Francesco Vettori, December 10, 1513, and Francesco Vettori to Machiavelli, December 24, 1513 (*Opere*, vol. VI, pp. 304-305, 312).

though Vettori was factually correct, Machiavelli was right in thinking that he owed the political prominence which he had enjoyed to Soderini. Without Soderini's influence Machiavelli would not have been sent on his more important diplomatic missions,[43] nor would he have been able to suggest the introduction of conscription and to draft the appropriate legislation. But the preferment given to the secretary by the *Gonfaloniere* had the consequence of making the *Gonfaloniere's* enemies also the enemies of Machiavelli; a number of aristocrats contemptuously characterized Machiavelli as "Soderini's lackey."[44]

The failure of the republican cause, the collapse of the republican regime, Soderini's subsequent flight into exile, and the return of the Medici placed Machiavelli in a lonely, almost hopeless, situation. That Machiavelli was the only chancellery official whom the Medici dismissed was their recognition of the close relationship between Machiavelli and the *Gonfaloniere*. The aristocrats who supported the Medici shared their notion of the influence which Machiavelli exerted during the republic. Other aristocrats, though opposed to the return of the Medici, saw no reason to lift a finger for the creature of Soderini. Still others of the aristocrats felt so insecure under the Medici that they would not risk speaking in favor of a man whom the Medici regarded as their enemy. The attitude of Francesco Vettori towards his once close friend is illustrative. The friendship between Machiavelli and Vettori blossomed in the course of a lengthy diplomatic

[43] With exception of Machiavelli's first mission to France in 1500 his three other missions to France, his two missions to Rome, his mission to Germany took place after Soderini had become *Gonfaloniere a vita* in 1502.

[44] ". . . detto Niccolo essendo suo mannerino. . . ," Cerretani, *Historia Fiorentina*, Ms. B.N.F., II.III.74, f.458.

mission to Germany in 1507/08 and they remained friends after their return to Florence. But when Machiavelli, after 1512 , turned to Vettori (who was then a Florentine ambassador to Rome) for assistance in achieving the grace of the Medici, Vettori seemed to be hard of hearing. Thus, the *Prince* and the *Discourses*, written at the nadir of Machiavelli's political fortunes, are permeated with resentment and bitterness which had resulted from the political conflicts in which their author had been involved—on the losing side.

In a number of passages in the *Prince* and the *Discourses* Machiavelli denounced aristocratic influence and policy; he held the aristocrats responsible for the destruction of Florentine republican freedom.[45] But he never denied the need for the existence of a ruling group. Like his contemporaries, Machiavelli believed that each political body consisted of different groups; each society had rulers and the ruled, those who were the leaders and those who were led.[46] Machiavelli's censure of the Florentine ruling group stemmed from what he considered to be the wrong criterion for determining its composition: to Machiavelli, membership in the Florentine ruling group appeared to depend chiefly on wealth.[47] This was a fateful flaw. In this context it is possible to understand Machiavelli's views on the relation between economics and politics. Machiavelli has been criticized for not comprehending the importance of economic factors in politics. Actually, he was a conscious opponent of the notion

[45] See *Discorsi* I, chapt. 52 (*Opere,* vol. I, p. 247), or III, chapt. 3 (*Opere,* vol. I, p. 386); but also the remarks about the Grandi in *Discorsi* I, chapt. 37 (*Opere,* vol. I, p. 218), without mentioning explicitly the Florentine aristocrats, clearly aim at them; and there are many similar passages.

[46] See below, p. 187.

[47] *Discorsi* I, chapt. 49 and III, chapts. 28 and 46.

that economic factors were useful forces in politics, and he expressed his objections to this idea in his chapter in the *Discourses* on money not being the sinews of war.[48] Machiavelli's whole conception of Roman history is based on the view, which he adopted from Sallust, that money and wealth are evil. To Machiavelli, the decline of Roman freedom and power began with the agrarian law of the Gracchi which gave rise to factions and internal strife.[49] Desire for riches made the conflict between the Senate and the people irreconcilable. About honors, both the people and the nobles had been able to reach agreements, "but when it came to a question of property, then the nobility resisted with so much pertinacity that the people, to satisfy their thirst for riches, resorted to . . . extraordinary proceedings."[50] In the *Prince* he gave trenchant expression to his view that seeking after wealth was evil: a man might be willing to forgive the murder of his brother or of his father, but he would not forgive the violation of his property.[51] This opinion contains a

[48] *Discorsi* II, chapt. 10 with the title: "I danari non sono il nervo della guerra, secondo che è la comune opinione."

[49] *Discorsi* I, chapt. 37.

[50] "Vedesi per questo ancora, quanto gli uomini stimano piú la roba che gli onori. Perché la Nobilità romana sempre negli onori cedé sanza scandoli straordinari alla plebe; ma come si venne alla roba, fu tanta la ostinazione sua nel difenderla, che la plebe ricorse per isfogare l'appetito suo a quegli straordinari che di sopra si discorrono", *Discorsi* I, chapt. 37 (*Opere*, vol. I, p. 218); but see also *Discorsi* III, chapt. 25 (*Opere*, vol. I, p. 457) for the thesis that "la piú utile cosa che si ordini in uno vivere libero è che si mantenghino i cittadini poveri," or chapt. 16 (*Opere*, vol. I, p. 437) on the need to "mantenere i cittadini poveri, acciochè con le ricchezze sanza virtú e' non potessino corrompere né loro né altri." The whole thesis of the corruption of Rome through the increasing wealth of her citizens comes, of course, from Roman historians, from Sallust and Livy's Praefatio.

[51] ". . . perché li uomini sdimenticano piú presto la morte del padre che la perdita del patrimonio," *Il Principe*, chapt. 17 (*Opere*, vol. I, p. 70).

note of moral indignation which is rather alien to Machia-velli. He seems to share the Christian condemnation of the sin of covetousness; striving for wealth takes on the character of original sin.

In the conventional terminology of Machiavelli's time it was customary to speak of "common good" and "private interest." It was assumed that following one's private interest was legitimate and natural but that in the case of a conflict between the common good and private interest, the common good would prevail. Machiavelli used these expressions—"common good" and "private interest";[52] but by identifying private interest with desire for wealth, which to him was evil, he destroyed the accepted principle that the common good and private interest were reconcilable and that the common good would ultimately triumph.

To Machiavelli, politics is an exacting mistress; man's whole behavior must be adjusted to her commands. Man ought to be purely *homo politicus*. It was not a weakness, but a matter of pride to Machiavelli that he could not "reason about the production of silk or of wool, or about gains and losses, but that it was—his—lot to reason about politics."[53] Although Machiavelli never expressed in a

[52] *Discorsi* II, chapt. 2 (*Opere*, vol. I, p. 280): ". . . non il bene particulare ma il bene comune è quello che fa grandi le città. E sanza dubbio questo bene comune non è osservato se non nelle republiche: perché tutto quello che fa a proposito suo si esequisce; e quantunque e' torni in danno di questo o di quello privato, e' sono tanti quegli per chi detto bene fa, che lo possono tirare innanzi contro alla disposizione di quegli pochi che ne fussono oppressi." It must be added that, to Machiavelli, the contrast between "common good" and "private interest," unavoidable in a corrupt republic or a princeship, does not need to come out into the open in a young free republic, see *Discorsi* I, chapt. 18 and II, chapt. 2 (*Opere*, vol. I, p. 284).

[53] ". . . la fortuna ha fatto che, non sapendo ragionare né dell' arte della seta, né dell' arte della lana, né de' guadagni né delle

theoretical formulation the view that politics are autonomous, his writings imply that politics are separate from
all other spheres of human activity and that for those
who take part in politics the demands of politics must
be placed above all others.

In the modern world this view has resulted in the idea
of the state as a living organism which encompasses individuals as integral but subordinate components. It has
been said that Machiavelli gave this meaning to the word
stato, thereby introducing this concept in political literature. But when Machiavelli wrote, the word *stato* was
not new. It had been frequently used in Italian political
literature of the fifteenth century to signify the power
and the apparatus of power of a ruler or a ruling group;
for instance, *lo stato de'Medici* and *lo stato di Francesco
Sforza.* This is also the most usual meaning of *stato* in
Machiavelli's writings. Sometimes, writers contemporaneous with Machiavelli used *stato* to designate a geographical area. This use of the word can also be found in the
works of Machiavelli; for example he called the Venetian
terra-ferma a *stato.* The term could also serve to indicate
the form of a government like *stato libero.* Thus,
when Machiavelli wrote, the meaning of *stato* was
flexible; it was beginning to be used to convey a more
abstract meaning than previously had been ascribed to it.
Soon the word assumed its modern meaning: it came to
be used to denote everything that belongs to a body
politic. *Stato,* in this latter sense, can seldom, if ever, be
found in Machiavelli's works. Nevertheless, Machiavelli
will have had an influence in promoting a wider use of

---

perdite, e' mi conviene ragionare dello stato, et mi bisogna o
botarmi di stare cheto, o ragionare di questo." (*Opere,* vol. VI,
pp. 239-240).

of the word in its more abstract, modern sense because his idea of a political society as a collective body having its own laws of existence was novel; there was no word in the existing vocabulary which conveyed this idea. With the dissemination of Machiavelli's views a word to express this idea was needed; the meaning of the word *stato* could be, without difficulty, extended to fill this need.

Because opposition to the aristocrats was a concomitant of his political influence in the republican period, Machiavelli was a firm advocate of a popular regime. He was convinced that the best form of government was a regime in which the great mass of citizens had the controlling power. He justified this belief in various ways: not only did he refute the usual objections to a popular regime,[54] but he advanced the cause of the people by more systematic considerations. He explained that few, if any, political societies could exist securely in isolation; almost all societies were involved in competition with others, and the alternative was to expand or to perish. The greatest need of any political society was an army, and the people alone provided the manpower to settle conquered areas and to guarantee the permanency of conquests.[55]

Within the dimensions of the political situation in which Machiavelli lived and wrote, he favored the Great Council.[56] Like Soderini who, to counter the aristocrats, worked to maintain the Great Council in its orig-

---

[54] See above, p. 156.

[55] *Discorsi* I, chapts. 1 and 6.

[56] Machiavelli's preference for the Great Council is most explicitly stated in his "Discorso delle cose fiorentine dopo la morte di Lorenzo," but the usefulness of the participation of the people in government is one of the principal themes of the *Discorsi*; see above, notes 10-13.

inal form with its established functions, Machiavelli stressed the usefulness and necessity of this institution. Even after 1512 he remained certain that the institutional arrangements of 1494 were essentially sound, and therefore he was faced with the problem of why a regime which embodied the right principles had met with failure and collapsed. In attempting to solve this problem he came to the conclusion that the well-being of any political society depends less on its institutions than on the spirit which stands behind them. To present this idea he used the word *virtù*. The meaning of this term in his writings has many facets; basically it was an italianization of the Latin word *virtus* and denoted the fundamental quality of man which enables him to achieve great works and deeds. In the ancient world man's *virtus* was placed in relation to *Fortuna; virtus* was an innate quality opposed to external circumstance or chance. *Virtù* was not one of the various virtues which Christianity required of good men, nor was *virtù* an epitome of all Christian virtues; rather it designated the strength and vigor from which all human action arose. In his writings Machiavelli used this concept to reflect the insight, which he shared with his contemporaries, that political success depends not on the righteousness of the cause nor on the use of intelligence, but that victory could come "against all reason" to those who were inspired by single-minded willpower or by some undefinable inner force.

Virtù was the prerequisite for leadership. Every leader, whether he was captain of an army or the head of a state needed *virtù*. But, according to Machiavelli, *virtù* could be possessed by a collective body as well as by individuals. For example, an army must have *virtù*. Undoubtedly Machiavelli's application of *virtù* to collective bodies in general was instigated by the belief that military bravery is the prerequisite for military success. But the bravery of an army is not, according to Machiavelli, a natural endowment; it is rather the result of training and of discipline, to which education, religion, and the dispensing of justice must contribute. Military *virtù*, therefore, reflects a spirit which permeates all the institutions of a political society and is an aspect of a more general *virtù* which is to be found in well-organized societies.

Machiavelli's concept of *virtù* postulates the existence of coherence among the institutions of a political society. Moreover, in its widest sense his concept of *virtù* implies that certain fundamental elements of strength and vitality have to be present in any well-organized society regardless of its particular form of government. Some forms of government—in Machiavelli's opinion it was a popular government—might be superior to others, but none could function without *virtù*. Details of Machiavelli's concept of *virtù* might seem quaint and contradictory, but his concept was eminently fruitful for it contains the suggestion that in every well-organized society a spiritual element pervades all its members and institutions tying them together in a dynamic unit which is more than a summation of its constituent parts. By separating politics from other human concerns Machiavelli made one contribution to the genesis of the modern idea of the state; his concept of *virtù* represents another.

That laws exist which govern the world of politics, that man must live for politics to the exclusion of all else, that *virtù* must be present in the individual and in well-organized societies—these were the ideas which had grown in Machiavelli's mind in the years of his political and literary apprenticeship. Looking upon past events with a comprehension sharpened by distance and a concentration enhanced by passion, Machiavelli felt that disregard of those tenets had brought about the defeat of his city as well as his own failure.

Like most of his contemporaries, Machiavelli regarded the history of the ancient world as a guide which showed how man ought to act. The image of the past comprises the program of the future. But by basing his interpretation of history and his recommendations for action on a few fundamental insights gained from personal experiences, Machiavelli was able to expound political concepts which differed from those which are found in contemporary political literature. In his references to the ancient past he used material from both Greek and Roman history, from classical writers of the most different periods. But the exemplary character of antiquity is for him chiefly embodied in the history of Rome.[57] Although many of his contemporaries shared his view that the period of history from which man could learn most about the true nature of politics was the history of Rome, Machiavelli's picture of Rome contains nuances which distinguish it from those of his contemporaries. In the minds of his contemporaries the Romans were superior to all other peoples because of their political valor. But in Roman history Machiavelli saw more than the example of a society with good institutions and dutiful and heroic citizens. The significance of Roman history lay in Rome's success. Rome presented the unique phenomenon of a

---

[57] For Rome as example, see, for a general statement, *Discorsi* II, proemio, or I, chapt. 17 (*Opere*, vol. I, p. 178): ". . . questo esemplo di Roma sia da preporre a qualunque altro esemplo."

city-state which became the ruler of the world. To Machiavelli, the continuity of Roman conquests in a world of competing states raised Rome above all others. Rome alone had attained the aim to which every political society aspired. The reason for Rome's successes was the existence of an interdependence between institutions and individuals which had given vitality to Roman politics throughout the Republican period.[58] The individual Roman had been able to develop and to use his talents by means of the institutions, but the institutions had also restrained him and kept him within the bounds necessary for the well-being of the whole society. To Machiavelli, the necessary interaction between men and institutions was uniquely demonstrated in the history of Rome; this feature of Roman political life assured the possession and maintenance of *virtù*, on which the political success of a society depended.

For Machiavelli, Rome offered the pattern which ought to be adopted in modern political societies. The Florentines ought to do what the Romans had done. Machiavelli's application of the Roman example to the Florentine political scene has been somewhat overlooked because it has been assumed that he saw the future in terms of the great territorial states. It is true indeed that his diplomatic missions had widened immensely his views about the possibilities and varieties of political formations. He had become aware of the difference in strength between the large territorial states and the Italian city-states and principalities, and he was conscious that neither the wealth nor the cultural splendor of the Italian

---

[58] ". . . cosí come gli buoni costumi per mantenersi hanno bisogno delle leggi, cosí le leggi per osservarsi hanno bisogno de' buoni costumi. . . ," *Discorsi* I, chapt. 18 (*Opere*, vol. I, pp. 179-180). This idea can also be found in chapt. 58, et aliis.

city-states could compensate for their lack of military power and effective military organization. It has been supposed that Machiavelli's interest in the territorial monarchies inspired him to write the last chapter of the *Prince* in which he exhorts his compatriots to unite their forces and to liberate Italy from the barbarians. It has been taken for granted that Machiavelli longed to see Italy equal to the great European monarchies; he has been considered as the prophet of the modern national state. But such appeals to national feelings in Italy were frequent at the time; and those who made them did not envisage a permanent political unification of Italy.

An exact reading of the last chapter of the *Prince* shows that Machiavelli considered only a temporary alliance of the existing Italian rulers and city-states in order to get rid of the *oltramontani*. Moreover, this last chapter of the *Prince* is now believed to be a rhetorical exhortation which he added later to the text of the treatise.[59] It did not belong to the original text of the *Prince* and it cannot be regarded as the end for which the previous parts of the treatise were designed. Machiavelli's speculations on the European political situation which he sent to Vettori at the time he was writing the *Prince* are formulated in the traditional terms of rational calculations.[60] Nor do these speculations suggest any awareness on his part of living at the beginning of a new era of power competition. Despite his knowledge of the larger European states Machiavelli did not despair of the future of

[59] See the "nota introduttiva" to the *Prince* by Sergio Bertelli in *Opere*, vol. I, pp. 3-10, but see also the appendix for a discussion of the relevant literature.

[60] See the famous correspondence between Machiavelli and Francesco Vettori from the years 1513-1514, *Opere*, vol. VI, pp. 232-368.

the city-state. The situation of Florence, although serious, was not hopeless. The intensity with which Machiavelli discussed every detail of Roman politics was stimulated by his belief that Rome was what Florence might have been and perhaps might still become.

The primary question—in the sense that all further reflections on the relevance of Roman history to Florentine politics depended on the answer—which Machiavelli had to face was "whether in a corrupt state it is possible to maintain a free government."[61] There was no doubt in Machiavelli's mind that corruption had entered Florentine political life. There had to be a "reform," and, like his contemporaries, he thought that reform must be "a return to the beginnings";[62] but unlike some of his contemporaries, he did not believe that reform could be effected *only* by reconstituting the institutions which that society had had at the time of its beginnings. The particular turn which Machiavelli gave to the problem of reform is implicit in his ideas about the origins of political societies. Like his contemporaries, he regarded political societies as the creation of man, and thus he recognized the existence of lawgivers at the beginning of any society. But in his writings he endowed the lawgiver with powers more divine than human.[63] The lawgiver is a towering figure not only because he establishes the institutions of a political society, but also because he infuses the spirit which gives a society cohesion and strength.

[61] "Se in una città corrotta si può mantenere lo stato libero," *Discorsi* I, chapt. 18 (*Opere*, vol. I, p. 179).

[62] The crucial passages are in *Discorsi* III, chapt. 1, with the title: "A volere che una sètta o una republica viva lungamente, è necessario ritirarla spesso verso il suo principio," but also chapts. 8, 22, etc.

[63] *Il Principe*, chapt. 6, *Discorsi* I, chapts. 2, 9, 10.

Thus, to Machiavelli, "return to the beginnings" was a continuous process. It meant keeping alive the spirit which stands behind the institutions of a society. In a rapidly changing world it was necessary to subject institutions to frequent examinations to test the efficacy of their original purpose: development of *virtù*.

Although Machiavelli believed that eventual decline and final dissolution of any human society was inevitable, he was impressed that the Romans had been able to stave off their inescapable fate for centuries—longer than had any other political society. The Romans had established tribunes and censors for the purpose of investigating whether institutions fulfilled their function of preserving the vitality of the Republic,[64] and Machiavelli suggested that in Florence officials ought to be created and charged with the duty to undertake such examinations. But there was still a difference between the idea of keeping *virtù* alive and that of reviving *virtù* after it had disappeared. Machiavelli was never quite able to decide whether political *virtù* could be regained once it had been lost.[65] If *virtù* could not be restored, then there might not be any chance for ever establishing a strong republican regime in Florence. Machiavelli could not bring himself to admit this contingency. But his theoretical proposition that the functioning of institutions depended on the existence of *virtù* seemed to exclude the possibility of enacting reform purely by making institutional changes. Because

---

[64] *Discorsi*, III, chapt. 1, particularly p. 381 in *Opere*, vol. I.

[65] *Discorsi* I, chapts. 16-18; Machiavelli's pessimism about the prospects of a republican regime in Florence is also outbalanced by his view that Tuscany is especially suited for republics, see *Discorsi* I, chapt. 55 (*Opere*, vol. I, p. 257); on this notion, see Hans Baron, *The Crisis of the Early Italian Renaissance*, Princeton, 1955, vol. I, p. 361.

Machiavelli was unwilling to give up hope that Florence might be able to follow in the steps of Rome, his views on this issue remained ambiguous.

In the light of his knowledge of Florentine history and Florentine politics, two phenomena of Roman political behavior seemed to him especially pertinent and worth pondering: the internal tensions in Rome and the excellence of Roman political leadership. Ever since Dante had compared Florence to a feverish woman squirming around on her bed cushions from one side to another,[66] internal dissensions were regarded as the bane of Florentine politics. Machiavelli's own view of the obstructionist policy of Florentine aristocrats was in accord with this explanation of the causes of Florence's decline; he criticized factions quite as bitterly as did his Florentine contemporaries.[67] But party struggles had raged in Rome, and in the *Discourses* he declared that "the disunion of the senate and people renders the republic of Rome powerful and free."[68] It might appear that Machiavelli was inconsistent on this issue, but to him, condemnation of Florentine factionalism and approbation of Roman party struggles was not a contradiction. He regarded political divisions as dangerous and destructive if one group claimed special rights which were to be denied to other parts of the society, and if this same group used its influence in the government to promote its own interests. He feared that, as a consequence of directing policy in the interests of a particular group, a rigidification of positions would take

---

[66] "Vedrai te simigliante a quella inferma
    che non può trovar posa in su le piume
    ma con dar volta suo dolore scherma," *La Divina Commedia, Purgatorio,* canto 6.

[67] *Discorsi* I, chapts. 7 and 8.

[68] "Che la disunione della Plebe e del Senato romano fece libera e potente quella republica," title of *Discorsi* I, chapt. 4.

place which would paralyze the vitality of a society and in its final effects result in the establishment of a tyranny of an individual or of a small group.[69]

However, Machiavelli accepted as an established and necessary fact the existence of groupings within a political society.[70] According to their personalities men differed in their inherent potential; thus their political usefulness varied. Ambitious men should have a chance to use their talents for leadership; those men who lacked ambition and therefore were easily disciplined and obedient were essential for the execution of policy. Machiavelli believed that the division of the Roman citizenry into senators and people had its basis in these psychological distinctions.[71] When political groupings were determined by factors— such as wealth or birth—which had nothing to do with political effectiveness,[72] then the common good was threatened. On the other hand, when natural psychological differences became the criteria for distinguishing the two groups, each making a necessary but distinctive contribution to politics, then the government should be shared by both groups, each of which should fulfill strictly separate functions. Because the government of the Roman republic had been organized in this manner Machiavelli thought that party divisions in Rome had not been destructive; indeed, why he believed that they, by keeping alive the spirit of competition, had increased the vitality of the society.[73]

[69] *Discorsi* I, chapt. 18 (*Opere*, vol. I, pp. 180-181).

[70] *Il Principe*, chapt. 9 (*Opere*, vol. I, p. 45): "Perché in ogni città si truovano questi dua umori diversi . . . ," or *Discorsi* I, chapt. 4 (*Opere*, vol. I, p. 137): ". . . sono in ogni republica due umori diversi. . . ."

[71] *Discorsi* I, chapt. 5.

[72] *Discorsi* I, chapt. 60 and III, chapts. 16 and 25.

[73] See *Discorsi* III, chapt. 19: ". . . la plebe romana aveva in Roma equale imperio con la Nobilità," and, in particular, Ma-

But Machiavelli realized that factionalism was not the only reason for the collapse of the republican regime in Florence. As vehemently as Machiavelli denounced the opposition of the aristocrats to Soderini, Machiavelli was aware that Soderini had been weak and vacillating, trying to find a "middle way" instead of giving clear direction to Florentine policy.[74] In spite of his political indebtedness to Soderini, Machiavelli was not blind to the *Gonfaloniere*'s deficiencies. A stronger man might have made better use of the opportunities which his position gave him. Florence had been not only torn by dissensions; the city had also lacked political leadership.

The problem of political leadership was a principal concern of Machiavelli and a prominent issue in both the *Prince* and the *Discourses*. A great deal of discussion has centered on the question of how it was possible for the author of the *Prince*, "a handbook for tyrants," to write also the *Discourses*, the theme of which is the idealization of a free republic. Machiavelli's contemporaries would have found the seeming disparity of his subject matter less astounding and less objectionable than we do. They were accustomed to write under an external stimulus, often with the intention of gaining the favor of a patron; it was by no means rare for the literati of the time to write books on monarchies as well as on republics.[75] Moreover, the contrast between the *Prince* and the *Discourses* is more apparent than fundamental; in both works the problem of political leadership is clearly a basic issue. In the *Prince* Machiavelli's vantage point was from above. His "new prince" was the perfect leader who disciplined his

---

chiavelli's discussion of the role of people and nobility in Rome in *Discorsi* I, chapts. 4 and 5.

[74] *Discorsi* III, chapts. 3, 9, 30.

[75] See above, p. 90.

subjects and established a strong political organization. Throughout his writings Machiavelli stated the proposition that all men are evil,[76] and his supposition that all men shared an identical nature was a prerequisite for his belief in the existence of political laws of general validity. However, his opinion that all men are evil had a particular significance for the *Prince*, in which *virtù* is concentrated in the leader. Machiavelli's prince made human weaknesses serve the purpose of his policy. By purely rational calculations based on the assumption that men are dominated by egoistic interests, a prince could control his subjects. He could prevent them from uniting in opposition to his regime by playing on their selfish interests. The prince alone would embody the interests of the whole society, and those over whom he ruled would be mere instruments which he could use according to his will.

Machiavelli's construction of a perfect prince heightened his interest in outlining the picture of an equally efficient republic, but it also increased the problems involved in the task. It is evident that a political organization in which the whole society was inspired by *virtù* would be superior to one which depended on the *virtù* of a single leader.[77] But how could an entire society achieve *virtù*? It could happen only by the elimination of all motivations—such as the striving for wealth—which might prevent man from concentrating his energies on politics. According to Machiavelli, Roman history showed that uniform poverty, or at least economic equality was a pre-condition for the achievement of *virtù*.[78]

[76] See above, note 14.
[77] *Discorsi* I, chapts. 11 and 17.
[78] See above, note 50.

However, even in a political society in which men were inhibited from working for personal material gains, there remained a fundamental inequality between the leaders and the people. Machiavelli was aware that even if political groupings developed according to men's political usefulness, these groupings contained a potential danger. Machiavelli realized that those who belonged to the group of the leaders will always tend to monopolize power. "I agree that a republic cannot survive nor be governed at all well unless in it there are citizens of good repute. On the other hand, the reputation citizens acquire in a republic may bring about a tyranny."[79] Machiavelli believed that the Roman republic had demonstrated the solution of this dilemma. Rome had given to its leaders rewards which satisfied their ambitions but prevented them from becoming a threat to freedom. The tendency of the leaders towards usurpation had been kept in check by entrusting the people with the election of the leaders. Observance of religion and tradition had guaranteed the obedience of the people because they were fearful of violating hallowed customs and of breaking laws.[80] Most of all, a pitiless and equal application of law had inhibited the rise of tyranny.[81]

A kind of rational psychology, making use of man's inborn drives for the purposes of politics, is present in both the *Prince* and the *Discourses*. But the directing influence which a prince possessed in his state would in a republic have to be exerted by institutions. Whereas a

[79] ". . . dico che una republica sanza i cittadini riputati non può stare, né può governarsi in alcuno modo bene. Dall'altro canto, la riputazione de' cittadini è cagione della tirannide delle republiche," *Discorsi* III, chapt. 28 (*Opere*, vol. I, p. 463).

[80] *Discorsi* I, chapts. 11, 13.

[81] *Discorsi* I, chapts. 24, 45.

prince could permit free rein to man's egoistic interests because the prince could control and manipulate them for his own ends, in a republic social life had to be organized in such a way that all of man's drives would be directed towards the state. Men would respond instinctively to the demands of politics.

According to Machiavelli, actions, whether they were those of an individual or those of a collective group, could be the result of motivations which could be rationally explained, but they could also be instinctive. Of this there is testimony in Machiavelli's strange description of the pagan "sacrificial acts in which there was much shedding of blood and much ferocity, and in them great numbers of animals were killed. Such spectacles, because terrible, caused men to become like them."[82] The ideal at which Machiavelli aimed in his recommendations for a perfect republic was the creation of a unified body, which, by acting instinctively, generated the strength, single-minded will power, and vitality necessary for political success. Such a republic possessed *virtù*.

Although there was nothing new in Machiavelli's use of the Roman republic as a pattern for imitation, he differed from his contemporaries in what he believed the Roman example taught. Machiavelli's views made it easier than his contemporaries thought—as well as more difficult—to imitate Rome. To Machiavelli, political revival could not be achieved only by imitating Roman insti-

[82] "Qui non mancava la pompa né la magnificenza delle cerimonie, ma vi si aggiugneva l'azione del sacrificio pieno di sangue e di ferocità, ammazzandovisi moltitudine d'animali: il quale aspetto, sendo terribile, rendeva gli uomini simili a lui", *Discorsi* II, chapt. 2 (*Opere*, vol. I, p. 282). See also the famous passage in *Il Principe*, chapt. 18 (*Opere*, vol. I, p. 72) or see *Discorsi* I, chapt. 16: (*Opere*, vol. I, p. 173): the people as "animale bruto," etc., etc.

tutions or just by effecting a moral reeducation of individuals in order to produce obedience and self-sacrifice. But they were accompaniments and consequences of what was essential for a political renaissance. To Machiavelli, the imitation of Rome meant a return to a life according to man's inherent natural instincts.

To Machiavelli, man is one of the forces of nature and man's strength emerges in accepting this fate. This conception of man gave Machiavelli's political utopia its unique character. For Machiavelli *was* the creator of an utopia; with his image of Roman politics he made his contribution to the body of literature in which perfect societies are constructed. But whereas the architects of other utopias place man outside history in a social world free of political conflicts and tensions so that he can live in permanent harmony and peace, Machiavelli's ideal polical order was one in which man lives in time and is subject to its ravages. It was the test of a good political order to grow, to expand and to absorb other political societies, even to ward off decline for a while as Rome had been able to do. But decline was inevitable; everything on earth has to undergo the natural cycle of birth, flowering, decline and death.[83] Man's action remains tied to the specific, steadily changing circumstances of the situation in which he finds himself at the moment. It was of little relevance to consider man's qualities abstractly and in isolation; the interaction of man and his surroundings was the sensitive point at which the potentialities of man for political action were revealed.

[83] "Egli è cosa verissima come tutte le cose del mondo hanno il termine della vita loro," *Discorsi* III, chapt. 1 (*Opere*, vol. I, p. 379), or 6 (*Opere*, vol. I, p. 145) "sendo tutte le cose degli uomini in moto," or at many other places.

The crucial significance of this idea becomes evident when we go beyond a discussion of Machiavelli's political views and analyze the assumptions on which they were based. Machiavelli was not a philosopher. He intended neither to outline a philosophical system nor to introduce new philosophical terms. Here again what is characteristic is the particular turn which he gave to the commonly used concepts dealing with the problems of human existence. The great images through which Machiavelli tried to define the strength and weakness of man's position in the universe were the same as those used by his contemporaries: *Fortuna, virtù,* and *Necessità.* But a precise reading of Machiavelli's works reveals distinctive variations. Like others who wrote before him, Machiavelli recognized *Necessità* as a factor determining actions but outside man's control. However, in Machiavelli's view *Necessità* is not just a hostile force which makes man's actions purely automatic.[84] *Necessità* may coerce man to take an action which reason demands; *Necessità* may create opportunities. In whatever situation man finds himself the final outcome depends on his response to the conditions which *Necessità* has produced. Thus, according to Machiavelli, rarely is there a situation which ought to be regarded as entirely desperate. At most times there are possibilities for men to turn circumstances to their advantage. As long as man uses all the capacities with which nature has endowed him he is not helpless in the face of external pressures.

The view that man has the possibility of controlling

---

[84] See particularly *Discorsi* III, chapt. 12 (*Opere,* vol. I, p. 425): "Altre volte abbiamo discorso quanto sia utile alle umane azioni la necessità, ed a quale gloria siano sute condutte da quella. . . ," but also I, chapt. 3 or 6: ". . . a molte cose che la ragione non t'induce, t'induce la necessità" (*Opere,* vol. I, p. 145).

events also shaped Machiavelli's idea of the relation between *virtù* and *Fortuna*. In general Machiavelli's ideas on this topic were again those commonly held in his time: he believed that man can exert a certain counterweight against *Fortuna*, and that there is a certain balance between *virtù* and *Fortuna*: "I think it may be true that *Fortuna* is the ruler of half of our actions, but that she allows the other half or thereabouts to be governed by us," he writes in the twenty-fifth chapter of the *Prince* on "How much *Fortuna* can do in human affairs and how it may be opposed."[85] At the end of the same chapter he wrote the famous statement that "*Fortuna* is a woman, and it is necessary, if you wish to master her, to conquer her by force; and it can be seen that she lets herself be overcome by the bold rather than by those who proceed coldly."[86] Others before Machiavelli had said that *Fortuna* was capricious and smiled only on those who were her favorites. The assumption of *Fortuna*'s preference for the bold re-echoed the Latin adage that "*fortes fortuna adjuvat.*" However Machiavelli's formulation modified these common views. In contrast to the static quality inherent in the belief in the existence of *Fortuna*'s elect, Machiavelli's formulation presumed the dynamism of a constantly changing scene in which sudden action can bring about the assistance of *Fortuna*.

[85] ". . . iudico potere esser vero che la fortuna sia arbitra della metà delle azioni nostre, ma che etiam lei ne lasci governare l'altra metà, o presso, a noi," *Il Principe*, chapt. 25 (*Opere*, vol. I, p. 99) with the title: "Quantum fortuna in rebus humanis possit, et quomodo illi sit occurrendum."

[86] ". . . la fortuna è donna; et è necessario, volendola tenere sotto, batterla et urtarla. E si vede che la si lascia piú vincere da questi, che da quelli che freddamenta procedono," *ibid.*, p. 101. For an application of this view to the course of history, see *Discorsi* II, chapt. 1, but also chapt. 29, 30, and III, chapt. 31.

A further implication in Machiavelli's simile of the relation between *virtú* and *Fortuna* also expressed his belief that this constant change takes the form of a struggle; continuous strife is an abiding condition of political life. His insistence on the decisive importance of power in politics can be regarded as the counterpart of this fundamental attitude to the nature of politics. His image pitting *virtù* and *Fortuna* against each other in a struggle for superiority indicates that he believed that the chance of controlling external events is offered to man only in brief, fleeting moments. Therefore man must make use of a singular conjuncture in which there must be a meeting of circumstances and individuality.[87]

This demand for coincidence of individual *virtù* with favorable circumstances pointed to the most striking and revolutionary feature of Machiavelli's political thought. No special human quality will guarantee success in politics; the qualities by which man can control events vary according to the circumstances. The impetuosity with which Julius II conducted his policy was appropriate to the situation in which the Church State found itself in the time of his reign. In less turbulent years the careful, almost timid rationalism of Soderini might have prevailed and saved Florence.[88] This kind of relativism pervades all the chapters of the *Prince* in which Machiavelli discussed the qualities required for political leadership.

These chapters of the *Prince* contain the essence of Machiavelli's thought in the sense that they exhibit most strongly his view that political action cannot be kept within the limits of morality. Although he indicated that amoral action might frequently be the most effective

---

[87] See above, note 20, and *Discorsi* III, chapt. 9.
[88] *Discorsi* III, chapt. 9 (*Opere*, vol. I, p. 418).

measure which can be taken in any situation, he never showed a preference for amoral actions over moral actions. He was not a conscious advocate of evil; he did not want to upset all moral values. But it is equally misleading to maintain the opposite: that Machiavelli wanted to replace Christian morality by another morality and that he encouraged politicians to disregard customary morality because their motives for acting ought to be the good of the political society which represented the highest ethical value. Just as Machiavelli admitted that it might be possible to found political societies which could exist in peaceful isolation, he also believed that men could arrange their lives in such a manner that they could follow Christian morality.[89] But when men joined the game of politics they had to follow its rules; and these rules did not contain a distinction between moral and amoral actions.

Because Machiavelli felt that Christian morality frequently formed an obstacle to actions dictated by the rules of politics, he criticized Christian morality and the Church. On the other hand, because he realized the usefulness of religion for disciplining the members of society, he envisaged a religion, perhaps even a true Christianity, which broadened the concept of morality in such a way that it would encompass not only the virtues of suf-

[89] "Sono questi modi crudelissimi e nimici d'ogni vivere non solamente cristiano ma umano; e debbegli qualunque uomo fuggire, e volere piuttosto vivere privato che re con tanta rovina degli uomini; nondimeno colui che non vuole pigliare quella prima via del bene, quando si voglia mantenere conviene che entri in questo male," *Discorsi* I, chapt. 26 (*Opere,* vol. I, p. 194), but on Machiavelli's views on Christianity and Church see also *Discorsi* I, chapt. 12. On the issue of political isolation, see *Discorsi* I, chapts. 6 and 19; Machiavelli was skeptical about the possibility of keeping a state permanently out of power competition.

fering and humility, but also that of political activism.[90] But such observations were incidental rather than basic to Machiavelli's thinking. The central point of his political philosophy was that man must choose: he could live aside from the stream of politics and follow the dictates of Christian morality; but if man entered upon the *vita activa* of politics, he must act according to its laws.[91]

Finally Machiavelli's image of man's need to conquer *Fortuna* by force—corresponding to man's sexual drive—suggests the tension which Machiavelli regarded as a necessary accompaniment of political action. The need to concentrate on a brief moment, the need to use all possible weapons, and the need to choose from a variety of methods the one best suited to the given situation—all this implied that political action demanded not only awareness of one's aim but also intensity in pursuing it. Similar to the passage in the *Discourses* in which he saw men becoming animals, he suggested in the *Prince* that the ruler should be a lion or a fox, or best, both.[92] He did not refer to animals because they symbolize human qualities; to Machiavelli, animals possess the pristine genuineness which, in men, is weakened by reason. Man's control over his world depends on his attaining a level of instinctiveness where he becomes part of the forces surrounding him. This identification is prerequisite for man's mastery of political life.

Machiavelli believed in the creative power of man in the world of politics. Man's political potentialities com-

---

[90] "[Men] hanno interpretato la nostra religione secondo l'ozio e non secondo la virtù," *Discorsi* II, chapt. 2 (*Opere*, vol. I, p. 283).

[91] See above, note 84.

[92] "Sendo adunque uno principe necessitato sapere bene usare la bestia, debbe di quelle pigliare la golpe et il lione.", *Il Principe*, chapt. 18 (*Opere*, vol. I, p. 72).

prised two aspects. Like many of his contemporaries Machiavelli believed in the rational nature of man; to him man was an instrument which had a rationally definable purpose and he could be employed in a calculable way. But at the same time, Machiavelli also saw man as an animal, driven by instincts which made him disregard obstacles and rational interests and which enabled him to exploit incalculable forces. But the opportunity when man could exert his power was rare, the moment brief and fleeting. Man was placed in a constantly changing world in which new forces and new situations were thrown up at any moment.

This recognition of the supreme challenge inherent in the ceaseless movement of history was a reflection of what Machiavelli had seen happening in Italy and all over Europe. And what had happened was becoming increasingly evident to greater numbers of Italians. Although Machiavelli's political proposals were aimed at answering questions raised by specific problems of the Florentine city-state, he was aware—and because of his experience as a diplomat he was certainly quite as well aware as anyone—of the relation of the Florentine crisis to the appearance of foreign armies on Italian soil. Since the French invasion of 1494, whatever happened in Italy was dependent on the struggles among the great powers beyond the Alps. The Italians had lost control over their fate, and every order, every peace was put in jeopardy again and again by new waves of invaders. The crises which had been shaking the Italian states since 1494 made it clear that every political action in Italy was circumscribed by forces originating at great distances. It was natural for Machiavelli to draw the conclusion that the dimension in which politics worked was history and that every political action had to be fitted into the context of historical change.

If, as we set forth at the beginning of this chapter, it was Machiavelli's intention to startle his readers with novel and contrary statements, his success was greater than ever he could have expected. To the religious of his age and of the following centuries his teachings—especially his proposition that man must choose between the rules of political activism and the precepts of Christian morality—were thought to be machinations of the devil. For his insistence on struggle and force as the quintessence of politics he was anathematized by those who believed in the harmony existing between enlightened self-interest and the common good. In more recent times he has been called the prophet of the national state and he has been credited with the discovery of the role of the ruling group in politics. There has been no generation since the time of the Renaissance which has not found some aspect of Machiavelli's writings repulsive or prophetic, puzzling or revealing. But the individual theses which he propounded would hardly have provoked such a furore had they not formed parts of a vision of politics, relevant and valid. Machiavelli expressed what men were slowly coming to realize: it is impossible to establish one permanent social order which mirrors the will of God or in which justice is distributed in such a way that it fulfills all human needs. Machiavelli clung to the idea that politics had its own laws and therefore it was, or ought to be, a science; its purpose was to keep society alive in the ever-moving stream of history. The consequences of this view—a recognition of the need for political cohesion and the proposition of the autonomy of politics which later developed into the concept of the state—have made Machiavelli's writings a landmark in the history of political thought. We can never return to concepts of politics which existed before Machiavelli wrote.

But Machiavelli is not merely a figure who contributed to the evolution of modern Western political thought. When we read his works we find that they still speak to us directly, immediately, in a strangely compelling way. Many of his examples are antiquated, many of his proposals exaggerated and unreal. But there are insights which disclose an apposite truth, there are passages which touch us like an electric shock. In placing politics in the stream of history, in demonstrating that every situation is unique and requires man to use all his forces to probe all the potentialities of the moment, Machiavelli has revealed— more than anyone before or after him—that, at any time, politics is choice and decision. Tanto nomini nullum par elogium.

PART II

History

Chapter 5 THE THEORY AND PRACTICE OF HISTORY IN THE FIFTEENTH CENTURY

• I •

Before the beginning of the sixteenth century historical writing had been given a definite form and shape by the humanists. Although many works on historical subjects were written in the Middle Ages, the humanists were the first in the post-classical world to conceive of historical writing as an important and independent literary genre. An episode which occurred in 1495 provides us with an excellent illustration of the humanist view on the writing of history.

Bernardo Rucellai, whom we have encountered as a prominent Florentine aristocrat and a patron of humanists, was on a mission to Naples. He was planning to write a history of the French invasion which had just taken place, and he made use of his stay in Naples to consult the great humanist Pontano.[1] Rucellai was invited to at-

[1] The following is based on Rucellai's description of his meeting with Pontano in a letter to Roberto Acciaiuoli, published in *Sylloges Epistolarum a viris illustribus scriptarum*, ed. Petrus Burmannus, Leyden, 1727, vol. II, pp. 200-202; the original of this letter seems to be lost. The letter is published without date. The meeting must have taken place in 1495, because this was the only time that Rucellai visited Naples after the French invasion of 1494. Fontius, in a letter to Bernardo Rucellai from March 1512, published in Bartholomaeus Fontius, *Epistolarum Libri III*, ed. L. Juhasz, Budapest, 1931, pp. 60-64, mentions that he had seen

tend one of the meetings of Pontano's academy which convened regularly in a garden at the foot of Vesuvius. Because of Rucellai's historical project, the theme of the meeting was the writing of history. It was characteristic of the humanist approach that the debate focussed on the problem involved in the imitation of classical models. First, some dispute arose over the question whether the modern historian should take one outstanding classical historian as his model, or whether he should study a number of ancient historical authors and select from each, for use as a pattern, those features in which the classical author excelled. The advocates of the synthetic method of procedure won the day. The next issue was to decide which of the classical historians deserved to serve as models. The result of the discussion made the task of a synthetic method much more manageable because only a very few classical historians were accepted as possible patterns. None of them was Greek because it was believed that the Romans had advanced beyond the Greeks, and also because Roman literature had an indubitable climax, the Augustan Age. No writer before or after had equalled the achievements of the Roman writers of that

---

Rucellai's description of the discussion with Pontano. This would indicate that Rucellai's letter to Acciaiuoli was meant to be a literary treatise rather than a personal letter, but it raises also the question whether Rucellai composed this piece immediately after his visit to Naples or much later, perhaps only after reading Pontano's "Actius." Fontius, in his letter to Rucellai, made some interesting, slightly critical, remarks on Pontano's theories: "Non enim semper eodem modo et ordine neque iisdem sententiis aut verbis utendum est. Nam locorum, temporum personarum et cuiusque fortunate auctoritas gradusque ratio est habenda." To Fontius, Livy was the one classical historian whom historical writers ought to imitate: "Caeterum in poetis maxime imitandus Vergilius, in oratoribus Tullius, in historicis Livius . . . De dicendo et imitandum . . . Nuthianum judicium. Quod probabis, si placuerit. Aut in Pontanico permanebis, si contra senseris."

period. Tacitus already was "far removed from the earlier dignity and grace."[2] It was established that there were only three perfect models: Caesar, Sallust, Livy. Among them the greatest praise was given to Livy: he is "equal to the Greeks whom he imitated, and superior to those who came later."[3]

It was not by accident that Rucellai turned to Pontano for advice on the writing of history, for the Neapolitan was one of the few humanists who, as his dialogue *Actius*[4] shows, had a serious and systematic interest in this subject. For the most part, statements on the nature of history are dispersed in letters, in dedications, and in speeches and lectures. Thus the letter in which Rucellai reported on the discussion of Pontano and his friends is one of the few brief statements of the common and accepted humanist notions on the writing of history.

The probable reason for the paucity of theoretical treatises on history by the humanists is that there is no special work or systematic treatment of the theory and methods of history in classical literature. The distinction which Aristotle in his *Poetics* had drawn between poetry and history,[5] the emphasis which Cicero in his *De Oratore*[6] had placed on the differences between the historian

[2] ". . . longe abest a pristina dignitate et gratia," Rucellai in *Sylloges*, vol. II, p. 202.

[3] ". . . par Graecis quos ille aemulatus est, supraque posteros," *ibid.*, p. 202.

[4] Published in Giovanni Pontano, *I Dialoghi*, ed. Carmelo Previterra, Firenze, 1943, pp. 127-239.

[5] Aristotle, *Poetics*, chapt. 9; for a recent comment, see A. W. Gomme, *The Greek Attitude to Poetry and History, Sather Classical Lectures*, vol. XXVII (1954).

[6] Cicero, *De Oratore*, book II, chapt. 15: "Videtisne, quantum munus sit oratoris historia? Haud scio, an flumine orationis et varietate maximum. Neque tamen eam reperio usquam separatim instructam rhetorum praeceptis: sita sunt enim ante oculos. Nam

and the rhetorician, and the few remarks on the special style appropriate for the writing of history by Cicero in *Orator*[7] represent the major sources for the views of the ancients on the theory of history.[8] Discussions by humanists on this problem derive from these passages of Aristotle and Cicero. The humanists, following Aristotle, compared poetry and history and placed poetry above history; and in accordance with Cicero the humanists characterized truth as the basic requirement for historical writings. The humanists also explained the particular features of historical style and elaborated on Cicero's suggestions for the contents of histories: military campaigns and topographical details. Moreover, the humanists illustrated Cicero's brief remarks by referring to examples from the writings of classical historians.

The preeminence of Sallust and Livy was generally acknowledged. Caesar, as the author of commentaries on events in which he himself had participated, was not regarded as a typical historian; the true historian was not expected to have been personally involved in the histori-

---

quis nescit, primam esse historiae legem, ne quid falsi dicere audeat? Ne qua suspicio gratiae sit in scribendo? Ne qua simultatis? Haec scilicet fundamenta nota sunt omnibus; ipsa autem exaedificatio posita est in rebus et verbis"; for the rest of Cicero's chapter see below, p. 273.

[7] Cicero, *Orator*, chapt. 11 (on special style of speeches in histories), chapt. 20 ("Huic generi historia finitima est. In qua et narratur ornate et regio saepe aut pugna describitur; interponuntur etiam contiones et hortationes. Sed in his tracta quaedam et fluens expetitur, non haec contorta et acris oratio"); chapt. 34 ("Quid enim est aetas hominis, nisi ea memoria rerum veterum cum superiorum aetate contexitur?"); chapt. 61 (fluency of historical style).

[8] Also Quintilian's statements on history, although clearly derivative from Aristotle and Cicero, were used, see particularly Quintilian, *Institutio Oratoria*, bk. X, chapt. 1, 31, and the comparison of Greek and Latin historians in bk. X, chapt. 1, 101-102.

cal situations about which he was writing.[9] But the paradigmatic character of Livy and Sallust was regularly stressed. For instance, Gregory of Trebizond said he would try to "explain what history is, with Sallust and Livy, who, I believe, should today be used as models in the writing of history."[10] Or Sabellicus, in a speech on the praise of history, declared that in his opinion "there would never be a history which could better instruct about political institutions than the one which Livy had written."[11] The most comprehensive and systematic justification of this view is contained in a lecture which Bartolomaeus Fontius gave in Florence and which might be regarded as the first brief history of historical writing.[12] Fontius began with an evaluation of the chief Greek historians; he then discussed the Roman historical writers, and this was the place where he established the exemplary character of Livy's history. Livy excelled all other historians in his eloquence, his comprehensiveness, his

[9] See Pontano, "Actius," *loc. cit.*, p. 231: ". . . tamen scribendi genus historicum ex omni parte minime complexus est Caesar, quippe qui materiam et praebere et relinquere maluerit aliis de se scribendi." This notion comes from Cicero, *Brutus*, chapt. 75: "Sed dum voluit alios habere parata, unde sumerent qui vellent scribere historiam. . . ."

[10] "Sallustii e T. Livii quos his diebus in historia solum imitandos censeo, genus dicendi, quale sit, enodabimus," Georgii Trapezuntii, *Rhetoricum Libri V*, Aldus, 1523, f. 82v. (in Leyden edition of 1547, p. 512).

[11] ". . . neque ut arbitror, futura est historia, quae melius vitam possit in omnes civiles disciplinas instruere quam haec quam Livius scripsit . . . ," Sabellicus, "Oratio de laudibus historiae in Titum Livium," *Opera*, Basilea, 1560, vol. IV, p. 482.

[12] On Fontius' *Oratio in Historiae Laudationem*, see Charles Trinkaus, "A Humanist's Image of Humanism: the Inaugural Orations of Bartolommeo della Fonte," *Studies in the Renaissance*, vol. VII (1960), particularly pp. 99-105. Trinkaus states, p. 105: ". . . this oration manages to see historical writing in a historical perspective and to present the rudiments, at least, of a conception of the nature of history."

clarity of organization, and his style. Fontius admitted
that later historical writers, like Eutropius, Orosius, or
Aegidius Colonna might give some valuable information.
Nevertheless the decline of Latin style in these later
times prohibited the writing of a worthwhile historical
work. Only in Fontius' own age, since Petrarch had
"brought the Latin language back in its fatherland,"[13]
had history, together with all the other literary genres,
come again into its own; and Fontius referred for proof
of his statement to Biondo, Bruni, and Poggio. They had
imitated the historical writers of the time of Rome's
greatness—as historians ought to do.

The allusions to the works of Biondo, Bruni, and Poggio illuminate the problem inherent in the humanist considerations on the writing of history. The humanists believed that writers of histories ought to follow the same
principle which the humanists applied to all their literary
efforts: the principle of "imitation." But the events with
which the humanist historians dealt had happened after
the fall of the Roman Empire; to a large extent, their subject matter was "modern." Considering the necessary difference in content which controlled their work, how was
it possible for a humanist historian to imitate classical
authors?

First of all, the counsel to take Livy and Sallust as patterns meant that historical writers should imitate the form
and style of these Roman authors. Like Livy's *History
of Rome*, each history ought to be divided in a number of
books, and each of them ought to begin with some general reflections. The narration should proceed from year
to year. Moreover, these classical writers had used cer-

[13] "His primus profecto fuit qui Latinam linguam . . . reduxit in
patriam."

tain stylistic devices which were especially suited to the writing of history. In *Actius*, Pontano mentioned particularly *brevitas* and *celeritas*; he explained these terms by quoting passages from Sallust and Livy, and he declared that, by using these stylistic means, the author could provide both knowledge of background and detail, and the impression of a rapid development of events.[14]

But historical writers were also to learn from classical authors what aspects of history were worth describing. Sallust's themes had been single wars, and so humanist historians wrote about single wars. Pontano wrote on Ferdinand of Naples' war against his Barons, Sanudo wrote on the Ferrarese war, Simonetta on the war of Sforza against Naples, and Rucellai on the war of Charles VIII. Livy's masterpiece was the history of Rome, of a city-state. Thus the humanists followed him in composing the histories of the city-states of their own times. The outstanding works were the histories of Florence written by Bruni, Poggio, and Scala, and the *Deche* of Venetian History which Sabellicus wrote; but Genoa, Milan, Bologna, Verona, all had humanist historians trying to create for their city a monument equal to that which Livy had erected for Rome.[15] Whatever time or places the humanist historians chose, Sallust and Livy taught them that their exclusive concern was politics. Although—as Livy had shown—internal struggles and the development of institutions deserved some attention, the principal topic ought to be foreign policy, especially wars and military actions. "Res gestae plerumque sunt bellicae."[16]

[14] Pontano, "Actius," *loc. cit.*, pp. 209-217.
[15] For details, see Eduard Fueter, *Geschichte der neueren Historiographie*, rev. edition, Munich and Berlin, 1936.
[16] Pontano, "Actius," *loc. cit.*, p. 218.

Cicero had said that the historian is to show "not only what was done and said, but also how and why,"[17] and this phrase was frequently echoed by the humanists.[18] Because the humanist historians dealt with the same aspects of history with which classical historians had dealt, the manner in which the ancient historians had proceeded in describing the "what" and the "how" was considered to be applicable to the treatment of the modern events with which the humanist historians were concerned. There was a fixed pattern, derived from classical histories, for the narration of a war. It might begin with a survey of the character and the history of the peoples which were involved, followed by an explanation of the negotiations which preceded the war. Only then could the historian embark on his proper task: the narrative of military events. Quite logically, a description of a battle dominated the historical work. Pontano suggested that the historian begin the story of a battle with an account of the omens presaging the outcome of the struggle.[19] The next requirement was a precise topological explanation of the area where the battle took place; that should be followed by brief character sketches of the chief military leaders, a detailed recital of the way in which the troops on the opposing sides were arranged, and a description of the war machines of the two armies.

[17] "Non solum quid actum aut dictum sit, sed etiam quomodo . . . ," Cicero, *De Oratore*, book II, chapt. 15; for the entire passage see above note 6 and below, p. 273.

[18] "In rebus gestis non solum quid actum aut dictum sit sed etiam quomodo et cur demonstrabit," Georgii Trapezuntii, *op. cit.*, f. 82v (in Leyden edition of 1547, p. 509). Similar statements are frequent, see, for instance, Guarino Veronese, *Epistolario*, ed. Sabbadini (*Miscellanea di Storia Veneta*, serie III, vol. 11, Venezia, 1916), vol. II, p. 463 et seq.

[19] Pontano, "Actius," *loc. cit.*, p. 221, and also for the following.

Such an elaborate construction made the battle the high-point. Likewise, the instrument by which humanist historians were to interpret the psychological motivation behind the course of events was of classical origin: the insertion of speeches in the text. Speeches served to emphasize the importance of an event. They were regularly placed in the narrative at the beginning of a battle when each captain was described as addressing his troops and stating the issues for which the war was being fought. Speeches served also as a means for indicating to the reader the alternatives of a given moment; often speeches were presented in pairs, one advocating the pros and the other the cons of a possible course of action.[20] The humanist historians were not concerned whether or not such deliberations had actually taken place. Since it was believed that the speeches in classical historical writings had been invented by their authors, the humanists felt entitled to the same prerogative.[21]

We have begun this discussion of humanist views on the writing of history with the meeting of Pontano's Academy which Bernardo Rucellai attended and in

---

[20] "Ipsis autem causis suscipiendi sive negocii sive belli coniuncta sunt consilia et hominum qui agendum quippiam decernunt sententiae ac voluntates; quae quod saepenumero sunt diversae, exponendae eae sunt a rerum scriptore in partem utranque . . . ," Pontano, "Actius," *loc. cit.*, p. 218.

[21] For an amusing example of the method which the humanists used for writing speeches, see Lorenzo Valla, *De rebus a Ferdinando Aragoniae Rege gestis* in [Schottus] *Hispaniae Illustratae . . . Scriptores varii*, Frankfurt, 1603, vol. I, p. 752: "Eorum primus fuit episcopus Conserranensis, qui orationem habuit, illa tempestate inter suos omnis juris divini humanique consultissimus, denique eloquentissimus. Nam ita constat inter eos qui affuerunt, nullum se literate loquentem, eloquentiorem, nec ante nec postea audisse. Quam tamen orationem, nemo eorum qui laudant, memoria tenet ad verbum, sed sententias aliquas et praecipua capita quae commodius in oratione regis, ne bis dicantur, a me ponentur."

which the problems of the writing of history were debated. The outcome, Rucellai's book on the *History of the French Invasion*,[22] illustrates the close connection between humanist historical theory and humanist historical practice. It is a notable example of this relationship because Rucellai, the ambitious and active Florentine statesman, was a dilettante rather than a professional literator; for this reason, he was eager to follow the prescripts which the humanists had set and to avoid any deviation from the recognized pattern lest he expose himself to obvious criticisms.

Rucellai chose a Sallustian theme, the history of one war, and his style, in the use of words and in sentence structure, was modelled on Sallust. Erasmus complimented Rucellai by saying that his book "was written by another Sallust or at least in Sallustian times."[23] Rucellai began his work with some general reflections; he is unhappy that he has to report not about glorious and virtuous deeds, but about stupidities, weaknesses, and crimes. Then he outlined the attitude and policy of the

[22] The book was printed in London in 1724, with the title Bernardus Oricellarius, *De Bello Italico Commentarius*, and then reprinted in London in 1733. I have used the edition of 1733.

[23] "Novi Venetiae *Bernardum Ocricularium*, civem Florentinum, cujus Historias si legisses, dixisses alterum Sallustium, aut certe Sallustii temporibus scriptas," Erasmus, *Opera Omnia*, vol. IV, Leyden, 1703, p. 363. Rucellai's work enjoyed a high reputation in his time. The author circulated the manuscript, or parts of the manuscript, widely; see the remark by Petrus Delfinus in a letter to Paolo Giustiniani, printed in Martène and Durand, *Veterum Scriptorum et monumentorum . . . amplissima collectio*, vol. III, Paris, 1724-33, p. 1173: "Confert cum multis scripta sua." We know from this letter that the manuscript was read by Delfinus and Paolo Giustiniani, and from other letters that Rucellai had shown the manuscript to Francesco da Diacceto (see *Sylloges*, vol. II, p. 199) and to Fontius (see Fontius, *Epistolarum Libri III*, p. 49). On the use of Rucellai's manuscript by later historians, see below, note 54 on p. 265.

chief Italian states—Florence, Venice, Naples, the Church State, and Milan—and he explained why the French King was called into Italy and why Charles VIII was receptive to these appeals. Rucellai's account of further diplomatic moves is interrupted by a lengthy description of the sea battle of Rapallo. Then, when the French land forces were finally on the march and approaching Italy, he punctuated this decisive event by a speech. Confronted by the Alps and terrified by the hazards of traversing them, the French leaders hesitated, but their reluctance was overcome when Giuliano della Rovere, in a passionate address, pointed out to them the advantages—the increase in power and wealth—which they would reap from control over Italy. With exception of a detailed account of the expulsion of the Medici from Florence and of the negotiations of the Florentines with Charles VIII, Rucellai's work becomes the narration of a military campaign. The climax of his history is a description of the battle of Fornovo, which was written strictly according to humanist prescripts. First Rucellai explained the topography of the battle field, then he reported on the councils of the leaders and their admonitions to their troops, and he recounted in detail the strength and order of the opposing armies. In order to evoke the confusion of the struggle he deliberately used a style of accentuated terseness throughout the battle narrative. The book ends with a description of the sieges in which the French garrisons, left behind in Naples, were overcome.

Bernardo Rucellai had taken an active part in many of the events about which he reported in his history. He had opposed Piero Medici's policy of aligning Florence with Naples against Milan; he had been Florentine ambassador to Charles VIII when the French King had stood before

Florence, and again when he had conquered Naples; and he was in personal contact with many of the political leaders of the time. Thus he had excellent sources of information. Some details of his story seem to be based on personal experiences and information; for example, his analysis of the policy of Lodovico Moro. Rucellai's view that Lodovico Moro was surprised by Charles VIII's eagerness to accept his invitation to come to Italy and that Lodovico tried desperately to reverse this decision, is probably more correct than the rather simple characterization of Lodovico—that he was a victim of blind ambition—held by many of Rucellai's contemporaries. The intimate knowledge of events which Rucellai possessed or could have acquired makes all the more astonishing his disregard for factual accuracy at many places in his work. Even if we keep in mind that historians were thought to have the right to invent speeches, it is quite impossible that Giuliano della Rovere addressed the French troops before they were crossing the Alps.[24] It might have been Rucellai's vanity that he exaggerated the importance of his embassy to Charles VIII when the French King approached Florence, but the contents of the speech which he reports that he himself gave to the King was a collection of examples of classical *clementia* and seems remarkably inappropriate to the situation in which Florence found herself. Furthermore, Rucellai described the political changes in Florence without ever mentioning Savonarola; the appearance of the Christian Frate was incompatible with Rucellai's aim of transposing the account

[24] For the facts, see H.-François Delaborde, *L'Expédition de Charles VIII en Italie,* Paris, 1888; it is characteristic that Guicciardini, *Storia d'Italia,* book I, chapt. 9, stresses the importance of the intervention of Giuliano della Rovere, but does not claim that he addressed the troops with a speech.

of contemporary events into the form of a classical history. This is a typical example of Rucellai's efforts to modify and tone down diplomatic and military events in such a way that they could be related in the forms and words, used by classical authors.

As we have indicated, Rucellai was inclined to be overly concerned about producing a history which could be read as if it were the work of a classical author. Scala, the Florentine Chancellor and a member of the same intellectual group as Rucellai, made some objections to those "who want to trace everything back to antiquity and omit with silence much that has been changed or innovated since then," but Scala insisted on the value of "adding the splendour of style" to the available accounts of the past.[25] And Pontano, Rucellai's great authority in things historical, although freer in his characterizations of the main figures involved in the Neapolitan war which he described and in which he himself had participated, adhered rigidly to classical prescripts in presenting his battle pieces. Thus, Rucellai followed the procedure which the writer of histories was expected to adopt.

How could this procedure be reconciled with the demand which Rucellai and all the humanist writers of history regarded as the fundamental law of history: that history should contain "nothing false."[26] Why simplifi-

---

[25] "Quamobrem non mediocri reprehensione dignos putarem nonnullos, qui dum omnia ad antiquitatem referre volunt, multa quae ut sint, immutata ac penitus innovata jam sunt, aut taciti praetereunt, aut insomnia quaedam vel monstra potius edere compelluntur," Scala, "Vita Vitaliani Borrhomaei" in Graevius' *Thesaurus Antiquitatum et Historiarum Italiae*, vol. VIII, part I, Leyden, 1723, p. 84. "Non vereor autem, si his quoque decorem addere orationis possimus . . ." can be found in Scala, "Historia Florentinorum," printed in Graevius, *loc. cit.*, p. 37.

[26] "Nam cum prima lex sit, ne quid falsi dicere, ne quid veri

cation and stylization of historical events was for the humanists compatible with truth becomes understandable if we relate their prescription for the writing of history to their general ideas about the purposes of historical work. Because the most important classical statements about the writing of history were contained in Cicero's *De Oratore*, the humanists regarded history as a branch of rhetorics, as an instrument by which the accepted doctrines of moral philosophy would be presented in such a persuasive manner that people would act according to the tenets of moral philosophy. The humanists frequently referred to classical sayings or commonplace statements which express the view that the value of history lies in the moral guidance which it gives to man: "History is useful because it makes man wiser since history helps him to build on experience extending far beyond the span of an individual life,"[27] "history teaches by example,"[28] "history inspires man to act virtuously and inflames him to deeds of glory."[29]

If history teaches by example, the purpose of history does not require completeness in facts or concreteness in

---

tacere audeamus . . . ," Oricellarius, *op. cit.,* p. 1. For the Ciceronian origin of this much used formula, see above, note 6.

[27] "Quanto enim plura exempla rerum longi diurnitatis temporis, quam unius hominis aetas complectitur: tanto est prudentior censendus is qui non suae tantum gentis aetatisque, sed omnium nationum et temporum memoriam accurata lectione complectitur . . ." Fontius, *Oratio in Historiae laudationem.*

[28] ". . . per exempla docet," very frequently, for instance, Valla, *op. cit.,* p. 728. See also Pontano, "Actius," *loc. cit.,* p. 229 for a longer discussion of the importance of the examples which history provides.

[29] "Primus nanque historiae finis et unica est intentio utilitatis, scilicet quae ex ipsius veritatis professione colligitur, unde animus ex praeteritorum notitia scientior fiat ad agendum et ad virtutem gloriamque imitatione consequendum inflammatior . . ." Guarino, *Epistolario, loc. cit.,* vol. II, p. 462.

detail. A certain amount of discussion took place among the humanists about how far historians ought to go in reporting what happened; they were bothered because history illustrated not only heroic and virtuous actions, but it also provided examples of meanness and vice. A limitation in historical works to accomplishments of virtue was rejected, however, because history's purpose was not only to exhort man to good deeds but also to deter him from bad ones.[30]

Rucellai's history and the works of other humanist historians were full of moral judgments. The importance of this aspect of the historian's work was the chief issue in a famous polemic between Facius and Valla.[31] In his history of King Ferdinand of Aragon Valla indulged in a graphic realism; he wrote of a queen trembling with fear, of a king falling asleep during diplomatic negotiations. Facius found Valla's presentation of human foibles and weaknesses not only superfluous, but a violation of the dignity of history. "The historian writes in one way, the satirist in another."[32] The historian must always be aware of his ethical responsibility, of being a judge and an educator.

In the Middle Ages and in the times of humanism, the

[30] The question raised by Cerretani in the Proemio of his *Historia Fiorentina*, Ms. B.N.F., II.II.74, ff. 21-23. But also the formulation of the generally accepted view by Fontius, *Oratio in Historiae laudationem:* "Nam et infamiae metu a scelere ac turpitudine vitae deterret improbos, et aeternae laudis cupiditate ad virtutem accendit probos."

[31] For details about this controversy, see Roberto Valentini, "Le invettive di Bartolomeo Facio contro Lorenzo Valla," *Atti della R. Accademia dei Lincei,* Classe di Scienze morali, storiche, e filologiche, serie quinta, vol. XV (1906), pp. 493-550. For Valla's concept of history, see also Franco Gaeta, *Lorenzo Valla. Filologia e Storia nell' Umanesimo Italiano,* Napoli, 1955, pp. 169-192.

[32] "Aliter enim historicus, aliter satiricus scribit," Facius, quoted by Valentini, *loc. cit.,* p. 536.

events happening on the earth were placed in relation to a permanent order of values that men ought to recognize and follow. But whereas in the Middle Ages history served to show the power of God, the humanist concept according to which history taught man to strive for virtue and to avoid vice emphasized the power which man could exert. Certainly the humanists recognized that man's control over events was limited and that much depended on *Fortuna*. But to the humanist there remained an area within which history was a man-made process.

• II •

The peculiar features of the humanist concept of history stand out strikingly if we turn to an examination of the historical method of the humanists and investigate the question of what kind of "research" they undertook, what they did to ascertain the facts they described in their histories. A problem of historical method did indeed exist for the humanists. Although the educational aims which historical writings were to serve permitted a stylization and manipulation of facts and events, history remained tied to a factual content. In accepting Aristotle's view that poetry is superior to history, the humanists agreed that although both poetry and history taught man how to act morally, poetry developed moral rules from the actions of an imagined world whereas history drew its lessons from the way in which men had actually behaved. Thus factual basis was a prerequisite for achieving the purposes of history.

Moreover, in the composition of historical works, practical aims were frequently combined with the general educational purposes of humanist activities. Humanists might want to gain the favour of a prince by giving an account of his rule. Or they might write the history of a city-state in order to secure employment by the government; Sabellicus' *Deche* of Venice won him a lectureship at the School of San Marco and the position of custodian of the books bequeathed by Cardinal Bessarion to the republic of Venice. From that time on the Venetian government regularly appointed a "public historiographer", who would present the records of the Venetian past in a literary form; Sabellicus was followed by Navagero, Navagero by Bembo.[33] In Florence the writing of Florentine histories was connected with the chancellorship; the holder of this office was expected to compose a history of the city. Bruni, Poggio, Scala, Machiavelli—all were chancellery officials and authors of Florentine histories. Histories served to strengthen loyalty to a ruler or a ruling family or to stimulate feelings of public spirit and civil pride, and these practical aims demanded a certain amount of factual detail and accuracy.

The elaboration of a special historical method placing the establishment of facts on a scientific basis is regarded as one of the most significant steps in the development of modern historiography. Historians of historical writings are inclined to use as a yardstick for measuring the development of historiography the progress made towards the evolution of a critical historical method. The value of historians and of schools of historiography is seen to be determined by the degree to which they evaluated the various available sources according to critical principles and realized the superiority of documentary sources over narrative accounts. The attitude of the humanist histo-

[33] The works of the Venetian "public historiographers" are collected in *Degli Istorici delle Cose Veneziane i quali hanno scritto per Pubblico Decreto*, Venezia, 1718, etc.

rians to this problem seems strangely inconsistent. In general, they relied rather uncritically on narrative accounts, but in some of their works there are fine critical investigations; and in some, too, we find the use of documentary sources. For instance, the investigation in which Bruni destroyed the popular legend of Florence's foundation by Caesar and established as the time of its origin the republican Rome of Sulla, has been called a "remarkable achievement of the new historical method."[34] Similarly the foundation of Venice was treated by some historians with great critical sense. In Bruni's work there are large portions based on material from the archives, and Lorenzo de Monaci proceeded in his Venetian history quite similarly.[35]

It ought to be noted, however, that those sections in which the humanists applied modern critical methods were those in which they described the foundation of a city. The story of the origin of a city was usually presented as a prologue or short dissertation, not as an integral part of the narrative. The reason for this is the special importance which the beginnings of a city had for determining the nature of its institutions throughout the course of its history. Because most of the Italian cities

---

[34] Nicolai Rubinstein, "The beginnings of political thought in Florence," *Journal of the Warburg and Courtauld Institutes,* vol. V (1942), p. 225, and, in general on Bruni's notion of the foundation of Florence, see Hans Baron, *The Crisis of the Early Italian Renaissance,* Princeton, 1955, particularly the chapter entitled "A New View of Roman History and of the Florentine Past," vol. I, pp. 38-60; but the importance of this notion is discussed throughout Baron's entire work.

[35] Printed as appendix to Muratori, *Rerum Italicarum Scriptores,* vol. VIII, under the title *Chronicon de rebus Venetis,* ed. by F. Cornelius, Venezia, 1758; on Monaci, see also Lino Lazzarini, *Paolo de Bernardo e i primordi dell' Umanesimo in Venezia,* Genève, 1930, pp. 109-110.

went back to Roman times, their early history had a special attraction in the age of the revival of classical antiquity. Moreover, since the sources for these early times were classical authors, it was natural to use techniques which had been developed for the understanding and interpretation of classical texts. Likewise, those humanists who did make use of documentary sources in their historical narratives were mostly chancellors or chancellery officials. Perhaps Bruni used archival material to check information which he found in narrative accounts.[36] If so, he was an exception. In general, if humanist historians used documentary sources, they did so because they were, for them, the most accessible means for finding out about the events which they treated in their histories. They did not believe that they were adopting principles which ought to be generally followed in the writing of history. The historians who used documentary sources were not considered to be innovators, nor did they claim to be.

In composing their histories, humanist historians usually followed a single source. They were not inclined to examine all available reports and to construct their own picture as a result of this investigation. When Merula, with whom Sabellicus was conducting a bitter feud, crit-

---

[36] Bruni's *Historiarum Florentini Populi Libri XII* (published in Muratori, *Rerum Italicarum Scriptores,* nuova edizione, vol. XIX, part 3) is certainly the outstanding work of fifteenth-century humanist historiography; it is carefully discussed by E. Santini, "Leonardo Bruni Aretino e i suoi 'Historiarum Florentini Populi Libri XII,'" *Annali della R. Scuola Normale Superiore di Pisa,* vol. XXII (1910), Filosofia e Filologia pp. 3-169. Santini certainly shows that Bruni used material from the archives in the later parts of his work, but he does not seem to prove to me that Bruni relied on archival material when an authoritative chronicle was available; for a further discussion, see bibliographical appendix.

icized Sabellicus' *Deche* because it was based exclusively on Venetian authors, Sabellicus countered by saying that "Sallust, Livy, and Dionysius and others had not followed Punic but Roman accounts,"[37] and he certainly expressed the generally accepted view.

In consequence, there was really only one problem of critical method with which the humanists were concerned, and that was to establish criteria for distinguishing, among various narrative sources, the one narrative source which was the most reliable and on which the humanists' history was to be based. They failed to find an elaborate system for determining these criteria. The one point on which they agreed was that the reliability of a narrative source was dependent on the temporal proximity of the author to the events he wrote about.[38] Thus Villani was the recognized authority for the earlier centuries of Florentine history, and Dandolo was the standard source for Venetian history; the humanists who wrote Florentine histories or Venetian histories seemed never to tire of re-writing, on the classical pattern, the chronicles of these authors. But whereas the humanist historians regarded as sacrosanct every word of a classical author, they lacked respect for narratives from the Middle Ages, which were sometimes characterized as "base scribblings

[37] "Criminabatur me in Veneta historia, quum diceret non oportuisse sequi me Venetos annales: ceu Crispus, Livius, Dionysius et alii Punicos secuti sint, non Romanos," quoted by Apostolo Zeno, "Marci Coccii Sabellici Vita," *Degli Istorici delle Cose Veneziani i quali hanno scritto per Pubblico Decreto,* vol. I, Venezia, 1718, p. XLI.

[38] See Scala, *Historia Florentinorum,* printed in Graevius, *op. cit.,* vol. VIII, part 1, p. 22: "Nos quae vero sunt vita propinquius sequuti summus," or Johannis Simonetae "In Commentarios Rerum Gestarum Francisci Sforziae Mediolanensium Ducis Praefatio," printed in Muratori, *Rerum Italicarum Scriptores,* nuova edizione, vol. XXI, Parte II, p. CXII. Some humanist historians stressed that

of monks."[39] They felt not only that they could question the validity of statements contained in the accounts of such obscure writers, but also that they could correct them. But, as Giustiniani's history of Venice shows, the basis for such corrections was not the application of a critical historical method, but common sense or practical knowledge.[40]

Thus the examination of the humanist attitude to the problems of historical method reveals that the humanists knew of two kinds of historical writings: the true history which was to be composed on the pattern of Livy or Sallust; and the reports about historical events which provided the material from which the true history would be constructed. The humanists felt justified in this assumption because they believed that these two genres of historical writings had existed also in the classical world: in addition to histories, the ancients had produced annals or commentaries.[41] The humanists expected that, in the fu-

---

they tried to lay their hands on all available reports; a few, for instance Bernardo Giustiniani, read widely in historical materials. But in general the humanists were concerned with establishing one author as the authority which they ought to follow and not with constructing a version of their own on the basis of their readings. An interesting study on the use of sources by a "typical" humanist historian was made by Ruggero Bersi, "Le fonti della prima decade delle Historiae Rerum Venetarum di Marcantonio Sabellico," *Nuovo Archivio Veneto*, N.S., vol. XIX (1910), pp. 422-460, vol. XX (1910), pp. 115-162.

[39] For Sabellicus' expression ". . . ignobilibus fraterculorum commentariolis . . ." see Zeno, "Sabellici Vita," *loc. cit.*, p. XLII.

[40] See Bernardo Giustiniani, *De origine urbis gestisque Venetorum historiae Libri XV* (first printed in 1492), in Graevius, *Thesaurus*, vol. V, part 1, libro III, pp. 25 et seq. as an example of this kind of criticism.

[41] The notion that the main purpose of historical commentaries was to collect and present the material for the true historian, can be found quite regularly; see for instance, Johannis Simonetae "In Commentarios . . . ," *loc. cit.*, p. CXI: "Equidem omnia in Commentarios, et eo ordine, quo gerebantur in dies,

ture, commentaries, patterned after those of the ancients, would preserve the main facts of contemporary events and that eventually chronicles, for which there was no ancient counterpart, would disappear.

This humanist distinction between two forms of historical writings—one containing chiefly facts and thereby providing the material from which the other, the true his-

---

singula celeri stilo deprompsi, si minus eleganter minusque ornate, at vera et incorrupta fide." Bruni also distinguished between histories and commentaries; he seems to have regarded brief factual statements, lacking details, as the main characteristic of commentaries. See Bruni, *Rerum suo tempore gestarum Commentarius*, published in Muratori, *Rerum Italicarum Scriptores*, nuova edizione, vol. XIX, part 3, p. 456: ". . . quae particulariter referre contra propositum esset nostrum, cum summam tantum rerum notemus, non historiam describamus"; see also E. Santini, "Leonardo Bruni Aretino e i suoi 'Historiarum Florentini Populi Libri XII' ", *loc. cit.*, p. 22. The humanists recognized 'Annals' as a genre of historical literature, but humanists differed about the distinctions among "Histories," "Annals," and "Commentaries." For Pontano, there was no difference between "histories" and "annals": history was a Greek word which replaced the Latin word 'Annals' which the Romans had originally used; see Pontano, "Actius," *loc. cit.*, p. 193. Fontius, in his *Oratio in Historiae Laudationem*, seems to have identified 'annals' with 'commentaries,' in the sense that annals are works which present brief factual data; Fontius' "Annales Surorum Temporum," printed in Philippi Villani, *Liber De Civitatis Florentiae Famosis Civibus*, ed. G. C. Galletti, Florentiae, 1847, pp. 153-159, is limited to a brief enumeration of the chief events of the years 1448 to 1483, but it can be questioned whether Fontius himself gave the title 'Annales' to his composition. The most frequent distinction seems to have been the one which Guarino made; see Guarino Veronese, *Epistolario, loc. cit.*, vol. II, p. 460: "Historia, ut plerisque placet auctoribus, earum rerum et temporum descriptio est, quae nostra vidit aut videre potuit aetas; . . . Annales autem eorum annorum expositio qui a nostra remoti sunt aetate." This distinction comes from Verrius Flaccus, as transmitted by Gellius; the humanists were undecided about the terminological differentiation between 'Annals' and 'Histories' because "There never was a general agreement about the two words in the Roman writers"; see M.L.W. Laistner, *The Greater Roman Historians, Sather Classical Lectures*, vol. XXI (1947), p. 167, note 3 and the literature indicated there.

tory, could be constructed—placed the true historian far above those who just collected and described facts. Not factual completeness and accuracy, but moral guidance was expected from the true historian, and he was therefore permitted to select and to stylize the events of the past. The order of values in historical writings which the humanists had established found a strange but striking illustration in the relation between Sanudo and Bembo.[42] In the last years of the fifteenth century Sanudo decided to set down in the form of annals the memorable events which were happening in Venice. Sanudo was aware that he had undertaken an immense task of great importance. Nevertheless, with a certain amount of regret and resentment, Sanudo suspected that people might regard his activities as not being of the highest literary order; people might deprecate his work because it was written in the vernacular. Sanudo said in justification that a work in Italian would have a greater impact than a work in Latin, but the frequency with which he returned to this point suggests that he himself needed to be convinced. Sanudo knew that annals were not history and that a "true history" demanded a more conscious composition, an elimination of material not concerned with war and foreign policy, and a more elevated style. He himself regarded his annals as the raw material on which later he would build a "true history" of Venice. However, because Sanudo felt that the times in which he lived were so important, he never found the right moment to stop his annals and to start transforming them into history; he went on

[42] For the following see Carlo Lagomaggiore, "L'istoria Veneziana di M. Pietro Bembo," *Nuovo Archivio Veneto*, N.S., vol. VII (1904), pp. 5-31, 334-372; vol. VIII (1904), pp. 162-180, 317-346; vol. IX (1905), pp. 33-113, 308-340, particularly IX, pp. 48 et seq.

gathering material and continuing his diaries. It was a shattering blow to him when Bembo was appointed "public historiographer" of the Venetian Republic and in that position then proceeded to persuade the government to force Sanudo to place his annals at Bembo's disposal. To Sanudo it appeared that his life-work had been done in vain. He despaired that his name would soon be forgotten because his diaries would be absorbed into a history which posterity would know under the name of Bembo.

It is sad that Sanudo could not know that 450 years later his annals are treasured as one of the great sources of information about the life of the Renaissance, whereas few will ever look at the lifeless, rhetorical exercise of Bembo's Venetian history.

· III ·

Humanist historical works formed only a part of the great number of writings in this period which were intended to give posterity knowledge of what had happened in the past. To the humanists, history was a literary genre which was assimilated with their over-all aims. Other historical writings express simply and directly the eternal human wonderment and curiosity about the world in which man lived; men wanted their descendants to know about any kind of memorable event which they had experienced or of which they had heard. Keeping of records was desirable also for practical reasons.[43] The family was a recognized unit in the society of a city-state, and the role which the members of a family had played in

---

[43] Paul Joachimsen, *Geschichtsauffassung und Geschichtschreibung in Deutschland unter dem Einfluss des Humanismus,* Leipzig, 1910, particularly pp. 11-14, still provides the best analysis of the nature of historical works written by "laymen."

the past enhanced the position of its living members. Participation in the government was frequently dependent on proving that an ancestor had held office, and families kept an exact record of the political activities of previous generations. Moreover, the conduct of government required an understanding of the developments which had brought about any current situation. Brief historical résumés summarizing the course of affairs were put together in the chancelleries.

The Florentines used a variety of means to keep the memory of the past alive. The *priorista*, containing a list of the members of a family who had ever held high office, was carefully continued from generation to generation. Sometimes these *priorista* were developed into family histories, in which the careers and attainments of the family's more prominent members were described. There were also the books of memories (*ricordi*), in which an individual noted down, from year to year, or from event to event, the most important occasions of his life: marriage, births of children, financial transactions, professional activities, and achievements. Finally diaries were kept by men of the most different social background and status, and they were replete with miscellaneous information: political changes and wars, famines, hurricanes and heavy snowfalls, strange acts of nature like the birth of a calf with two heads, the construction of important buildings, the celebration of festivals, the prophesies and sermons of itinerant preachers.

But, at the beginning of the sixteenth century, the conviction had become widespread among Florentines that the uses of history went beyond providing knowledge of the strange happenings which might occur in this world, and beyond the demands for personal advancement or the satisfaction of civic pride. It is certainly true that the emergence of a new view of the purposes of history was due to the influence of the humanists. They had infused into the concern with the past a new significance by recognizing history as an important literary genre which could give man guidance in his actions. But to many of those living in the troubled times of the Florentine republic the lessons to be drawn from history were specific rather than general. History moved closer to politics because it was expected that history could teach men about political behavior, about the functioning of institutions and the conduct of government. Neither the conventional forms in which Florentines were accustomed to set down a record of the past for the enlightenment of their descendants, nor the pattern which the humanists prescribed for the writing of history were entirely compatible with the purpose of using history as a guide to politics. Illustrative are the historical works which, during the republican period, were composed by three members of the Florentine aristocracy: Piero Parenti, Francesco Guicciardini, and Bartolomeo Cerretani.

Parenti's purpose was to make a "simple and brief note of things worth preserving."[44] His work has the form of a diary. Beginning with the events of 1494, Parenti wrote down every two or three months what had happened in the intervening period.[45] But Parenti called his work a "history," and he had justification for believing that his

---

[44] "Nota semplice et breve di chose degne di memoria . . . ," Piero Parenti, *Historia Fiorentina*, Ms. B.N.F. II.IV.169, f. 1r. On Parenti's history see also the Appendix.

[45] Parenti's history begins with the assassination of Galeazzo Maria Sforza in 1476, but his treatment of the happenings between 1476 and 1494 is very spotty, and if not all, certainly some of the notices about events before 1494 are not contemporary with the events but composed quite a while afterwards.

work was not merely a diary. Omitting notes on natural catastrophes, miracles, or new building enterprises, Parenti concentrated exclusively on describing the Florentine political scene. He gave reports about what was said and decided in the meetings of the magistrates, he reproduced the contents of laws, and he discussed the views and attitudes of individual politicians and the shifting alignments among them. In its emphasis on political details and on the varieties of personal motivations, Parenti's manuscript indicates a realization that every political action and situation is the outcome of an interaction of manifold forces, and that the historian must try to reveal the causal connections which tie political events together.

Whereas Parenti's history came from the diary tradition, Francesco Guicciardini's work had its roots in the tradition of the *ricordi* and family histories.[46] It was written between 1508 and 1510. By then Guicciardini's years of study were over. He was established as a lawyer and a teacher of law in Florence. He was married and his first daughter had been born. Like most Florentines of his status and position, he had set his sights on a political career, but he had not yet reached the age required for holding office. Guicciardini used these years of waiting for literary work. He started by writing down notes of an autobiographical character, and he composed a family history. But he began also to compose a *Florentine History*. This work is closely related to his manuscript on the Guicciardini family. Guicciardini's history begins at the end of the fourteenth century, at the time when the

---

[46] See Nicolai Rubinstein, "The 'Storie Fiorentine' and the 'Memorie di Famiglia' by Francesco Guicciardini," *Rinascimento,* vol. IV (1953), pp. 171-225, and the evaluation of Guicciardini's *Storie Fiorentine* in Vittorio de Caprariis, *Francesco Guicciardini dalla Politica alla Storia,* Bari, 1950, pp. 27-62.

Guicciardini were becoming prominent in Florentine politics. The role which the various members of the Guicciardini family played in Florentine politics is emphasized throughout the entire work. Sometimes, passages from the family memoirs are taken over directly into the *Florentine History*. However, Guicciardini must have felt that in undertaking the larger task of a *Florentine History* he would be able to demonstrate certain truths which could not be derived from personal memoirs or from a family history.

On the other hand, although Guicciardini adopted the recognized pattern of the history of a city-state, he did not follow the humanist rules for historical writing. In his history there are no introductions with general reflections, there are no speeches, nor any of the paraphernalia such as omens and indications of celestial constellations. However, he did share the contemporary view that history taught by example. But he was not concerned with general rules of human behavior which history might teach. Like Parenti's history, Guicciardini's work dealt only with politics; the instruction which history provided was instruction in the art of politics. Guicciardini's purpose was to examine the concrete effects of the various types of government. His description of Florentine events at the end of the fourteenth century and the beginning of the fifteenth was intended to show the working of an oligarchic form of government; the discussion of the political developments since 1494 was to illustrate the functioning of a democratic regime.

Guicciardini's fascination with history was too strong to permit him to obliterate the variety and richness of the past by the imposition of a theoretical structure. He provided subtle characterizations of Cosimo and Lorenzo de'

Medici, of Savonarola, of Bernardo Rucellai, and when he approached his own time, his story increased in detail, revealing the importance of personal rivalries and ambitions. But Guicciardini was aware that if history is to serve as a guide to politics, its writing requires detail and factual accuracy. Guicciardini checked his facts and compared his information with that of others. Concreteness was concomitant with his aim of finding in history the criteria for a good government; this aim forced upon him new standards of factual accuracy.

Parenti and Guicciardini are valuable sources for the history of the republican regime, and Guicciardini's *Florentine History* is a work of literary distinction. In these respects, Cerretani's *Florentine History*, written almost simultaneously with that of Guicciardini, is much inferior. Moreover, Cerretani's work is fundamentally different from those of his two contemporaries, because he did not enlarge upon a conventional form of record keeping; rather, Cerretani intended to write a "true history" in the humanist sense. His work is not divided in books because "history is a whole,"[47] but otherwise he accepted humanist rules. Cerretani described the development of Florence from the foundation of the city up to his own time. His account is embellished with speeches full of allusions to classical writers; he reported signs from heaven presaging important events, and he declared his intention to "give good examples to the reader."[48]

Cerretani's *Florentine History* clearly falls into two parts. The second and longer part is devoted to a detailed

---

[47] ". . . storia non e altro che un tutto . . . ," Cerretani, *Historia Fiorentina*, Ms. B.N.F. II.III.74, proemio; the entire proemio—ff. 21-23—is interesting as a brief summary of the humanist theory of history.

[48] "dare a chi legge un' buono esemplo . . . ," *ibid.*

description of Florentine political developments in the years from the death of Lorenzo Magnifico in 1492 to the battle of Ravenna in 1512. As a member of the ruling group, Cerretani had interesting information about Florentine party groupings and struggles, about legislative measures and proposals, and about the financial difficulties of the government. The weakness of this part of Cerretani's work is that he seems to have made little attempt to collect information systematically; he wrote down what he remembered and what he had heard by chance or had read. Moreover, the carefully constructed classicizing speeches stand in jarring contrast to the concreteness of detail. The first part of Cerretani's history, which extends from the foundation of the city into the fifteenth century, was written after the second part, and evidences still more strongly the impact of the humanist theory of history. Cerretani himself stated that he would follow first the Latin and then the Florentine writers, and, indeed, this part of his work is nothing more than a rewriting of the conventional story. But this part has some interesting and distinguishing features. The past is seen in the light of the present and related to it. Behind the account of earlier events the experience of recent happenings is visible. To Cerretani, the situation in Florence after the overthrow of the tyranny of the Duke of Athens was parallel to that which existed after the overthrow of the Medici regime; in both times the *grandi*, having been instrumental in removing the tyrant, felt entitled to more than their due share in the government. Moreover, Cerretani was interested in describing the origin of institutions and procedures which played a role in the history of the republican regime; he emphasized the relation of the Great Council to previous councils and he gave great attention to the methods used in the past for the filling of offices.

Most remarkable, however, is the manner in which Cerretani connected the party struggles of his time with those of earlier centuries; he explained that the same contrasts and conflicts which disrupted the republican regime were present throughout the entire course of Florentine history. He had some justification for saying that "history is a whole" because he viewed Florentine history as an interconnected complex, and saw the present as the outcome of the past. Cerretani's intentions are more interesting than their execution, but they confirm what the Florentine histories of Parenti and Guicciardini had indicated: the interest in history had become pragmatic; history was to serve the understanding of the existing political situation and give guidance in political action.[49] The concomitant of this pragmatic interest in history was that the writers of history were to place stress on two aspects of history which previously had been neglected, factual accuracy and causal connections.

The problem was that this pragmatic approach could not be expressed in the accepted forms of historical writing. Diaries, family histories, and autobiographical memoirs could hardly do more than provide raw material for such a pragmatic treatment of history. At the same time, the recognized patterns for more comprehensive works of historical literature were equally unsuited. The "true histories," in the humanist sense, were political histories; but the political content of these "true histories" sub-

---

[49] Earlier writers tended towards this pragmatic approach; see Hans Baron, *op. cit.*, pp. 141 et seq., but the political reasoning in the works of Parenti, Guicciardini, and Cerretani is on a quite different, incomparably higher level.

served the humanists' aim of moral instruction. The patterns, rules, and methods, which humanists had established, defined and restricted the writing of history in such a way that analyses of the details of practical politics could hardly be fitted to the humanist mode of historical literature.

The consequence was that history became subordinated to politics also in the sense that historical investigations became embedded in political treatises. The most characteristic example of integrating history in a work of political theory is Guicciardini's *Dialogo del Reggimento di Firenze*.[50] When Guicciardini had returned from Spain, in 1514, he found the Medici established as rulers of Florence. The political reality was very different from the situation which he had envisaged when, in Spain, he had outlined his ideas about the establishment of a well-organized government in Florence. Moreover, to a man of Guicciardini's pride and ambition the prospect of remaining in Florence where his political career would be completely dominated by the Medici was not especially attractive. Serving the Pope—albeit a Medici Pope—was preferable; as administrator in the Church-State he would have a freer hand and greater scope for his talents. He advanced quickly in the Papal service. In 1516 he was appointed Governor of Modena, then Reggio and Parma were added to his jurisdiction, and in 1524, he became President of the Romagna. But by then the situation in Florence had changed. With Giuliano and Lorenzo de' Medici dead, it

[50] Printed in Francesco Guicciardini, *Dialogo e Discorsi del Reggimento di Firenze*, ed. R. Palmarocchi, Bari, 1932, pp. 3-172; for this work see also above, pp. 117 et seq. It might be mentioned that also Cerretani's history was followed by a historical dialogue, see above, pp. 147 et seq.

seemed doubtful whether the Medici could remain in control. The future of Florence had become again uncertain, and many plans were made for the restoration of a republican regime.

In this situation Guicciardini undertook to set down his ideas about the form which a republican regime in Florence should take, and the outcome was the *Dialogo del Reggimento di Firenze*. The second part of the *Dialogo* contains, in a slightly revised and extended form, the ideas which he had previously developed in the *Discorso di Logrogno*. But the first part was new. Instead of discussing theoretically the virtues and vices of the various forms of government, in particular of a monarchy or a democracy, Guicciardini presented a historical study, illustrating both the defects of one-man rule by describing and analyzing the system of government of Lorenzo Magnifico, and the weakness of democracy by examining the regime which followed the overthrow of the Medici. From a concrete and detailed investigation of the past, Guicciardini deduced the norms for an ideal government of Florence, which he then explained in the second part of the *Dialogo*. Like many of his contemporaries, Guicciardini regarded history as a man-made process; by use of his reason, man should be able to discover the laws which determine the course of politics and then apply these laws in such a way that he would be able to control events. Historical investigation was an instrument to disclose the laws of politics.

Chapter 6 BETWEEN
HISTORY AND POLITICS

The problem of embodying a pragmatic view of history in accepted literary forms created the danger of a bifurcation of historical expression. On one hand, histories of a literary genre could be written according to humanist prescripts; on the other hand, the material of political history might be presented in political treatises. The result would have been that the contents of the literary histories would have no political relevance and the information about the past contained in political treatises would not be history. It is one of the crucial facts in the development of modern historiography that such a division into a rhetorically and a politically oriented use of the past did not take place. In the following chapter we shall attempt to analyze more closely the particular issues which created this "crisis in historiography," and we shall discuss the intellectual developments which might explain why this "crisis" was overcome.

• I •

In the years between 1520 and 1525 Machiavelli wrote the *Florentine History*;[1] it was his last large literary work and it deserves attention in this context not only because of the intellectual importance of the man who wrote it, but because it is a striking example of the difficulties arising

[1] For bibliographical details on Machiavelli and on problems of his *Istorie Fiorentine*, see the appendix.

from the contrast between the humanist concept of history and a pragmatic approach to the past. Machiavelli undertook the *Florentine History* not because he especially wanted to write a history, but rather because it had been commissioned by Cardinal Giulio Medici, the head of the Florentine Studio. Machiavelli expected that this commission might lead to others from the Medici rulers, so he was anxious to please his employers. He framed his history according to the accepted humanist standards. As he stated explicitly in his foreword, he had studied Bruni's and Poggio's histories of Florence, "in order to see the forms and methods which they had adopted in writing their works,"[2] and although he wrote in the vernacular, he otherwise adhered to humanist prescripts and patterns. Machiavelli divided his work into a number of books, and each began with general reflections on a topic to which the events described in the following chapters referred. The narrative is studded with a large number of carefully wrought speeches. Important events are announced by signs from the heavens, and battle scenes are painstakingly related. In his method, Machiavelli also adopted humanist principles; he followed one author at a time, re-writing his account in a more elevated style.

But there are indications that Machiavelli considered the humanist prescripts as a literary convention rather than as an appropriate form for the writing of history. After he described the battle of Anghiari in the ornate manner required by humanist historical theory, he commented that in this long and famous struggle only one man was killed and he did not die from enemy action but

---

[2] ". . . per vedere con quali ordini e modi nello scrivere procedevono . . ." *Istorie Fiorentine*, proemio (*Opere*, vol. VII, p. 68).

from falling from his horse and landing on his head.[3]
With this remark he satirized the elaborate battle pieces
of the humanist historians.

The humanist pattern was for Machiavelli a framework
onto which he hung, almost arbitrarily, his political message. The *Florentine History* is colored by Machiavelli's
political interests and by the political problems of his
time. Rather than covering evenly all the events in the
history of Florence, he proceeded selectively. Single
scenes are full of minutia and worked out at length, but
the narrative itself does not comprise a connected history. Events which Machiavelli believed contained valuable historical lessons—such as the tyranny of the Duke of
Athens[4] and the revolt of the Ciompi[5]—are recited in great
detail, whereas the happenings of the intervening decades
are hardly mentioned. In the introductions to the various
books and in the speeches Machiavelli set forth his favorite political theses: the problem of factions in a republic,[6] the importance of colonies,[7] the difficulties involved
in conspiracies against tyrants.[8] One of Machiavelli's
most persistent political concerns—the inadequacy of the
mercenary system—is frequently stressed in the *Florentine History*.

One might say that in his *Florentine History* Machiavelli adhered to the humanist principle that "history
teaches by example," only the "examples" which Machiavelli adduced were intended to demonstrate the existence
and the functioning of political laws. Furthermore, the

[3] Libro V, chapt. 33 (*Opere*, vol. VII, p. 383).
[4] Libro II, chapts. 33-37 (*Opere*, vol. VII, pp. 188-204).
[5] Libro V, chapts. 9-18 (*Opere*, vol. VII, pp. 227-250).
[6] Libro III, chapt. 1 (*Opere*, Vol. VII, pp. 212 et seq.) and Libro
VII, chapt. 1 (*Opere*, vol. VII, p. 451 et seq.).
[7] Libro II, chapt. 1 (*Opere*, vol. VII, p. 137 et seq.).
[8] Libro VIII, chapt. 1 (*Opere*, vol. VII, pp. 508 et seq.).

events which Machiavelli recounted are stylized in order to evince these laws. Thus the protagonists of his history are types without individual reality. It has been said that Machiavelli was a political scientist, not an historian; and it may be added that since Machiavelli was carrying out a prescribed task in writing the *Florentine History*, he might have been satisfied to use this opportunity for presenting a few of his ideas to a wider audience. However, because his political ideas and laws were bound to particular historical situations, they appear more massive and much less subtle and convincing than in the works—the *Prince* and the *Discourses*—in which he could freely concentrate on assembling all possible arguments for practical recommendations. On the other hand, the humanist pattern which Machiavelli felt constrained to adopt led him to dissolve the historical process in single episodes which he considered as exemplary and instructive, and forced him to neglect the causal connections which tie single events together to form a coherent unit.

It must be admitted that the difficulties which Machiavelli encountered in writing the *Florentine History* were not only those of combining a pragmatic political concept of history with humanist ideas of history; he hesitated to express frankly his political views. When, in 1524, he came to that part of his history which was concerned with the developments of the fifteenth century, he wrote a letter to Francesco Guicciardini saying that he would give ten soldi to have Guicciardini at his side while writing his history because he would like to have Guicciardini's opinion whether he offended either by exaggerating or understating the facts.[9] Clearly Machiavelli was reluctant to praise the rule of Cosimo and Lorenzo but he

[9] August 30, 1524 (*Opere*, vol. VI, p. 417).

feared that their descendants, with whom he wanted to ingratiate himself, might resent his lack of enthusiasm for the Medici of the fifteenth century. Machiavelli solved this problem by focussing on foreign policy and writing little about Florentine domestic events in the times of Cosimo and Lorenzo.

• II •

Machiavelli's turning to Guicciardini for advice is a sign of the intimacy which had developed between them. Among the many people with whom Machiavelli corresponded there were only two with whom there was a steady exchange of letters extending over many years: Francesco Vettori and Francesco Guicciardini. Machiavelli's friendship with Vettori went back to the years of the republican regime, when, in 1508, they had been together on a diplomatic mission to Germany. The pinnacle of their correspondence is the letters which they exchanged in the years following the return of the Medici. Vettori, Florentine ambassador in Rome, mixed information about political events with anecdotes about the life at the Papal court, and Machiavelli responded with speculations about politics, with descriptions of his rustic existence, and with a report telling his friend about the progress he was making in composing the *Prince*.

Machiavelli's correspondence with Guicciardini began only in 1521. Of course, they had known each other in the times of the republic but then Guicciardini, a member of the aristocratic group opposing Soderini, was full of distrust for the man who enjoyed the *Gonfaloniere's* favors.[10] But after 1512 these differences in political out-

---

[10] In Guicciardini's *Storie Fiorentine*, Machiavelli is primarily mentioned as an instrument of Soderini; see Guicciardini, *Storie Fiorentine*, ed. R. Palmarocchi, Bari, 1931, pp. 277, 297.

look were probably overshadowed by common dislike of the Medici rule in Florence, and when in 1521 Machiavelli, on a mission to the Chapter General of the Franciscans in Carpi, passed through the area which Guicciardini was administering for the Church, they got along well with each other. Between Machiavelli and Guicciardini there was never the easy familiarity which existed between Machiavelli and Vettori; Guicciardini remained the grand seigneur whose interest in Machiavelli was that of a patron. But Guicciardini clearly appreciated Machiavelli's intellectual versatility, enthusiasm, and inventiveness, and Machiavelli admired Guicciardini's political clarity and executive ability. Their relations became very close in the last year of Machiavelli's life when the identity of their views about the Italian situation brought them together in a common political effort. After the victory of the forces of Charles V over the French in the battle of Pavia in 1525, both Guicciardini and Machiavelli were convinced that whatever views one held about the future of Florence and the rule of the Medici, the basic requirement for political action by any Italian state was to break the hold of Charles V over Italy. Guicciardini, as Papal adviser, was the driving force behind the attempts to form a coalition against Charles V, and after the League of Cognac with Francis I had been finally concluded, he went to North Italy as the Papal representative among the allied commanders directing the military campaign. Machiavelli fully supported this policy, and he was used by the Pope as well as by Guicciardini for missions to make preparations for military action. Without any reservation Machiavelli accepted Guicciardini's political leadership. In one of his last letters to Francesco Vettori, written only two months before his death, Machiavelli stated: "I love Messer Francesco Guicciardini, I love my fatherland more than my soul."[11]

Machiavelli died before the complete failure of the anti-Hapsburg policy had become evident. It is a puzzling question to what extent, if he had lived to realize the full triumph of Charles V, he would have modified his political and historical ideas. There is no doubt that the events of 1527 and their aftermath—the restoration of a republican regime in Florence and then the slow succumbing of this regime to the united forces of Pope and Emperor—deeply influenced the views of his two great friends—Vettori and Guicciardini—on politics and history. As long as Machiavelli lived, Vettori and Guicciardini had remained rather apart, the one active in politics in Medicean Florence, the other living away from Florence as Papal administrator. But at the time when Machiavelli died, in the summer of 1527, Vettori and Guicciardini found themselves in a very similar position. Both had been willing to serve the Medici; when they had a choice, however, they preferred a republican regime to the rule of the Medici, although, as Florentine aristocrats, they were convinced that a republic in Florence could function effectively only if the aristocrats had a decisive share in the government. Thus, when the republic was restored in Florence, both Vettori and Guicciardini were eager to play their part in the new regime. But because both had served the Medici in important positions, they were distrusted. They received no official positions in Florence, though as long as Niccolò Capponi, a moderate aristocrat, was *Gonfaloniere* they were consulted on some mat-

---

[11] "Io amo messer Francesco Guicciardini, amo la patria mia piú dell' anima," Machiavelli to Francesco Vettori, April 16, 1527 (*Opere*, vol. VI, p. 505).

ters. However, when a more radical group seized power in Florence and Capponi was replaced as *Gonfaloniere* by Francesco Carducci, both Guicciardini and Vettori felt threatened and they retired to their estates.[12]

In this most critical time Guicciardini and Vettori rightly thought that their experiences and personal contracts might be of the greatest value to the Florentine republic, but both were eliminated from the political scene and became impotent observers. To make some use of their involuntary freedom from political activity, both turned to literary work. Among the writings which Guicciardini undertook in this period of his life was a history of Florence which might be called a second *Florentine History*, in order to distinguish it from the account of Florentine events which he had written in 1508/09.[13] Vettori also composed a historical work, a *Summary of Italian History from 1511 to 1527*.[14] If Machiavelli's *Florentine History* had demonstrated the difficulties of combining a pragmatic view of history with the humanist concept of history as a part of rhetorics and ethics, the historical works which Guicciardini and Vettori attempted in the period between 1527 and 1530 show that

[12] In May 1530, Guicciardini and Vettori together were asked to justify themselves before Court, see Roberto Ridolfi, *Vita di Francesco Guicciardini*, Roma, 1960, p. 493, note 29.

[13] Francesco Guicciardini, *Le Cose Fiorentine*, ora per la prima volta pubblicate da Roberto Ridolfi, Firenze, 1945; the title "Cose Fiorentine" was given to this work by Ridolfi. For bibliographical details, see the appendix.

[14] Francesco Vettori's *Sommario della Storia d'Italia dal 1511 al 1527* is published in *Archivio Storico Italiano*, Appendice, vol. VI (1848), pp. 283-382. The biography of Francesco Vettori by Louis Passy, *Un ami de Machiavel, François Vettori, sa vie et ses oeuvres, 1474-1539*, Paris, 1913, 2 vols., is not fully satisfactory. About him, see the careful analysis by R. von Albertini, *Das Florentinische Staatsbewusstsein im Uebergang von der Republik zum Prinzipat*, Bern, 1955, pp. 242-260.

Guicciardini and Vettori had begun to realize that these difficulties were not only formal and technical, but derived from the incompatibility of what the humanists considered as appropriate subject matter with the facts and problems in which the pragmatic political historian was interested. An analysis of the historical works written by Guicciardini and Vettori in this period will show that there was a true crisis in historical thinking.

The historical piece on which Guicciardini worked in these years, his second *Florentine History* was never finished. The work raises two questions: why did Guicciardini undertake it, and why didn't he complete it? The first question is puzzling because the second *Florentine History* overlaps the *Florentine History* which he had written in his youth. It is true indeed that in the second *Florentine History* he intended to cover the entire Florentine past, but he condensed the account of the foundation of the city and of its earlier history into one introductory book. He began a circumstantial description of events only with the end of the fourteenth century, which was the time when he had begun the narrative in his first *Florentine History*. In the second *Florentine History* he treated the last decades of the fourteenth century and the first half of the fifteenth century more extensively than in his previous work, and although the narrative in the second *Florentine History* was not fully worked out beyond the events of the middle of the fifteenth century, Guicciardini's notes show that he planned to continue in the same detailed and comprehensive manner. He wanted to deal at length with the same events on which he had focussed in his first *Florentine History*. Apparently his reason for discussing the same happenings again was that he regarded his second *Florentine History* as a work different in character from his first one.

In his second *Florentine History* Guicciardini was attempting to write the history of a city-state in the traditional classical pattern. This is indicated by the inclusion of the account of the city's foundation and early history, and by the insertion of meticulously fashioned speeches which were frequently presented in couples, the one stating the positive, the other the negative side of a proposed action. He took great care with these speeches; that he considered them as independent essays is shown by the fact that the manuscript contains speeches belonging to parts of the story which he never got around to writing. His use of speeches in the second *Florentine History* constitutes one of its differences from his earlier history, which is a bare report without rhetorical embellishments.

Guicciardini intended the second *Florentine History* to be a "true history" in the humanist sense, but that it is not. His concern with the causal connections of political events resulted in significant deviations from the practice and method of humanist historians. Guicciardini designed his speeches to throw light on the attitude of prominent historical figures or provide factual information which had not previously been given in the narrative; and thus they are much more functional than those of a typical humanist historian. For instance, in Guicciardini's report of the debate as to whether or not Florence should undertake the war against Lucca, Rinaldo degli Albizzi and Niccolò da Uzzano, the two main opponents, used the same arguments which Poggio Bracciolini, in his history, had put into their mouths.[15] But there is an important difference in the way in which these arguments were

---

[15] Guicciardini, *Cose Fiorentine*, pp. 204-210.

worked into rounded speeches. Poggio elaborated the arguments by linking them with general philosophical reflections; Guicciardini strengthened them by adding factual details on the political situation under discussion. To this extent Guicciardini was much more concrete and realistic.

Guicciardini's interest in discovering the causal connections which link political events together demanded a factual accuracy which the method of the humanist historians could not guarantee. At the outset of his second *Florentine History* Guicciardini adopted the humanist method of basing his account on that of a previous author who was recognized as the authority for the period. But soon Guicciardini began to check his authority's facts against the reports of other authors. Guicciardini was a shrewd judge of the prejudices and weaknesses of an author;[16] he considered Marchionne Stefani to be reliable on foreign policy because he had been an ambassador, but he regarded him to be biased on domestic affairs. Guicciardini was conscious of the derivative nature of Machiavelli's *Florentine History;* he doubted the veracity of its facts, and therefore he did not use it much.

Guicciardini's concern for factual accuracy led him to change his method. When he arrived in his narrative at the fifteenth century he began to use documents which he had found among the papers of his and other patrician families. In the later parts of his manuscript statements based on documents increase, whereas those taken from narrative accounts diminish. Clearly he considered documentary sources to be particularly reliable. Corre-

---

[16] For the following see the careful analysis of Guicciardini's use and evaluation of sources by Roberto Ridolfi, in his introduction to the *Cose Fiorentine*, pp. XXVIII-XXXV.

sponding to this shift in his method there was a change of focus; his notes show that he was becoming more and more involved with the affairs of the whole of Italy. He seems to have recognized that the history of Florence could be understood only as a part of the entire Italian scene.

We have suggested that Guicciardini embarked on writing a second *Florentine History* because he realized that his first one failed to meet the accepted standards for a "true history." However, at the same time, he could not free himself from the idea that history should be of use in practical politics and contribute to an understanding of the emergence of the existing political situation. But an explanation of the interconnection of political events required more labor and study than the re-writing of previous historical accounts in an elevated style, which the humanists regarded as the task of a historical writer. Moreover, the examination of the complexity of factors which determined the course of Florentine history made the pattern of the history of a city-state, which the ancient historians had established and the humanists adopted, a restrictive and almost deceptive structure. For it seemed to deny the pertinent hypotheses that politics is reaction quite as much as action, and that no state can exist in isolation.

Guicciardini's second *Florentine History* remained a fragment. The return of the Medici to Florence in 1530 brought Guicciardini back into public life, but even later when he had leisure he did not resume work on this manuscript. He chose other subjects for historical treatment. It seems most likely that he was discouraged from finishing his second *Florentine History* because he had become aware that a history of Florence, written in the conventional form of a "true history," would lack all political relevance.

Vettori's *Summary*, which, like Guicciardini's second *Florentine History*, was written in the critical years of the struggle of the Florentines against the forces of Charles V and the Medici Pope, grew out of a practical political concern; Vettori wanted to discover how the current situation of Florence and of Italy had come about. Vettori's work covers the years from 1511 to 1527. By emphasizing the inner unity of this period, by discussing the European framework into which the Italian developments belonged, by stressing the dynamism of political life, by creating psychological protraits which illuminated the leading personalities and their purely secular and egoistic interests, Vettori wrote the first European diplomatic history. Actually, Vettori concentrated on the same topics which the humanists held in such esteem: diplomatic negotiations and wars. In the letter of explanation which Vettori placed at the head of his manuscript, he suggested that the difference of his work from a "true history" in the humanist sense was relative rather than fundamental, and was caused by his deficiencies as a writer. He wrote in the vernacular, not because he did not admire those who could compose in the Latin language, but because he felt he could produce a better work in Italian. Vettori insisted that his "intention was not to write a full history."[17] His work lacked "that elegance and perhaps carefulness which it ought to have."[18] He was aware that he had written about matters

---

[17] ". . . il proposito mio non è suto di scrivere intera storia," Vettori, *Sommario*, p. 285.

[18] "E benchè io non abbi scritto con quella eleganzia e forse diligenzia che si converrebbe," *ibid.*, p. 284.

which did not belong in a "true history," and that he had omitted those details which a historical work ought to contain: "the order of battle, the number of men killed in them, the proper names of the places where the conflicts took place, the speeches in which the captains addressed the soldiers."[19] But there is more than a hint of irony in Vettori's deprecatory remarks about his own work in comparison to histories written by humanists or in the humanist pattern. The low repute in which the humanists held the unlettered chroniclers of historical facts seemed to be matched by the contempt of the man of action for impractical intellectuals.

Vettori's exclusive concern with foreign policy and war was not stimulated by the belief that these were particularly dignified subjects showing man at his heroic best. Questions of domestic policy which were crucial for other Florentine historians were, in Vettori's eyes, of little relevance. He explained his attitude by stating that free governments existed only in the utopias which Plato and Thomas More had invented; they had never existed in reality.[20] Actual governments were based on force;

[19] "Potrei avere descritto più distintamente l'ordine delle battaglie, notato il numero delli uomini morti in esse, i nomi propri de' luoghi dove siano suti li conflitti, l'orazioni fatte da' capitani alli soldati; ma (come ho detto) il proposito mio non è suto di scrivere intera istoria, nè ancora sono si arrogante, che quando volessi pigliare tale provincia, mi persuadessi di posserla perfettamente assolvere," *ibid.*, p. 285.

[20] *Ibid.*, p. 293: "Ma parlando delle cose di questo mondo sanza rispetto e secondo il vero, dico che se si facesse una di quelle repubbliche scritte e imaginate da Platone, o, come che scrive Tommaso Moro inglese, essere state trovata in Utopia, forse quelle si potrebbono dire non essere governi tirannici: ma tutte quelle repubbliche o Principi de' quali io ho cognizione per istoria, o che io ho veduti, mi pare che sentino di tirannide. Nè è da maravigliarsi che in Firenze spesso si sia vivuto a parti ed a fazioni, e che vi sia surto uno che si sia fatto capo della città; perchè è

thus all governments were tyrannical and man's concern with the problems of government was merely an indication of his failure to understand the situation into which he was placed. To Vettori, Italian politics consisted of a struggle on the part of the various states to maintain their political independence.

It would appear that Vettori's original intention was to deal with Florentine history during the Medicean regime of 1512 to 1527, and it is even possible that the basis of his work were personal *ricordi*. The *Summary* is somewhat disproportionately detailed about events in which Vettori was personally involved—the return of the Medici to Florence in 1512, and the actions and campaigns of the younger Lorenzo de 'Medici to whom Vettori had been a political adviser and a close friend. His experiences at the centers of Italian political life, as ambassador at the court of the Medici Pope in Rome and as a confidante of two of the leading members of the Medici family, Lorenzo and Cardinal Giulio, had made him aware how erroneous was the belief that a single Italian state could follow an autonomous policy, or direct or control the course of events. The policy of a single state became comprehensible only in the context of what was happening all over the Italian peninsula. The framework of Vettori's historical treatment of the preceding fifteen years was necessarily enlarged to encompass the whole of Italian and even European policy; events in France and Spain, Germany and England had to be taken into account.

---

città popolata assai, e sonovi di molti cittadini che arebbono a partecipare dello utile, e vi sono pochi guadagni da distribuire: e però sempre una parte si è sforzata governare ed avere gli onori ed utili; e l'altra è stata da canto a vedere e dire il giuoco. E per venire agli esempli, e mostrare che, a parlare libero, tutti i governi sono tirannici. . . ."

A feeling for the interdependence of all historical events is the most distinctive feature of Vettori's views on history. He did not regard "what had occurred in Italy from the year 1511 to the beginning of the year 1527" as a finite subject of investigation. "One has to speak also about what has occurred outside Italy because the affairs with which one deals are so interconnected that one can hardly write about those of Italy and leave out the others."[21] Thus the varied, complicated, and almost unfathomable causal connections which lay behind every political event dwarfed the influence which an individual could exert. Vettori had no confidence in man's virtue; to Vettori, *Fortuna* was all-powerful, and man a toy in *Fortuna's* hands.

The first sentence of the *Summary* reports the victory of the French under Gaston de Foix over the Papal and Spanish troops at Ravenna and it ends with the comment "*Fortuna,* unstable as always, suddenly changed."[22] Soderini was a good, intelligent, practical, and just man, but all these qualities were of no avail because of "bad fortune."[23] The most famous illustration of Vettori's notion of the power of *Fortuna* is his characterization of the two Medici Popes, Leo X and Clement VII. Leo X committed one mistake after another, but he was always saved

[21] "Onde trovandomi questa primavera alla villa ozioso, pensai di scrivere non intera e giusta istoria, ma brieve ed eletto Sommario delli successi dal fine dell' anno MDXI, insino al principio del MDXXVII in Italia: quantunque cognosca non essere possibile non parlare ancora di quello che è occorso fuori d'Italia; perchè le cose delle quali si tratta, sono in modo collegate insieme, che male si può scrivere di quelle d'Italia, omettendo l'altre interamente," *ibid.*, p. 284.

[22] ". . . la fortuna, come instabile, subito si mutasse . . . ," *ibid.*, p. 287.

[23] "homo, certo, buono e prudente ed utile . . . ma la mala fortuna . . . ," *ibid.*, p. 289.

by *Fortuna;* towards Clement VII, *Fortuna* was hostile. Although Clement foresaw dangers and acted cautiously, all his plans misfired and he had to suffer the transformation of his reputation "from a great and renowned Cardinal into a little and despised Pope."[24] What, according to Vettori, man can learn from history is not rules for action, but a realization of the "changeability of fortune."[25]

As different as Guicciardini's and Vettori's work are in subject matter, in intent, and in state of completion, they have certain elements in common. We observed that Guicciardini tried increasingly to place the Florentine events in the larger context of developments in Italy, and we suggested that he lost interest in continuing his manuscript because this Italian dimension was too unwieldy to be worked into an account of a city-state from the time of its foundation. Although Vettori might have originally intended to write a history of the most recent Florentine events, he soon realized the impossibility of limiting his work to Florence and thus he embarked on a description of the general developments in Italy and Europe. For both Guicciardini and Vettori the traditional humanist pattern of the history of a city-state was artificial and meaningless; its application prevented history from being politically useful.

Yet both Guicciardini and Vettori wanted to write "true histories"; they acknowledged that historians had to follow certain rules if they expected their product to

[24] ". . . di grande e riputato Cardinale, piccolo e poco stimato Papa," *ibid.,* p. 348; see also about Leo X, *ibid.,* p. 339: ". . . quanti più errori fece, a tanto più rimediò la fortuna."

[25] "E certo, in questi quindici anni si sono trattati negozii importantissimi e da considerare in essi la varietà della fortuna. . . fortuna, alla quale sono tutte le azioni umane sottoposte . . . ," *ibid.,* pp. 284-5, but this notion appears frequently in the work.

be considered as a part of the recognized literary genre. Guicciardini would not have begun to compose a second *Florentine History* if he had not regarded his earlier work as deficient in literary merit, and Vettori would hardly have made so many apologies for his work's failure to fulfill the standards of a "true history" if he had not believed in history as a legitimate and valuable literary genre. But although Guicciardini and Vettori were aware of the distance between the humanist pattern of history and political reality, and although both were unable to fit their works into this pattern, neither was willing to abandon the writing of history; nor was either willing to subordinate history to politics and to use the past exclusively as material for proving a political thesis. They believed that historical writings could disclose insights which could be expressed in no other way.

This realization of the particular and unique value of history might be regarded as a result of the experiences in the critical years from 1525 to 1530, ending with the fall of the Florentine republic and the firm establishment of the power of Charles V in Italy. The interdependence of all Italian events and their dependence on foreign powers had rendered obsolete the traditional themes of history. But the experiences of these years had also revealed the limitations of human planning and human power and had demonstrated the uncertainty of what man could achieve in politics by his own volition. Uncontrollable forces were ruling events. Vettori gave expression to this insight by emphasizing that *Fortuna* was the mistress of this world. The investigation and description of the power of *Fortuna* became the task which was peculiar to the historian and which he alone could fulfill.

Guicciardini and Vettori were not the only ones who

had become aware of the dominating role of uncontrollable forces. Their thinking reflected the existence of a new historical consciousness which took hold over the minds of men. But it would be wrong to assume that the increased interest in history based on a new estimation of the forces determining the course of politics suddenly emerged as a result of the dramatic events which occurred between the battle of Pavia in 1525 and the surrender of Florence in 1530. One might say that these events brought about the break-through of this new historical consciousness; nevertheless, it had been slowly developing since 1494 when the French invaded Italy. The immediate impact of this latter event had been a stimulus to new advances in political thought because the changes in governments and the fall of rulers which resulted from the French invasion necessitated a search for the means of recreating political stability by political reforms. The effect of the French invasion on historical thought was much less evident at first and came to be noticed only later. As a matter of fact, men had to undergo a series of recurring shocks and invasions before they realized that they were exposed to uncontrollable forces which prevented a return to the past and the restoration of stability. Only then did men view the invasion not as an ephemeral phenomenon, but an epochal event. By investigating the changes which took place between the years 1494 and 1527 in the contemporary evaluation of the nature and importance of the French invasion of Italy, we shall see the background from which Vettori's and Guicciardini's ideas about history evolved. We shall also be able to define more exactly what constituted the crucial features of the new historical consciousness which began to come to the fore at the end of the first three decades of the sixteenth century.

• III •

Before 1494 the Italian view about the position of Italy in Europe was clear and simple: there was Italy; and there was the indistinct mass of all the other nations of Europe which the Italians regarded as culturally inferior. The Italians of the Renaissance liked to repeat the classical adage that God—or Nature—had placed the Alps as a protecting wall around Italy.[26] People living beyond the Alps were foreigners and it was unnatural for the *oltramontani* to interfere in Italian affairs.

When Charles VIII of France took up his claims against Naples and began to make serious preparations for an invasion of Italy, Pontano, the great humanist who was then the first statesman of the Aragonese rulers of Naples, tried to promote the formation of a united front of all the Italian states against the French. The notion of the natural separation of Italy from the rest of Europe represented his main argument. It was in the interest of each Italian state to prevent a disturbance of the "common calm."[27] "To preserve Italy and her states in freedom,"[28] Pontano thought "the union of Italy," would be the "remedy for all accidents."[29] The French "never came

[26] The classical model of this statement was Cicero's phrase in *De Provinciis Consularibus Oratio:* "Alpibus Italiam munierat antea natura non sine aliquo divino numine"; for examples of the use of this notion in fifteenth-century Italy, see my article "The Concept of Nationalism in Machiavelli's 'Prince,' " *Studies in the Renaissance,* vol. I (1954), p. 41.

[27] ". . . reposo commune . . . ," Pontano to Antonio de Gennaro [Neapolitan Ambassador in Milan], January 1st, 1493, *Codice Aragonese,* ed. Francesco Trinchera, vol. II, part 1, Napoli, 1868, p. 249.

[28] ". . . ad volere conservare Italia, et li stati di quella in libertate . . . ," Pontano to Luigi de Palladinis [Neapolitan Ambassador at the Papal Court], September 16, 1493, *ibid.,* vol. II, part 2, p. 250.

[29] ". . . la unione de Italia, cio e lo remedio de tutti li incon-

to Italy without bringing destruction and their coming is of such a nature that the ruin will be general."[30] If the invasion is begun, it will be impossible to control it; it is not "in the power of the one who has started such a move to stop things at his will. Consider what has happened in the past and think how frequently foreign powers, called and led into Italy because of our dissensions, have oppressed and tyrannized Italy."[31]

In retrospect, Pontano's admonitions were prophetic. However, his exhortations did not suggest that the coming of the French would be an epoch-making event such as had never occurred before. To Pontano, the threatening French enterprise was similar to the many foreign invasions of Italy which had happened in the past. Nor did the situation appear unique to the Italian powers to which Pontano addressed his appeals. The rulers of the Italian states saw no reason to follow Pontano's advice and to take recourse to the extraordinary measure of forming a general Italian alliance. They regarded Pontano's arguments as inspired by the particular interests of the Aragonese whom he served and who were most immediately threatened by the French. The Italian powers considered his warning as a case of special pleading couched in the language of humanist rhetorics, and they were loath to listen to his alarms. Venice refused to believe that the

venienti . . . ," Pontano to Luigi de Palladinis, December 5, 1493, *ibid.*, p. 330.

[30] "Francesi mai vennero in Italia che non la ponessero in ruina. et questa venuta e da natura che . . . portara ruina universale," Pontano to Luigi de Paladinis, January 17, 1494, *ibid.*, p. 431.

[31] ". . . pense etiam non essere in fine in potesta di quillo che move in principio una tanta procella, ad farla tranquillare ad sua posta. Considere bene le cose passate, et veda quante volte per le interne dissensione se sonno chiamate, et conducte in Italia potentie ultramontane, che poi l'hanno oppressa, et tiranizata . . . ," Pontano to Antonio de Gennaro, April 24, 1493, *ibid.*, vol. II, part 1, p. 379.

French would carry out their threat to invade Italy. Lodovico Moro in Milan expected that he could handle the French king like previous Italian rulers had been able to manage foreign princes—the German Emperors or the Kings of Provence—who had come into Italy.

This false optimism was not even dispelled by the complete success of Charles' enterprise when, thrusting lightly aside all opposition, he marched the length of the Italian peninsula and conquered Naples. The military superiority of the French and the rapidity of their advances caused astonishment; some felt the French triumph to be a punishment which God handed out to the Italians for their sins, particularly for the vice of sodomy which was rampant in all Italian states, but especially in Naples.[32] However, after the quickly formed Italian League had forced Charles VIII back over the mountains, it seemed obvious to the Italians that this French invasion, like previous ones, was a passing event.[33] This opinion was expressed by Marin Sanudo who composed a history of the French invasion immediately after the retreat of the French. As a Venetian he praised the Venetian government which he presented as having been the driving force behind the coalition against Charles VIII, but he stated explicitly that the war must be seen as a repetition of previous history: the Italians always succeeded in expelling the foreigners who disregarded the natural wall of the mountains which God had placed around Italy.[34]

---

[32] For instance, *I Diarii di Girolamo Priuli*, ed. Arturo Segre, vol. I, p. 14 in Muratori, *Italicarum Rerum Scriptores*, nuova edizione, vol. XXIV, part 3.

[33] In general see Emilie Herbst, *Der Zug Karl VIII nach Italien im Urteil der italienischen Zeitgenossen*, Berlin and Leipzig, 1911.

[34] ". . . gente gallica, la qual, secundo l'antiche hystorie, mai hanno potuto longamente dominar in quella, nè mantenir alcuno Stato acquistato da loro, ma sempre sono stà scacciati vituperosa-

Nevertheless, a feeling of discomfort and anxiety persisted because the evinced military impotence of the Italians would seem to invite foreign armies to Italian soil. All Italians were eager to decline responsibility for having called Charles VIII into Italy in 1494. The Florentines, despite their alliance with France, liked to emphasize in their transactions with other Italian powers that "we have never provoked the French to come into Italy";[35] Lodovico Moro was apologetic about having once been "a good Frenchman," and claimed to have expiated this sin by fathering the league which forced Charles VIII out of Italy.[36]

The view that Charles VIII's campaign had been an ephemeral episode similar to many such events in the past was decisively shaken when the French returned into Italy in 1499 and, as an accompanying event, the Spaniards conquered Naples in 1501. In retrospect the invasion of 1494 appeared as the first trembling of an earthquake which shattered the foundations of Italian political life. The first two historical writers who presented the campaign of 1494 as an epoch-making event were Corio in his *History of Milan,* and Rucellai in his *History of the French Invasion.* Both wrote in the first

---

mente. Perchè havendo l'eterno Iddio posto le Alpe per termene, che barbari e tal generazione fussero divise dalla italica gente . . . cussi mai non ei ha lassato Iddio molto in questa parte prosperare. . . ," Marin Sanudo, *La Spedizione di Carlo VIII in Italia,* ed. R. Fulin, *Archivio Veneto,* suppl., 1873, p. 16.

[35] ". . . che noi non havevamo mai provocati li francesi in Italia . . . ," from a report of the Florentine ambassador Gualterotti about a conversation with Lodovico Moro, April 7, 1496, A.S.F., *Lettere di X di Balia. Responsive,* vol. 46, c. 100.

[36] "Et che altra volta Sua Eccellentia era buono Francese, ma conosciuti li modi loro se n'era ritracto . . . ," a remark made by Lodovico Moro according to a report of Gualterotti, April 17, 1496, *ibid.,* c. 125. See also Herbst, *op. cit.,* p. 30.

years of the sixteenth century. Rucellai characterized the campaign of Charles VIII as "by far the greatest event of this age, which has had an impact on the entire human race."[37] Corio, the official historian of Milan, stated that the coming of Charles VIII "had lighted an unquenchable fire which ruined not only the Sforza family, but the whole of Italy."[38]

In recognizing the magnitude of the chain of effects unleashed by the French invasion of 1494, both Corio and Rucellai were forced to ask why the Italian rulers had not been able or willing to prevent the coming of the French, and they had to explain this astounding instance of political shortsightedness. Corio had made his career in the service of Lodovico Moro and he painted a favorable picture of him as ruler of Milan; Corio praised Lodovico's intelligence and his consummate political skill. Lodovico had been "the arbiter of Italy and her stabilizer."[39] His political gifts were such that it was almost incomprehensible that he had instigated the French invasion. How could he have forgotten that God had set the mountains between Italy and other states "so that one nation would not have to mix with another"?[40]

[37] ". . . rem hujus aevi longe omnium maximam, neque sine motu maximo generis humani . . . ," Oricellarius, *De bello Italico*, London, 1733, p. 3.

[38] ". . . vi ha destato un tanto inestinguibile incendio, che la famiglia Sforzesca non solo ma quasi tutta l'Italia, come intenderai, o lettore, ha ruinato," Bernardino Corio, *Storia di Milano*, eseguita sul edizione principe del 1503, ridotta a lezione moderna, ed. Egidio de Magri, Milano, 1855, vol. III, p. 457 (the modernization is lingual, a change of Corio's Lombard dialect). A strong statement about the extension of the crisis to the entire globe can be found in Jovius, *Historiarum sui temporis Libri XLV*, beginning of Libro I.

[39] "Lodovico Sforza era stimato veramente l'arbitro d'Italia ed il conservatore," Corio, *op. cit.*, vol. III, p. 470.

[40] ". . . si reo o pessimo consiglio, non ricordandosi che il

Corio's only explanation was that the immeasurable ambition which led Lodovico to his fateful step was the work of God. God had blinded Lodovico. God wanted to punish us "for our sins."[41]

For Rucellai, the first link in the chain of events which resulted in the catastrophe of 1494 was the demand of the Pope for French support. Thus "the origin of the calamity" was Alexander VI, "distinguished by crimes of every kind,"[42] "the most vicious of criminals whom our centuries have seen."[43] Rucellai had still another target: Piero Medici. In deciding to support Naples against Milan, Piero had neglected to consult the experienced statesmen of Florence.[44] Lodovico Moro appeared to Rucellai as a wise ruler who had been driven into political isolation by Alexander VI and Piero Medici, and this situation compelled Lodovico to ask the French for support. According to Rucellai, the other Italian rulers had been stupid and they had lacked political foresight. He contrasted this gloomy picture of human folly in the years immediately preceding the coming of the French with the happy times in earlier years. Then affairs had been conducted with intelligence and sagacity. From 1484, when the Venetian expansion had been halted, Lorenzo Magnifico and Ferdinand of

---

Creatore di ogni cosa fece tutto rettamente, creò i monti per confini tra gli oltramontani e gli Italiani, a ciò che una nazione non avesse a frammischiarsi coll'altra. . .," Corio, *ibid.*, p. 470.

[41] ". . . io penso che Lodovico fosse destinato a codesto male pei nostri peccati . . . ," Corio, *ibid.*, p. 471.

[42] Alexander VI "initium calamitatis" "facinore omni insignis," Oricellarius, *op. cit.*, p. 5.

[43] "Alexander nequissimus omnium, quos saecula nostra viderunt," Oricellarius, *op. cit.*, p. 68.

[44] ". . . neque in Senatu, neque cum veteribus amicis, quibus communicare de maximis rebus Laurentius consueverat. . . ," Oricellarius, *op. cit.*, p. 9.

Aragon maintained the peace in Italy.[45] Corio also characterized the years before 1494 as a time of unusual splendor and wealth. He described at length the prosperity of Milan in the years from 1490 to 1493; "All over there were festivals and delights and Jupiter ruled in peace; everything seemed more stable and firm than it had been at any other time."[46] Corio even suggested that the immense contrast between the previous well-being and the following ruin was God's intention; it would engrave more deeply on men's hearts the misery which came from sinful actions.[47]

Thus, at the beginning of the sixteenth century some fundamental features had been established for the historical evaluation of the French invasion of 1494. It had had far-reaching consequences for Italy and the whole of Europe. It represented a historical turning point, because

[45] "Verum ubi Ferdinandus Aragonius et Laurentius Medices vita excessere, quorum alter Neapolitanum regnum ab Alfonso patre Hispano rege, alter a majoribus suis principatum acceptum apud Florentinos retineret, cuius auctoritas, civitatisque majestas gravis habebatur, perturbari miscerique cuncta cepere. Hi longe prudentissimi omnium Italiae Principum, quum ad protegendam communem libertatem, pacemque, et otium intendissent animum, consociassentque consilia, iam inde a parentibus veluti jure hereditario relicta, ac per manus tradita, ea assidue agitare, monere, niti, quibus res Italiae starent, ac (ut illorum verbis utar) examine aequo penderent. Verebantur enim gravissimi homines, ac longe animo in posterum prospicientes, ne sociorum, atque amicorum labefactata imperia ad se reciderent: neque ruere illa posse existimabant, quin sua quoque eodem motu concussa prolaberentur. At liberi (ut interdum res humanae se habent) parentibus longe dissimiles, patrum consiliis spretis, ea primum moliti, deinde aggressi sunt, unde calamitas Italiae simul et sui exitium oriretur," Oricellarius, *op. cit.*, pp. 4-5.

[46] "Erano in campo le feste ed i piaceri, e Giove trionfava colla pace, per cui tutto sembrava si stabile e fermo più che in qualunque altro tempo," Corio, *op. cit.*, vol. III, p. 456.

[47] ". . . sembrava possibile poter ancor più in alto attingere, acio credo con maggiore ruina si avesse a precipitare . . . ," Corio, *ibid*, p. 457.

it ended an era of stability and peace, and opened an era of war and sudden changes. The responsibility for the event lay with the Italian rulers, whether their mismanagement of affairs derived from personal deficiencies or from God's inscrutable will.

Yet, these ideas were still embryonic, and their systematic development was chiefly the work of Florentine writers and politicians. In other parts of Italy interest in this question was less pronounced because life still continued in its old forms. For instance, although Conti, the historian of the Church State, felt obligated to defend Alexander VI against the accusation of having brought the French into Italy, he did not consider this event as a turning point in history.[48] In Florence, however, the coming of the French into Italy had started an internal revolution and the restoration of political stability seemed to be inextricably connected with the establishment of peace. Thus, the causes of the French invasion became a vital political issue rather than a theoretical question.

With perverse pride the Florentines held Piero Medici responsible for creating the situation in which the French invasion had become unavoidable. On the other hand, they insisted that the peace which had reigned in Italy before the French invasion had been due to Lorenzo Magnifico and the ensuing distress was the fateful consequence of his premature death.[49] The analysis of the

[48] Sigismondo dei Conti, *Le Storie de' suoi tempi dal 1475 al 1510*, 2 vols., Roma, 1883; the defense of Alexander VI in book 10; printed in vol. II, pp. 51-97; see particularly p. 60.

[49] For instance, Parenti, *Historia Fiorentina*, Ms. B.N.F. II.IV.169, f. 163v: ". . . giudicandosi che la nostra citta el bilico fussi di tanta rivolutione . . . ," or also Cerretani, *Historia Fiorentina*, Ms. B.N.F., II.III.74, ff. 227-232.

causes of the French invasion which Guicciardini gave in his first *Florentine History* was centered on this contrast between the contentment in the times of Lorenzo Magnifico and the unrest after his death. During his lifetime Florence flourished because her political life was stable and her citizens were prosperous. Other powers held her in high esteem. Everything was transformed by the French invasions which brought into Italy "a fire and a plague changing not only the political regimes but also the manner of ruling and of war."[50] The result of the French invasion was both an overthrow of political regimes and a complete breakdown of political morals; instead of thinking of the common good of Italy, each ruler turned to his own particular interests.

The two sections in Guicciardini's first *Florentine History*—the one dealing with an Italy peaceful and united in purpose, and the other with an Italy torn and dominated by petty rivalries and ambitions—were separated by a section in which Guicciardini described how this change had come about. He wanted to trace "not only general effects and causes, but in a manner as detailed as possible, the origins and the sources of all these evils."[51] The section pivots on the actions of Piero Medici, Alexander VI, and Lodovico Moro. According to Guicciardini, Piero had made two mistakes: he had created enemies in Florence, and he had alienated Milan. Guicciardini emphasized that these mistakes were the result of political

---

[50] "Ed era entrata in Italia una fiamma ed una peste che non solo mutò gli stati, ma e' modi ancora del governargli ed e' modi delle guerre . . . ," Guicciardini, *Storie Fiorentine*, pp. 92 et seq.

[51] "Nella quale cosa io mi ingegnerò di mostrare non solo gli effetti e le cagione in genere, ma ancora, quanto più particularmente potrò, le origine e le fonte di tutti e' mali." Guicciardini, *ibid.*, p. 84.

miscalculations but they had their origin in human deficiencies—in jealousy, pettiness, meanness, and vanity. Human failings and vices led to the constellation which resulted in the appearance of the French in Italy. Guicciardini's examination of the causes of the French invasion and of the changes it wrought was more closely argued and more impressively presented than Rucellai's, but in its decisive features Guicciardini's analysis was similar to Rucellai's. Guicciardini did not even follow up Rucellai's suggestion that the French invasion was not only an Italian but a European event with consequences for "the entire human race."[52] Although Guicciardini delineated the differences between the world of the fifteenth and the world of the sixteenth century, his *Florentine History* was focussed on Florence and Italy, and he viewed the invasion of Charles VIII primarily from the point of its impact on Florence.

In order for the causes and the consequences of the French invasion to be understood, it had to be seen in the context of European politics; this conception was fully realized only in the third decade of the sixteenth century. Then Italy was the main theatre for the struggle between Charles V and Francis I. With the recognition that the campaigns on Italian soil were part of a general European war, men began to see that the invasion of Charles VIII had to be evaluated as an event of European history. This was done by Girolamo Borgia whose *History of the Italian Wars* might be considered as the first historical work which fully evidences the proposition of the invasion of Charles VIII as a European event.[53] Borgia's work forms

[52] See above, note 37.

[53] Hieronymii Borgii, *Historiae de bellis Italicis ab anno 1494 ad 1541*, Ms. Bibl. Marc. Cod. Lat. 3506. The manuscript has never been published. A note on the first page of the manuscript states

an important link in the evolution of the ideas on the importance of the French invasion. Borgia used Rucellai's manuscript extensively as was his own later used by Guicciardini for his *History of Italy*.[54] In the 1520's, when Borgia began to write his history, the notion was widespread that the year 1494 had been a turning-point. This Borgia took for granted, and he started his work with a detailed survey of Italy in the period before the French invasion, emphasizing the flourishing condition of Italy[55] but in 1494 the gates of Italy were opened to foreigners

---

that on June 22, 1544, Borgia has given the completed manuscript "in novo palatio apud aram celi" to the Pope (i.e., Paul III Farnese) "et obtuli quam ore benigno legit et probavit." In the foreword to the sixteenth book Borgia also states that Jovius had shown him in Naples that part of the manuscript of his *Historiarum sui temporis Libri XLV* which dealt with Charles V's expedition to Tunis of 1535. A note at the end of the seventeenth book of Borgia's manuscript shows that this book was completed in March 1538, but since only one more book follows, it seems possible that the work was completed some time before Borgia gave the manuscript to the Pope in 1544. However, the manuscript was written in sections, which have dedications to different people; the first of these dedications is dated August 1526; then the first six books, reaching from 1494 to roughly 1520, were completed. Thus the sections on the origin and importance of the invasion of Charles VIII were written in the third decade of the sixteenth century, although the possibility of later revisions cannot be excluded. On Borgia, see Raffaele di Florio, *Girolamo Borgia*, Salerno, 1909 and also E. Percopo, "La Vita di Giovanni Pontano," *Archivio Storico per le Provincie Napolitane*, vol. LXI (1936), pp. 227-28, and Benedetto Croce, "Per la biografia di Girolamo Borgia," *La Critica*, vol. XXXII (1934), pp. 149-151. Borgia was a member of Pontano's circle and lived in Naples until 1503; he became then secretary to the condottiere Bartolomeo d'Alviano, and went after Alviano's death to Rome, where he was patronized by the Farnese. In 1544, Pope Paul III made him Bishop of Massalubrense.

[54] The evidence that Borgia used Rucellai's manuscript is internal; excerpts from Borgia are preserved among the Guicciardini papers. Guicciardini also used Rucellai's work.

[55] "Erant tunc res Italiae florentes; atque omnes Italiae urbes immensis opibus abundantes; tanto deditae luxui et ocio ut mole jam sua laborare viderentur," Borgia, *op. cit.*, f. 5v.

for the first time in two hundred years.[56] Borgia distributed responsibility for the origin of "all the evils of Italy" among Alexander VI, Lodovico Moro, and Alfonso of Naples.[57] And he regarded as the decisive reason for all further calamities the failure of the rulers of Florence and Naples to maintain the alliance system of their "wise fathers."[58] To Borgia, the conflict which had broken out in 1494 had two aspects: it brought Italy under the rule of foreigners, and it started a conflagration all over Europe. "It was the work of human nature or of fortune that, after a long and happy peace, long and cruel wars broke out, not only in Italy but all over the world."[59] To Corio and Rucellai, Italy had been the target at which the European powers had aimed; to Borgia, the Italian wars were a function of the general power struggle among the great European states. Italy was but a pawn in their game of power politics.

In the earlier attempts to write the history of the French invasion of 1494 great attention was given to the question of personal guilt. Rucellai, Corio, and Guicciardini ascribed the disasters of Italy to the vices of the people or to the weaknesses, deficiencies, and moral shortcomings of individual rulers. The authors of this interpretation were influenced by the humanist notion that the purpose

[56] "[Lodovico Moro] portasque Italiae primus nostro aevo post ducentesimum annum Gallis patefecit," *ibid.*, f. 5v.

[57] "Principio omnibus constat Alexandri sexti pontificis, Ludovici Sfortiae quem Maurum ob colorem vafrumque ingenium appellabant, et Alfonsi secundi Neapolitanorum regis regnandi libidinem immanissimam fontem originemque omnium Italiae fuisse malorum," *ibid.*, f. 4r.

[58] ". . . qua Laurentius et Ferrandus prudentissimi patres diu inter se aluerant," *ibid.*, f. 5r.

[59] "Antiquum sive naturae humanae sive fortunae vitium est, non Italiae solum, sed et omnibus fere terris post longam laetamque pacem diuturnum luctuosumque bellum exoriri," *ibid.*, f. 2r.

of history was to teach right behavior. But such an interpretation was also compatible with the assumption that Italy was separate from the rest of Europe, that it had an autonomous existence, and that the Italians were able, therefore, to control whatever happened on their peninsula. But the attribution of responsibility to the moral failure of individual Italian rulers made little sense if whatever occurred in Italy was determined by the conflicts among the great European powers and was dependent on developments in areas in which the Italian rulers had no influence. Borgia sat in judgment over the Italian rulers at the time of the French invasion,[60] but he was aware of the discrepancy between these interpretations, the one based on moral principles, the other on political causality. Thus to Borgia, the end of Italian peace was not only the doing of the foolish sons, Piero and Alfonso, who destroyed the work of their wise fathers, Lorenzo and Ferdinand, but it was an unavoidable celestial revolution in which Jupiter overthrew the golden reign of Saturn.[61]

• IV •

In the evaluation of the importance of the French invasion the present determined the image of the past. The

[60] "Sed cum principum nostrorum culpa et ignavia factum sit, ut terram omnium olim gentium Dominam in barbarorum potestatem iterum redactam videamus, non erit inutile eorum peccata notare, ut quoniam pleraque simultate atque ambitione principum magis quam bonis artibus gesta sunt, unde secuta imperia saeva, scelerata bella, strages, excidia horrenda posteris, atque iis ipsis qui ea viderint reformidanda, inde posteri vario memorabilique exemplo moniti capiant sibi suaeque reipublicae quod imitentur, inde quod turpe sit et exitiale caveant," *ibid.*, f. 2v.

[61] ". . . iamque ut Saturni regna illa a poetis celebrata nimio torpentia veterno ab Jove excitata legimus sic nostrum saeculum a Carolo excitum variisque agitatum calamitatibus vidimus," *ibid.*,

continuance of the invasions of Italy heightened the significance of the campaign of Charles VIII in 1494, and when, in the 1520's, Italy was the chief theatre for struggle between Hapsburg and Valois for European hegemony, it became apparent that the beginning had been the French campaign of 1494, which increasingly, was seen as an event of lasting impact and of significance for the entire course of European history. But it should be noted that, with the change in the evaluation of the importance of the French invasion, the views about the causes of this event changed also. As long as it was seen as an ephemeral event and as long as its significance seemed restricted to the Italian political scene, the responsibility could be placed on individuals or on the moral corruptness of the Italian people in general, whom God wanted to punish. But when the French invasion was viewed as the result of the rivalry between the great European powers, with the Italians as suffering victims as much as active promoters, the cause of this event was believed to have been far beyond human power; it had been decreed in the stars and the heavens. It was only a short step further to Vettori's notion of the omnipotence of *Fortuna.*[62]

---

f. 5v. See also *ibid.,* f. 89r.: "Consilium coeli horrendum procul intueor, incredibilem Europae vastitatem horreo. Quid, o Saturne, Quid, o Mars, tristia mundi sidera in unam sedem propere coistis. . . ."

[62] ". . . mutabilis aevi res gestas et fortunae varietates . . . ," was also Borgia's main theme, as he writes in the dedication, *op. cit.,* f. 1; but see also the introduction of his third book: "Fortunae varietatem et si in omni vita continentur videmus, nulla tamen in re saepius quam in regnorum conditione spectare solemus; ex qua rerum inconstantia pabet, quam fluxa sunt etiam regna quae stulti mortales tantopere mirantur vastisque conatibus expetunt . . . uno in regno intra triennii spatium sub quinque regibus variatum est. Quos fortuna velut in tragedia non ficta non tam cito ostentaverit, quam cito sustulerit. . . ."

The world of history was the realm of *Fortuna*. In recognizing the unlimited power which *Fortuna* holds over human affairs the idea of history as an independent force was symbolized. Certainly *Fortuna* had always been thought to play an important role in history. The theme of the struggle of man's *virtù* against *Fortuna* was one of the traditional topics of history. Military action, in particular, was regarded as an area in which *Fortuna* was especially powerful. Even in diplomatic correspondence, rulers were warned against undertaking wars because once one had started, the rulers had delivered themselves into the hands of *Fortuna*.[63] But whereas in earlier times *Fortuna's* influence was limited to special spheres or definite occasions, the *Fortuna* which emerged as the ruler of world history in the sixteenth century was the power behind everything that happened: it was an embodiment of the uncontrollable forces determining the course of events. This view of *Fortuna* was the outcome of the experience that no single event has a clear beginning, and the investigation of causal connections only exposes the vista of an infinite number of further relationships and in-

---

[63] ". . . la fortuna porta de stranie varietate et multo spisso se e veduto in le guerre essere stati perditori quelli che li hanno mossi, et che non e in potere el fin dela guerra de quilli la hanno mossa. . . ," Pontano to Luigi de Palladinis, January 17, 1494, *Codice Aragonese*, vol. II, part 1, pp. 423-424. Pontano's views on *Fortuna*, characteristically different from those of men like Vettori, Borgia, Guicciardini, are succinctly stated in a remark of Pontano's to King Ferdinand, October 12, 1493, published by Percopo, *loc. cit.*, p. 50: "Non fidate tanto in Dio, perchè non te aiuta senza te in li casi, dove l'huomini se possono aiutare. Non vogliate all'ultimo darve tutto a fortuna, perchè sôle ingannare, e puro li huomini hanno in bona parte lo libero arbitrio." In general, for the fifteenth-century view on the relation between *virtù* and *Fortuna*, which is still Machiavelli's, see Giovanni Gentile, "Il Concetto dell' Uomo nel Rinascimento," *Il Pensiero Italiano del Rinascimento*, Firenze, 1940, pp. 84-89.

terdependencies. Such a view of *Fortuna* destroyed the fifteenth-century belief in man's power to control, or at least to influence events. Yet this notion of *Fortuna* did not lead to a return to the medieval concept of a world directed according to God's plan. Italians of the sixteenth century saw no straight course or rational purpose in history; man was driven by forces which he could not fathom.

It may seem paradoxical, but this view of *Fortuna's* power and man's helplessness constituted a greater attraction for the consideration of the past and the writing of history. As long as it was believed that man could exert a formative influence on events, the search for rules of political conduct and for perfect political institutions was of paramount importance; but when man appeared to be unable to create lasting institutions which would withstand the forces of *Fortuna*, the chase after the laws of politics became futile. Explanations of how things came about seemed more relevant than prescriptions for what ought to be done.

If before 1527 the most lively minds were attracted to writing about politics, in later years it was the writing of history which became an exciting task. And the task was to write in a way which would mirror the political reality of the time as well as reflect the awareness that the historical perspective was unique. Despite the changes in form and content, history remained an independent literary genre.

Chapter 7 GUICCIARDINI

In 1538 when Francesco Guicciardini was fifty-five years old, he began to write a history of the preceding forty years.[1] In the course of his lifetime he had written family memoirs and autobiographical notes,[2] he had composed commentaries on works of others—for example, one on Machiavelli's Discourses[3]—he had outlined plans for an ideal constitution of Florence,[4] and twice he had undertaken to write a history of Florence.[5] But the *History of Italy* stands apart from all his writings because it was the one work which he wrote not for himself, but for the public. When Guicciardini embarked on this last and largest of all his literary enterprises his political career had ended. He was aware that what was for him the greatest fame which man can attain—the fame as a moulder of the political world—had evaded him. But he still yearned for immortality, and he turned to the writing of history be-

[1] For the dating of the composition of the *Storia d'Italia*, see Roberto Ridolfi, *Vita di Francesco Guicciardini*, Roma, 1960, pp. 398 et seq. For the literature on Guicciardini, see the bibliographical appendix, where I explain and justify my views on particular facts of Guicciardini's career and on debated problems of his concepts and thinking. The annotations of this chapter will be chiefly limited to documenting textual statements by references to Guicciardini's works.

[2] Published in the volume: *Francesco Guicciardini, Scritti Autobiografici e Rari*, ed. R. Palmarocchi, Bari, 1936.

[3] Published in the volume: *Francesco Guicciardini, Scritti Politici e Ricordi*, ed. R. Palmarocchi, Bari, 1933.

[4] Published in the volume: *Francesco Guicciardini, Dialogo e Discorsi del Reggimento di Firenze*, ed. R. Palmarocchi, Bari, 1932.

[5] See above, pp. 243 et seq.

cause he hoped that literary work might bring him the fame which had escaped him in politics. Although literary renown might not be of the highest order, Guicciardini held literary achievements in great esteem. In the *History of Italy*, which is exclusively concerned with matters of war and diplomacy, he commented that one of the members of a French diplomatic mission was Guillaume Budé, "a man with great knowledge of Greek and Latin, and in erudition almost unique among the men of our time,"[6] and he added to the story of the death of the Condottiere Bartolomeo d'Alviano the detail that the funeral oration was given by the Venetian humanist Navagero.[7]

Because Guicciardini was eager for his work to achieve a permanent place in literature, he wrote it with particular care: he deliberated over the choice of words, he invited criticisms of the humanist Giovanni Corsi,[8] and finally, he re-wrote large parts of the manuscript several times in order to perfect the style. An indication of the standards which he had set for this work can be found on a free leaf opposite the text of the manuscript. There he inscribed the sentences from Cicero's *De Oratore* containing the rules about the writing of history.[9]

[6] ". . . uomo nelle lettere umane, così greche come latine, di somma e forse unica erudizione tra tutti gli uomini de' tempi nostri. . . ," *Storia d'Italia*, Libro XII, chapt. 11 (vol. III, p. 344; here, as in the rest of this chapter, indications of volume and page, given in brackets, refer to the edition of the *Storia d' Italia* by Constantino Panigada, Bari, 1929).

[7] *Ibid.*, Libro XII, chapt. 17.

[8] Corsi's letter was published by E. Rostagno in his introduction to the *Storia d'Italia*, ed. A. Gherardi, vol. I, pp. LXXIII et seq.

[9] The translation from Cicero, *De Oratore*, II, chapt. 15, has been taken from the edition in the 'Loeb Classical Library,' but it should be noted that Guicciardini's excerpt from *De Oratore* has a few slight, purely stylistic variations from the Latin text

"The nature of the subject needs chronological arrangement and geographical representation: and since, in reading of important affairs worth recording, the plans of campaign, the executive actions and the results are successively looked for, it calls also, as regards such plans, for some imitation of what the writer approves, and, in the narrative of achievement, not only for a statement of what was done or said, but also of the manner of doing or saying it; and, in the estimate of consequences, for an exposition of all contributory causes, whether originating in accident, discretion or foolhardiness; and, as for the individual actors, besides an account of their exploits, it demands particulars of the lives and characters of such as are outstanding in renown and dignity. Then again the kind of language and type of style to be followed are the easy and the flowing, which run their course with unvarying current and a certain placidity, avoiding alike the rough speech we use in Court and the advocate's stinging epigrams."

Clearly Guicciardini felt that his *History of Italy*

---

given in the Loeb Classical Library. Guicciardini's excerpt was published by R. Ridolfi, *Genesi della Storia d'Italia Guicciardiniana,* Florence, 1939, p. 8, and runs as follows: ". . . Rerum ratio ordinem temporum desiderat, regionum descriptionem; vult etiam quin in rebus magnis memoriaque dignis consilia primum, deinde acta, postea eventus expectantur, et de consiliis significari quid scriptor probet et in rebus gestis declarari non solum quid actum aut dictum sit, set etiam quomodo, et, cum de eventu dicatur, ut cause explicentur omnes, vel casus vel sapientie, vel temeritatis; hominumque ipsorum non solum res geste, set etiam qui fama ac nomine excellant, de cuiusque natura ac vita. Verborum autem ratio et genus orationis fusum atque tractum et cum lenitate quadam equabili profluens sine hac iudiciali asperitate et sine sententiarum forensium aculeis prosequendum est . . ."

would be considered a work of literature only if it met the standards of a classical history. Guicciardini wanted to produce a "true history" in the humanist sense and this aim is evident on every page of the *History of Italy*. Guicciardini designated these rules and prescripts of the humanists as "laws of history." Whenever he included material which was not of a political or military nature he apologized for violating these "laws."[10] His accounts of military campaigns, particularly his descriptions of battles, conform exactly to the rules for writing "true history." He placed great emphasis on speeches, and he wrote them frequently in couples, representing opposite viewpoints. The organization of the *History of Italy* follows the humanist prescripts; Guicciardini divided the work into books and subdivided them according to years. Originally he planned to have the work consist of nineteen books, but he rearranged the manuscript so that there would be twenty books because twenty is a more perfect number.[11] But if in its formal aspects the *History of Italy* corresponds to humanist prescriptions, these are not the features which the reader considers as determining the character of the book. Rather it is a work which bears the imprint of the author's personality and mind, and as such it is a reflection of the Florentine political tradition and of the political experiences of the age.

At the time of the great crisis of Guicciardini's life, after the *Sacco di Roma* and the liberation of Florence

---

[10] "Ma ritornando al principale proposito nostro, dal quale il dolore giustissimo del danno publico m'aveva, più ardentemente che non conviene alla legge dell'istoria, traportato . . . ," *Storia d'Italia*, libro IV, chapt. 12 (vol. I, p. 381).

[11] ". . . come numero più perfetto," advice Corsi's to Guicciardini, see above, note 8.

from the Medici rule, when he did not have position or influence with either the Pope or the Florentines, he imagined that he might be called before the court which had been established by the Florentines to judge the enemies of the republic.[12] He composed, therefore, two speeches, one containing the accusations which a prosecutor might raise against his actions, the other the defense which he would present against these accusations.[13] The accusation to which Guicciardini considered himself most vulnerable was that of an overweening ambition; hence this was the main point of his accusatory speech. Even in his youth "his restlessness and ambitiousness was so well-known that he was called Alcibiades, indicating therewith that he possessed a demanding, restless, and dissatisfied spirit."[14] He had united with those who wanted to overthrow the republic. As a Papal administrator, he lived in "a house full of tapestries, of silver, of servants . . . he knew no superior . . . he went around with a guard of more than one hundred German mercenaries . . . considering the importance of his business, his unlimited authority, the great extent of the territory he administered, his court and his pomp, he appeared equal to dukes rather than to lesser princes."[15] That was the life he liked, and

[12] Actually, in 1530, Guicciardini was called into court and, in absentia, condemned, see Ridolfi, *Vita di Guicciardini*, pp. 322 et seq.

[13] Guicciardini, *Scritti Autobiografici*, pp. 193-245 (Oratio Accusatoria), pp. 249-281 (Oratio Defensoria). Ridolfi, *Vita di Guicciardini*, p. 484 emphasizes that these speeches were composed in 1527 and have nothing to do with Guicciardini's process in 1530.

[14] ". . . tra noi tutti era tanto nota questa sua inquiete ed ambizione che alcuni de' nostri lo chiamavano Alcibiade, volendo denotare uno spirito cupido, inquieto ed autore di cose nuove . . . ," Guicciardini, "Oratio Accusatoria," *Scritti Autobiografici*, p. 212.

[15] "E certo se voi avessi veduto . . . messer Francesco in Romagna . . . con la casa piena di arazzi, di argenti, di servidori,

that way of existence he obtained because he had always favored the Medici and had served them in every possible way. They had always protected him so that he had been able shamelessly to enrich himself at the expense of the people he ruled and the soldiers who served him.

In the speech which Guicciardini designed as a defense against these imaginary indictments he placed great emphasis on refuting the accusation that he had made use of his high position for the purposes of personal gain. The people had been secure under his rule and they had admired his impartial justice; he could point to many testimonies which showed the satisfaction of the people with his government. Moreover, the courtly splendor which had surrounded him had been necessary to maintain his authority. The reality behind this magnificent façade had been constant work and endless worries throughout days and nights. He had never taken part in any plans to overthrow a legally established government and was always willing to serve loyally those who ruled in Florence. His way of life and his actions in the past show that his mind "was never opposed to a free republic."[16] That was the regime which he preferred.

---

con el concorso di tutta la provincia, che dal papa in fuora, quale rimetteva totalmente ogni cosa a lui, non cognosceva altro superiore, con una guardia intorno di più di cento lanzchenech, con alabardieri, con altre guardie di cavalli andare per la città in mezzo sempre di centinaia di persone, non cavalcare mai con manco di cento o centocinquanta cavalli, affogare nelle signorie, ne' titoli, nello illustrissimo signore, non l'aresti ricognosciuto per vostro cittadino, per simile a voi; ma considerata la grandezza delle faccende, la autoritá smisurata, el dominio e governo grandissimo la corte e la pompa, vi sarebbe parso più presto equale a ogni duca che a altro principe," Guicciardini, *Scritti Autobiografici,* pp. 209-210.

[16] ". . . che tu non abbia lo animo alieno da uno vivere libero . . . ," Guicciardini, *ibid.,* p. 180; these words come from the "Consolatoria," but for the same meaning in the "Defensoria," see pp. 280-281.

Guicciardini was certainly not as evil as his speech representing the accusations of an imaginary prosecutor painted him, but he was also not quite as pliable and selfless as he maintained in his defense. There are elements of the true Guicciardini in both of these contrasting speeches. The accusation of personal enrichment was certainly unjustified; Guicciardini was incorruptible. He was almost fanatically concerned about his honor, which, as he once wrote, is a "burning stimulus" to action.[17] But he was a man of strong ambitions, and he was very conscious of his great gifts and talents. Occupation of important positions in politics he regarded as his right; his experiences as Papal administrator rigidified this disposition. He viewed politics from above. Order, security, justice were to him more important than forms of government. Instead of evaluating a system of government according to abstract values, one ought to consider its effects; that is the criterion which he used in the *Dialogo del Reggimento di Firenze*.[18] Moreover, Guicciardini clearly enjoyed the society of princes, rulers, and ministers, into whose company his administrative positions had thrown him. It is reported that when, in 1537, young Cosimo Medici became ruler of Florence, Guicciardini was most anxious to have one of his daughters married to him.[19] Guicciardini felt that he belonged to a small elite, and his interest in the members of this elite is fully reflected in the *History of Italy* in which all light is focussed on the leaders of states and governments.

[17] "A chi stima l'onore assai succede ogni cosa, perché non cura fatiche, non pericoli, non danari. Io l'ho provato in me medesimo, però lo posso dire e scrivere: sono morte e vane le azione degli uomini che non hanno questo stimulo ardente," Ricordo 118 in Guicciardini, *Ricordi*, ed. Raffaele Spongano, Firenze, 1951, p. 129.

[18] See above, pp. 119 et seq.

[19] See Ridolfi, *Vita di Guicciardini*, p. 387; Ridolfi doubts the veracity of this report.

Guicciardini's sense of superiority diminished the weight of his confessions of republican faith. Certainly he disliked having the Medici rulers in Florence and he wanted to see a republican form of government established. But he was a Florentine aristocrat and his goal was a republic in which the aristocrats would rule; and when he advocated a *Gonfaloniere a vita*, one has the feeling that he saw himself in this position. Freedom had for him no absolute value; it was not even a reality: "Don't believe those who so fervently preach liberty. Nearly all of them—probably every single one of them—has his own particular interests in mind. Experience proves beyond any doubt that if they thought they would be better off under an absolute government, they would rush into it as fast as they could."[20] Guicciardini had the family pride of the Florentine aristocrat. In addition to writing family memoirs, he set down rules of behavior which he collected in his *Ricordi;* they were intended for members of the Guicciardini family and were meant to instruct them on how to maintain their status and reputation.

Guicciardini had the aristocratic conviction that his class knew better than anyone else how to rule because they had been trained and schooled in the art of government. Experience is the quality most needed by the man of affairs. "Let no one trust so much in native intelligence that he believes it to be sufficient without the help of experience. No matter what his natural endowments any man who has been in a position of responsibility knows

---

[20] "Non crediate a costoro che predicano sì efficacemente la libertà, perché quasi tutti, anzi non è forse nessuno che non abbia l'obietto agli interessi particulari: e la esperienza mostra spesso, e è certissimo, che se credessino trovare in uno stato stretto migliore condizione, vi correrebbono per le poste." Ricordo 66 in Guicciardini, *Ricordi*, p. 76.

that experience attains many things that natural gifts
alone could never attain."[21] Or he emphasized "how different theory is from practice."[22] Thus "it is a great error
to speak of the things of this world absolutely and indis-
criminately, and to deal with them, as it were, by the
book. In nearly all things one must make distinctions and
exceptions, because of differences in their circumstances.
These circumstances are not covered by one and the
same rule. Nor can these distinctions and exceptions be
found written in books. They must be taught by discretion."[23] Guicciardini's principal objection to the theories
which Machiavelli advanced in the *Discourses* was that
Machiavelli put things "too absolutely."[24] Guicciardini
did not agree with Machiavelli's basic assumption that
Rome could serve as a perfect norm: "How wrong it is to
cite the Romans at every turn."[25]

---

[21] "Non si confidi alcuno tanto nella prudenza naturale che si
persuada quella bastare sanza l'accidentale della esperienza, perché
ognuno che ha maneggiato faccende, benché prudentissimo, ha
potuto conoscere che con la esperienza si aggiugne a molte cose,
alle quali è impossibile che el naturale solo possa aggiugnere,"
Ricordo 10, *ibid.*, p. 14.

[22] "Quanto è diversa la pratica dalla teorica! . . . ," Ricordo 35,
ibid., p. 42.

[23] "È grande errore parlare delle cose del mondo indistintamente
e assolutamente e, per dire così, per regola; perché quasi tutte
hanno distinzione e eccezione per la varietà delle circumstanze, le
quali non si possono fermare con una medesima misura: e queste
distinzione e eccezione non si truovano scritte in su' libri, ma
bisogna le insegni la discrezione," Ricordo 6, *ibid.*, p. 11.

[24] ". . . troppo assolutamente. . . ," "Considerazioni ai Discorsi
del Machiavelli" in Guicciardini, *Scritti Politici*, p. 8.

[25] "Quanto si ingannono coloro che a ogni parola allegano e
Romani! Bisognerebbe avere una città condizionata come era loro,
e poi governarsi secondo quello essemplo: el quale a chi ha le
qualità disproporzionate è tanto disproporzionato, quanto sarebbe
volere che uno asino facessi el corso di uno cavallo," Ricordo 110
in Guicciardini, *Ricordi*, p. 121, but see also "Considerazioni
intorno ai Discorsi," in Guicciardini, *Scritti Politici*, p. 11.

But Guicciardini's insistence on the value of practice and experience was not that of an unlearned man. On the contrary, he had been educated by some of the best minds of his time, and his intellectual interests were wide and lively. But experience provided the material on which man's reason ought to work. Guicciardini shared the pride of contemporaries in the power of man's reason. "Remember this: whoever lives a life of chance will in the end find himself a victim of chance. The right way is to think, to examine, and to consider every detail carefully, even the most minute. And even if you do, it takes great pains to make things come out right."[26] Guicciardini was guided by the belief, characteristic of the Florentine aristocracy, in a rational attitude and policy. He was scarcely touched by the idea that energy or will power or *virtù* could be more powerful than reason: "Only wise men are brave. Others are either temerarious or foolhardy."[27] Thus Guicciardini had no doubt that an intelligent man using the experiences of the past could construct a stable government or control the course of events. In his younger years, at least, Guicciardini did not question the validity of a policy of rational calculations, of which Lorenzo Magnifico was the admired symbol.

Because Guicciardini had been inspired by the belief in man's power to control events and in his own talent to manage his affairs, the shock caused by the events of 1527

[26] "Sappiate che chi governa a caso si ritruova alla fine a caso. La diritta è pensare, essaminare, considerare bene ogni cosa etiam minima; e vivendo ancora così, si conducono con fatica bene le cose: pensate come vanno a chi si lascia portare dal corso della acqua," Ricordo 187 in Guicciardini, *Ricordi*, p. 199.

[27] "Soli e savî sono animosi; li altri sono o temerarî o inconsiderati . . . ," Guicciardini, *ibid.*, p. 107.

was profound. As one of the chief advisers to the Pope, Guicciardini had urged Clement VII to conclude the ill-fated League of Cognac against Charles V, and the outcome demonstrated how wrong even the best considered decisions can be. As a result Guicciardini not only lost the confidence of the Pope but also he was rebuffed by the anti-Medicean regime in Florence. It was then that he wrote that "from the extreme height of honors and esteem, of important affairs and general renown" he had been "suddenly thrown down to the other extreme into an idle, abject, and private life without dignities, without business," and in his own city "inferior to any small citizen." Now finally he had learnt "what children and unlettered men know: that prosperity does not last and fortune changes."[28] "Neither fools nor wise men can ultimately resist what must be. Hence I have never read anything that I thought better said than: Ducunt volentes fata, nolentes trahunt."[29]

Guicciardini's further political career was an illustration of the manner in which man can become a tool in the hands of *Fortuna*. He made his way back into the graces of Clement VII, but because he had wavered in his loyalty to the Medici cause as long as the Pope had seemed helpless, he had to pay a price: he had to take a

[28] ". . . da uno estremo eccessivo di onori, di riputazione, di faccende grandissime e di notizia universale in che tu eri, ti truovi precipitato subito in uno altro estremo di uno vivere ozioso, abietto, privatissimo, sanza degnità, sanza faccende, inferiore nella tua città a ogni piccolo cittadino. . . . Sanno pure insino a'fanciulli, insino a quelli che non hanno elementi di lettere, che le prosperità non durano, che la fortuna si muta . . . ," Guicciardini, "Consolatoria" of 1527, *Scritti Autobiografici*, pp. 167, 174.

[29] "Né e pazzi né e savi non possono finalmente resistere a quello che ha a essere: però io non lessi mai cosa che mi paressi meglio detta che quella che disse colui: 'Ducunt volentes fata, nolentes trahunt'," Ricordo 138 in Guicciardini, *Ricordi*, p. 150.

leading part in the harsh persecution of the leaders of the republic after the restoration of the Medici regime in 1530 and he had to defend the odious Duke Alessandro before Charles V. Guicciardini hated the tyrannical procedures of the Medici rulers, but he was too experienced in diplomacy not to realize that in the existing circumstances their rule in Florence was unavoidable. He became a principal advisor of the Medici on Florentine affairs, and in the eyes of the Florentines he was one of the chief instruments of Medicean absolutism. However, he never gave up hope that he might be able to bring about a regime in Florence which corresponded more closely to his ideas about an ideal government. When, after the assassination of Alessandro, the young Cosimo Medici was called in to take over the rule in Florence, Guicciardini tried to impose on him conditions which would limit his power. Francesco Vettori mocked these attempts; promises on paper would be of little avail as long as Cosimo had command of the military forces.[30] And Vettori was right. Cosimo soon was firmly in the saddle, and Guicciardini's attempt to limit his power had only filled the Duke with suspicion. Under Cosimo Guicciardini was without any political influence and there was nothing left for him but to retire to his villa. Then he began to write the *History of Italy*.

The humanists believed that history taught by example. In Guicciardini's *History of Italy* there are hardly any examples which ought to be imitated. Among the many people whose natures and actions Guicciardini discussed, there is only one for whom he seems to have felt unlimited admiration: Gonsalvo da Cordova, the Gran Cap-

[30] See Ridolfi, *Vita di Guicciardini*, p. 511, note 16.

itano. Guicciardini regarded him as the embodiment of all the qualities which a great military leader ought to possess.[31] But in general, Guicciardini had a low opinion of military leaders; some of them had no knowledge of military science, some of them were cowards, and most of them were so concerned about their own fame—and so jealous of the fame of other captains—that they were more interested in preventing their rivals from enhancing their reputation than in defeating the common enemy.[32] Guicciardini's views of the statesmen of the sixteenth century were no less negative. He acknowledged Lodovico Moro's intelligence, but he presented him as driven by "megalomaniac ambition," which brought ruin to himself and to Italy.[33] Soderini lacked judgment, he was overconfident in good times and he lost his head at the first sign of danger.[34] Of the two Medici Popes, Leo X was frivolous, he spent his days with actors, musicians, and buffoons, he practiced unashamedly his unnatural sexual inclinations and he wasted his not inconsiderable political gifts in schemes to promote the fortunes of his family; Clement VII was so unable to make up his mind that all his plans came to nought.[35] Even those political figures whose actions, in the estimation of later historians,

[31] "Ma Consalvo, che da qui innanzi chiameremo più spesso il Gran Capitano, poichè con vittorie sì gloriose si aveva confermato il cognome . . . ," *Storia d'Italia*, libro VI, chapt. 10 (vol. II, p. 134), also libro XII, chapt. 19.

[32] *Storia d'Italia*, libro XIV, chapt. 4, or libro XV, chapt. 6, or libro XVII, chapt. 8, etc., etc.

[33] "Accresceva questi disegni e speranze fallaci la persuasione, nella quale poco ricordandosi della varietà delle cose umane si nutriva da se stesso, d'avere quasi sotto i piedi la fortuna, della quale affermava publicamente essere figluolo . . . ," *ibid.*, libro III, chapt. 4 (vol. I, pp. 230 et seq.), but also libro IV, chapt. 14.

[34] *Ibid.*, libro XI, chapts. 3 and 4.

[35] *Ibid.*, libro XVI, chapt. 12 contains the famous comparison of the character of the two Medici Popes.

controlled and transformed the European scene in the sixteenth century were in Guicciardini's eyes unequal to their positions and their tasks. Julius II was "an instrument destined to ruin Italy"; his passionate impetuosity prevented him from judging correctly the consequences of his actions. Only in reporting Julius' death did Guicciardini express some recognition of the Pope's energy in administering the affairs of the Church.[36] Francis I of France cared more for the trappings of royal power than its substance.[37] Charles V was presented as an inexperienced and helpless young man controlled by his counsellors. The first decision which Charles V made on his own—to release Francis I after forcing him to sign a harsh treaty—was wrong and it was taken against good advice.[38]

Guicciardini intensified this sordid picture of his own times by alluding to the existence of better times. A brief account of the effects of the discovery of America gave him the oportunity to suggest the possibility of a world not tormented "by avarice and ambition."[39] He made a few comparisons between his own time and antiquity, and in these passages he iterated the humanist notion of the unparalleled greatness of the classical world. In the sixteenth century one looked in vain for the magnanimity, virtue, and courage which characterized the Romans.[40] Guicciardini averred that perfection is possible

[36] ". . . fatale instrumento, e allora e prima e poi, de' mali d'Italia . . . ," *ibid.*, libro I, chapt. 9 (vol. I, p. 65), and also, libro XI, chapt. 8; the formulations which Guicciardini used in describing the dying Pope suggest that he used here the reports of the Florentine ambassadors (see below, p. 297).

[37] *Ibid.*, libro XV, chapt. 14 and libro XVII, chapt. 14.

[38] *Ibid.*, libro XVI, chapts. 14 and 15.

[39] ". . . quasi tutti gli abitatori, semplicissimi di costumi e contenti di quel che produce la benignità della natura, non sono tormentati nè da avarizia nè da ambizione . . . ," *ibid.*, libro VI, chapt. 9 (vol. II, p. 130).

[40] *Ibid.*, libro VI, chapt. 12 or libro XII, chapt. 8.

only at the beginning, and all things human are there-
after inevitably subject to corruption.[41] To the men of the
sixteenth century the proof of this surrounded them:
short-sighted people, vicious people, people of petty interests and aims dominated the political life of their
time. Guicciardini's pessimistic view of human nature
should not be interpreted as the primitive reaction of a
man who, because his own ambition had been frustrated,
took pleasure in belittling the achievements of all others.
His pessimism had deeper roots. In a secularized form the
History of Italy is concerned with the old theme of the
misery of the human condition.

This aspect of the meaning of the *History of Italy* has
been frequently overlooked because of the book's length.
The work is more often read in excerpts than studied in
its entirety. But if the *History of Italy* is viewed as a coherent whole, it becomes a tragedy, unfolding in a number of acts.[42] Against the background of a description of
the peaceful and prosperous times which had been assured
by the wise guidance of Lorenzo Magnifico and Ferdinand of Aragon, Guicciardini set an analysis of the vices,
stupidities, and restless ambitions of their sons which led
to the calling of the French King into Italy. The trium-
phal entry of Charles VIII in Naples, the formation of the
Italian League, and the Battle of Fornovo constitute the
rest of the first two books of the *History of Italy*. In this
opening section Guicciardini raised the question which is
the underlying problem of the work: was it possible to
restore the peace which had existed before the French in-

---

[41] ". . . era fatale che tutte le cose del mondo fussino sottoposte
alla corruzione . . . ," *ibid.*, libro II, chapt. 1 (vol. I, p. 119).

[42] This is not a purely modern formulation; sixteenth-century
historians sometimes regarded the events of history as a tragedy,
see above, note 62 on p. 268 and *ibid.*, libro VI, chapt. 16.

vasion, and, if so, why did the Italians miss the opportunity to recover their previous felicity?

The withdrawal from Italy of Charles VIII made the French invasion appear to have been an ephemeral event. But no historical event leaves a situation entirely as it was before. After the retreat of the French, Florence's loyalty to the French alliance and her refusal to enter the Italian League created political irritation and instability throughout Italy. The practical difficulties of appeasement were increased by the changes which took place in the minds of the men who directed affairs. The part which Alexander VI and Lodovico Moro had in inviting the French into Italy and in turning them out again had stimulated the ambitions of the Pope and the hopes and fears of the ruler of Milan: thus these two became the instigators of more unrest and further invasions. In the following three books of the *History of Italy* Guicciardini focussed on their plans and actions. The wretched end of Lodovico Moro, and the sudden death of Alexander VI appeared to be the just deserts for the miseries which they brought upon Italy. Yet the removal of these two men from the political scene did not stop the developments which they had started. The decisive role which the Venetians had played in the events of 1494/95 had made them arrogant and overconfident. Likewise the new Pope, Julius II, felt that he could command events according to his will and that nothing could stop him from realizing his audacious plans. The outcome of the clash between the Pope and the Venetians was unexpected: the humiliation of Venice and the firm settlement of the French in Milan and the Spaniards in Naples. According to Guicciardini, this was the time when there was the possibility of preserving the independence of those parts of Italy which the French and the Spaniards did not control, but this chance was destroyed by the ambitions of Leo X who wanted to establish his family as rulers of Urbino. The foreigners were then drawn even into the center of Italy.

Thus a new stage of developments began in 1521. To the events from 1521 to 1534 Guicciardini devoted the last seven books of the *History of Italy*. In content and in form these last seven books differ from the previous books. The events after 1521 are part of the general European struggle between the French King and the Hapsburgs; the Italian rulers were no longer initiators of events but rather were subject to them. Guicciardini's style of narration changed; it becomes more detailed and factual. Two books of this last part of the *History of Italy* are slightly revised versions of a book of memoirs which Guicciardini had begun to write in 1535 describing the years when he was Papal Commissioner in the war against the Spaniards. He was able to use this older manuscript because a purely factual recording of events was appropriate for conveying the impression of helpless submission —the condition into which Italy had fallen after 1521. Yet the tragic character of Guicciardini's work consists not only in the fact that he presented a description of the chain of causal connections which nobody was willing or able to break. He also showed that from event to event the crisis deepened so that with every missed opportunity the problem of re-establishing peace and prosperity became more complex and the loss of freedom and independence unalterable. As the first consequence of the foreign invasion, governments and rulers were overthrown, later the people suffered, and finally artistic treasures were destroyed, morals and customs were changed; and the Italy which had existed before 1494 was no longer.[43]

---

[43] See, particularly, *ibid.*, libro I, chapt. 9, libro VIII, chapt. 1, libro XVII, chapt. 8, and libro XVIII, chapt. 1.

How did Guicciardini explain the catastrophe which came over Italy? One of his explanations was that God was punishing man for his sins; some of his remarks seem to indicate that he believed that all humanity was corrupt and therefore deserved this fate.[44] Other statements point particularly to the sins of the rulers who indulged in vices, in boundless ambition, and senseless cruelty. In still other passages he attributed the disasters of Italy to human failings, most of all to lack of prudence; instead of taking reason as a guide, men preferred to follow their wishes and desires.[45] Nevertheless, sin and weakness were not the only determinants, nor were they even the most decisive factors in bringing about the ruin of Italy. Even if people had acted prudently and wisely, and even if they had considered all the relevant circumstances and had taken all possible precautions, events might have come out very differently from what men would expect. There is no way for man to make sure of success; on the contrary, it is more likely that he will be defeated. The master over the events of history is *Fortuna*. The strongest, most permanent impression which the *History of Italy* imparts—and was meant to impart—is that of the helplessness and impotence of man in the face of fate. Guicciardini began the *History of Italy* by stating that his work "will show by many examples the instability of all human affairs, like a sea whipped by winds." Those who guide the destiny of people must always be aware of the "frequent changes of *Fortuna*."[46] In addition man

[44] ". . . avendo patiti tanti anni Italia tutte quelle calamità con le quali sogliono i miseri mortali, ora per l'ira giusta d'Iddio ora dalla empietà e sceleratezze degli altri uomini, essere vessati . . . ," *ibid.*, libro I, chapt. 1.

[45] For instance, see *ibid.*, libro VII, chapt. 10.

[46] ". . . onde per innumerabili esempli evidentemente apparirà

might learn from history about the conduct of war[47] and the art of government,[48] and he might be reminded that he ought not to let his passions or ambitions reign over reason; but the one general truth which history—and only history—can teach is the inconstancy of all human affairs.[49]

What is the significance of history if it shows nothing but the inscrutable arbitrariness of *Fortuna?* Repeatedly in the *History of Italy* Guicciardini asserted that it was not "lost time or without value" to learn from the study of history about the vicissitudes of man.[50] Man ought to

---

a quanta instabilità, nè altrimenti che uno mare concitato da' venti, siano sottoposte le cose umane; quanto siano perniciosi, quasi sempre a se stessi ma sempre a'popoli, i consigli male misurati di coloro che dominano, quando, avendo solamente innanzi agli occhi o errori vani o le cupidità presenti, non si ricordando delle spesse variazioni della fortuna, e convertendo in detrimento altrui la potestà conceduta loro per la salute comune, si fanno, o per poca prudenza o per troppa ambizione, autori di nuove turbazioni", *ibid.*, libro I, chapt. 1 (vol. I, p. 1).

[47] ". . . il governo della guerra . . . cosa tra tutte l'azioni umane la più ardua e la più difficile . . . ," *ibid.*, libro IX, chapt. 17 (vol. III, p. 90). Reflections on the present state of the conduct of war and military science are frequent; for instance, see libro XV, chapt. 6, or libro XVII, chapt. 8.

[48] In this respect, the frequent references to the constitution of Venice are significant, see, for instance, *ibid.*, libro VIII, chapt. 10.

[49] An expression which Guicciardini used is the "ruota della fortuna" (*ibid.*, libro X, chapt. 14 [vol. III, p. 197]); he can say that "la fortuna, risguardando con lieto occhio le cose del Pontefice e di Cesare, interruppe il consiglio infelice de' Capitani . . ." (*ibid.*, libro XIV, chapt. 7 [vol. IV, p. 116]), or he can warn that "è da temere più da chi ha avuto sì lunga felicità la mutazione della fortuna," (*ibid.*, libro XVI, chapt. 5 [vol. IV, p. 288]), but the references to the power and influence of fortuna are so frequent that it is evident that Guicciardini really wanted to carry out the intention which he stated in the first chapter of the first book: to demonstrate the "spesse variazioni della fortuna."

[50] "Non è certo opera perduta o senza premio il considerare la varietà de' tempi e delle cose del mondo," *ibid.*, libro I, chapt. 4 (vol. I, p. 29).

realize that he cannot expect rewards for good behavior, nor success from the use of intelligence; man must fortify himself with strength to withstand the adversities which may befall him whatever he does. To Guicciardini, history provided not rules of behavior, but rather led toward a philosophical attitude. Guicciardini knew that Christianity did not indicate the path which man ought to follow in the world of politics. However, man ought to be aware that in the uncertainties of history he can never win as much as he would lose by tarnishing his name. In everything a man does he must consider the effect which that action might have on his dignity. In the last analysis the writing of history serves to maintain the dignity of man.[51]

The *History of Italy* is the work of a man whose mind was steeped in trust in the efficacy of a rational conduct of politics, but the *History of Italy* is also the work of a man who has experienced that the world is dominated and controlled by the unfathomable power of *Fortuna*. The assumption of the possibility of rational explanation and the acceptance of the domination of *Fortuna* are incompatible beliefs; however, Guicciardini's ability to combine these two disparate elements engendered the distinguishing and novel features of the *History of Italy*: more intensive psychological explanations of human motivations;

[51] Pontano, in accordance with ancient writers, regarded as one of the uses of history that history taught man to be armed against misfortune; see Pontano, "Actius," *Dialoghi*, ed. Carmelo Previterra, p. 229: ". . . ut fortunam, ut varietatem inconstantiamque rerum humanarum animadvertentes discant in adversis esse patientes ac firmi"; but Guicciardini implied a philosophical contempt for customary values rather than an appeal to courage, see also Guicciardini, "Consolatoria," *Scritti Autobiografici*, pp. 184 et seq.

a larger historical framework taking into account the interconnected nature of the European state-system; a more extensive application of critical methods.

Acknowledging the power of *Fortuna* and rationally interpreting the course of events was not inconsonant because *Fortuna*, by becoming more powerful, had also become farther removed from man. Because Guicciardini and his contemporaries had witnessed the triumph of *Fortuna* over reason, they considered the realm of *Fortuna* and the realm of reason as totally separate; in effect, *Fortuna* and reason were opposites. When in earlier times it had been believed that *Fortuna* was able to interfere in particular situations and to enhance or to destroy an individual, it could be questioned whether the outcome of an action was due to man's ability or to *Fortuna*'s favor. But when *Fortuna* was viewed as an embodiment of uncontrollable forces rather than as a whimsical goddess, man was left struggling for himself, and history was the means for studying the potentialities of man.

Although Guicciardini had to recognize the influence which *Fortuna* exerted over the world, his manner of demonstrating the extent of *Fortuna*'s power was to investigate precisely how far a rational explanation of events could lead: Guicciardini's direct concern was the rational explanation of cause and effect. The analysis of the psychology and the motives of the political leaders became an essential task of the historian. Previously it had been said that the historian ought to describe not only what happened, but also why things happened; in the *History of Italy* explanation of the "why" took precedence over narration of the "what." Guicciardini's rational concept of man gave him a criterion for judging man's motives; they always contain an element of his

particulare, of his personal interest.[52] But the special form
which man's drive to satisfy the *particulare* might take
was unique to each individual; it was dependent on a
great variety of factors and subjected to constant
changes. The conventional method which historians used
to describe a personality (and which Guicciardini used
in his first *Florentine History*), was to view the individual in relation to the recognized scheme of virtues and
vices so that the moral qualities of the individual in question would be clearly discernible to the reader. But in the
History of Italy Guicciardini presupposed that self-interest—the satisfaction of the *particulare*—was basic to
man's nature, and its only permanent element. Otherwise man's character is not fixed; it is not a definite sum
of good and bad qualities. According to Guicciardini,
man's personality is revealed only in the sequence of
events and can be changed and transformed by them.
By constructing his characterizations on observable actions in which an individual interferred in the course of
history, Guicciardini achieved a remarkable degree of
psychological realism in his characterizations.

The most brilliant example of Guicciardini's art of
psychological analysis is his characterization of the two
Medici Popes, Leo X and Clement VII.[53] Vettori, as we
have seen, had ascribed the opposite outcome of their actions—the success of the one, the failures of the other—to
Fortuna. Clement VII's great qualities of mind had been
of no avail because *Fortuna* had taken sides against him.

[52] "Una delle maggiore fortune che possino avere gli uomini
è avere occasione di potere mostrare che, a quelle cose che loro
fanno per interesse proprio, siano stati mossi per causa di publico
bene . . . ," Ricordo 142 in Guicciardini, *Ricordi*, p. 154; see also
above note 20.

[53] *Storia d'Italia*, libro XVI, chapt. 12.

Guicciardini, however, questioned the assumption that Clement VII's talents had been equal or even superior to those of Leo X. Guicciardini admitted that Clement VII had unusual intellectual gifts and that he showed an astounding perspicacity in judging a political situation. But Leo X had one supreme quality which Clement VII lacked: Leo was quick in making decisions. As long as Leo lived, the two cousins—the one discerning, the other resolute—complemented each other, but after Leo X's death, it could be seen that Clement's perspicacity led him to hesitate and waver. That Leo's success and Clement's failure were inherent in the natures of the two men became apparent in the effects which they could exert on the course of events.

Man makes his decisions on the basis of evaluating an existing situation, but because the outcome of an action is not always as man expects, he has ultimately to change his intention to conform to the unexpected result.[54] Guicciardini explored the devious process which leads from the reality of a factual occurrence to its psychological reflection in the mind of the actor which creates a new intention that will bring about further action.[55] Thus the *History of Italy* moves on both the level of factual events

---

[54] ". . . spessa variazione delle cose, variandosi secondo i progressi di quelle le speranze . . . ," *ibid.*, libro XII, chapt. 5 (vol. III, p. 318). See, as an example, Guicciardini's description of the effect of the battle of Pavia, libro XVI, chapt. 6.

[55] ". . . persuadendosi che, levata quella cagione di tanta alterazione, avesse con piccola fatica, anzi quasi per se stessa, Italia nello stato di prima a ritornarsi. Ma non sempre per il rimuovere delle cagioni si rimuovono gli effetti i quali da quelle hanno avuto la prima origine. Perchè, come spesso accade che le deliberazioni fatte per timore paiono, a chi teme, inferiore al pericolo, non si confidava Lodovico d'avere trovato rimedio bastante . . . ," *ibid.*, libro I, chapt. 3 (vol. I, p. 17). As an example, see libro IX, chapts. 1 and 2.

and of man's motivations. Guicciardini tried to show how events and motivations are continually acting and reacting upon each other. Facts, however, have not always the consequences which, as a result of a rational evaluation, they ought to have;[56] rather their effects become distorted by man's wishes and desires. Man's illusions and errors form an integral part of history.[57]

Guicciardini's aim of demonstrating how far a rational explanation of political events could lead contributed to another novelty of the *History of Italy:* its geographical and chronological extension and limits. We have referred to Guicciardini's work as the *History of Italy,* and that is how it is usually called. However, Guicciardini never used this title. He spoke of it as a history "concerned with the affairs of Italy,"[58] and there are reasons for his somewhat vague description of the contents. He regarded Italy as different from the other nations of Europe because of its cultural supremacy, but he did not think of Italy as a political unit, nor did he believe that Italy should be united. Therefore, the subject of the *History of Italy* is not Italy as a political unit, but the happenings on the Italian peninsula. The various powers which existed in Italy were not suitable subjects for separate histories because the developments within each state were inextricably entangled with those of all the others; likewise, all that occurred in Italy was related to events which

[56] Guicciardini never ceased to wonder that "da tante piccole cagioni dependono bene spesso i momenti di cose gravissime . . . ," *ibid.,* libro XIX, chapt. 15 (vol. V, p. 279).

[57] "Nelle cose degli stati non bisogna tanto considerare quello che la ragione mostra che dovessi fare uno principe, quanto quello che secondo la sua natura o consuetudine si può credere che faccia . . . ," thus justifies Guicciardini this procedure in Ricordo 128, in *Ricordi,* p. 139.

[58] ". . . cose accadute alla memoria nostra in Italia . . . ," *Storia d'Italia,* libro I, chapt. 1 (vol. I, p. 1).

took place in other parts of Europe. Guicciardini felt that he had to discuss that which happened in other nations "because deliberations and events there are frequently connected with events here."[59]

The subject matter of Guicciardini's work was defined by an inner logic; it extended as far as causal connections could be established between events, and by including the developments in Germany, France, England, and Spain in his discussion of Italian events, he demonstrated the degree to which Western Europe had grown together. Unquestionably his recognition of the greater size of the political scene derived from his knowledge of affairs gained as Florentine ambassador and Papal administrator and adviser. In giving literary expression to his experiences he was instrumental in making men of his own time as well as of later times conscious of the existence of an interconnected state-system. Guicciardini implied that the periods into which history can and must be divided ought to be determined by the immanence of the historical process, not—as previously—by philosophical or theological assumptions. At least this is suggested by Guicciardini's procedure in delimiting the *History of Italy*. In 1535 Guicciardini had started to write a book of memoirs in which he intended to give an account of his own activities as Papal adviser and military commissioner in the years surrounding the events of the League of Cognac

---

[59] "Parrà forse alieno dal mio proposito, stato di non toccare le cose succedute fuora d'Italia, fare menzione di quel che l'anno medesimo si fece in Francia; ma la dependenza di quelle da queste, e perchè a' successi dell'una erano congiunti molte volte le deliberazioni e i successi dell'altra, mi sforza a non le passare del tutto tacitamente," *ibid.*, libro XI, chapt. 6 (vol. III, p. 244); or see Guicciardini's justification for discussing the discoveries of the Portuguese and Spaniards as having "qualche connessità con le cose Italiane," libro VI, chapt. 9 (vol. II, p. 128).

(1526); he conceived of his work as commentaries such as those which Caesar had composed. When he reached 1526 in his *History of Italy* he inserted sections of the memoirs into the narrative and they form the sixteenth and seventeenth books.[60] Probably Guicciardini turned from the composition of commentaries to the writing of history because he expected that he would acquire a greater reputation from the authorship of a work of history. But by going as far back into the past as he did—to the French invasion of 1494—he indicated that events could really be understood only if they were traced back to the point where the lines of causal connection had started. Despite its immense length the *History of Italy* is a unit because its extension in time and space is dependent on the principle of causal connections.

Demonstration of the extent and limits of a rational explanation of events required factual accuracy. We have seen that Guicciardini, like most of the pragmatic writers of history, had been careful to provide a correct account of the events of the past. If Guicciardini's first *Florentine History* showed his concern for presenting an accurate factual report, and if his second *Florentine History* revealed his preference for using documentary material, his *History of Italy* testifies to the perfection of these methods. Among his papers we find numerous excerpts from the manuscripts of writers who had previously treated the events of this period: Rucellai, Corio, Commines, Borgia.[61] Guicciardini was not content to follow the account of one author, but rather he tried to get

---

[60] See Ridolfi, *Genesi,* particularly p. 14, and Ridolfi, *Vita di Guicciardini,* pp. 505-506.

[61] See Roberto Ridolfi, *L'Archivio della Famiglia Guicciardini,* Firenze, 1931, for Guicciardini's excerpts from sources, particularly pp. 71 et seq.

hold of all available reports about an event, and he weighed them carefully in order to establish what had actually happened.[62] A few chapters in the *History of Italy* are but sketches that contain notes of the raw material which he intended to use and to develop; these unfinished chapters show how he tried to compare the various reports which he had studied and how he looked for criteria to establish their veracity.[63] But a large part of his sources were documents. In 1530 when he had returned to Florence to mete out, on behalf of the Pope, punishment to the leaders of the republic, he brought the entire archive of the Board of the Ten, containing the records of diplomatic negotiations, to his house, and he kept it there. We can find many indications that he relied much on these diplomatic reports. For instance, he wrote about the death of Julius II in almost the same words with which the Florentine ambassadors had reported about it—"that the Pope retained in all things the same judgment and mental vigor which he had had before his illness."[64] Systematic collection of all available reports, critical examination of their value, reliance on documentary material when available—these were Guicciardini's methods in writing the *History of Italy*.

The *History of Italy* approaches the principles and methods of modern historiography, but the author intended it to be a "true history" in the humanist sense.

[62] Characteristic of Guicciardini's careful method is a "Nota delle cose delle quali s'ha a investigare la verità della Giornata di Vaila," published by E. Rostagno, *All' Autentica Edizione della Storia d'Italia di Francesco Guicciardini*, Firenze, 1919, p. 147.

[63] See *ibid.*, libro XV, chapt. 15, libro XIX, chapt. 5, etc.

[64] ". . . e ritenendo in tutte le cose la solita costanza e severità, e il medesimo giudicio e vigore d'animo che aveve innanzi alla infermità . . . ," *ibid.*, libro XI, chapt. 8 (vol. III, p. 257), and see above, p. 128.

Because the work reflects many of our own ideas about the writing of history, the features which result from Guicciardini's attempt to adjust the *History of Italy* to the humanist pattern have been considered as blemishes on what would otherwise have been a more perfect work. On the contrary, it should be recognized that Guicciardini's adoption of elements of humanist historical theory served to give intellectual unity to the *History of Italy* and to strengthen the impact of the work. First it cannot be denied that Guicciardini reaped advantages by using humanist rules and devices. One might wonder whether he would have concentrated so exclusively on the events which showed the emergence of a European state-system had not the humanists considered foreign policy and wars the most worthy subject for historical treatment. By organizing the study according to years, Guicciardini intensified the feeling of the powerlessness of man in relation to the crowding of events. Even the omens which he sometimes mentioned[65] suggested the external forces to which man is subjected. Most of all, Guicciardini would have hardly been able to create the impression he wanted to convey if he had not made use of the right which humanists had accorded to the historian: that of inventing speeches. In his second *History of Florence*, Guicciardini used speeches in a functional way, and in the *History of Italy* he employed them still more purposefully.[66] He used them to empha-

[65] For instance, *ibid.*, libro I, chapt. 9 or libro XI, chapt. 4, or libro XIV, chapt. 2.

[66] Like his contemporaries, Guicciardini was frank to acknowledge that his speeches were invented; see the passage in *ibid.*, libro VIII, chapt. 6 (vol. II, p. 279), where he states the one exception: ". . . non mi pare alieno dal nostro proposito . . . inserire la propria orazione avuta da lui innanzi a Cesare, trasferendo solamente le parole latine in voci volgari. . . ." Before most of

size facts or events which were particularly relevant to
the decision which a government had to make.[67] Moreover, he used them to characterize the attitude and aims
of social groups within a society;[68] to show how men mis-
judged events;[69] or to point out the difference between a
reasoned evaluation of events and the distortion resulting
from man's insistence on giving free rein to his desires
and passions.[70] By means of speeches the historian fulfilled the function of a judge: Guicciardini indicated how
policy was to be conducted if it were managed rationally, and how it was conducted in reality.[71] In the *History of Italy* speeches are devices to disclose the multi-
dimensional character of the historical process.

But the impact of the humanist concept of history
showed itself in a still more profound and more fundamental way. To the humanists, the purpose of history had
been to give man moral guidance. With the realization
that politics had its own rules and its own laws this belief was shaken, and to many the past became chiefly a
guide to successful political action. But the political catastrophe which showed the futility of all human calculations also dealt a blow to such pragmatic uses of the
past. In the *History of Italy* Guicciardini seems to deny
that there is any meaning in history; the work gives the
impression that history is aimless and without purpose.[72]

---

the battle scenes Guicciardini presented a speech of the captain;
these speeches are rhetorical rather than functional, and inserted
in accordance with classical patterns.

[67] See, for example, *ibid.*, libro XV, chapt 2.

[68] See, for example, *ibid.*, libro II, chapt. 2, or libro X, chapt. 4.

[69] See, for example, *ibid.*, libro VIII, chapt. 1.

[70] See, for example, *ibid.*, libro IV, chapt. 6.

[71] See, for example, *ibid.*, libro XVI, chapt. 14.

[72] "Esempio potente a confondere l'arroganza di coloro i quali,
presumendosi di scorgere con la debolezza degli occhi umani la
profondità de' giudicii divini, affermano ciò che di prospero o di

The *History of Italy* can be regarded as a variation on the great themes of the fight of man against fate and of the misery of the human condition.

However, the lesson contained in the *History of Italy* is not only that of human impotence; it is not only one of despair, but also of pride. Even if man could not dominate the external world, he remained ruler in his own realm—that of the intellect. Reason gave to man the strength to resist the seduction of false gods and to realize—as well as to show to others—the futility of most of his ambitions and the true worth of the things of this world. Thus although Guicciardini did not share the humanist view that history exemplifies general rules or guides man's behavior, he returned to the humanist concept of the moral value of history: history appeals to man to become conscious of his own intrinsic value.

This shift of the use of history from demonstrating the validity of general definable rules to teaching the need for a personal philosophy challenged the historian to new tasks. If the study of history did not reveal the existence of a permanent order behind the multiplicity of events, then the schemes which theology or moral philosophy had imposed upon the course of history were extraneous, and the historian need no longer concentrate on the search for recurring and generally valid patterns. He could turn his attention to the description of diverse and singular historical phenomena, he would aim at factual

---

avverso avviene agli uomini procedere o da' meriti o da' demeriti loro: come se tutto dì non apparisse, molti buoni essere vessati ingiustamente e molti di pravo animo essere esaltati indebitamente; o come se, altrimenti interpretando, si derogasse alla giustizia e alla potenza di Dio; la amplitudine della quale, non ristretta a' termini brevi e presenti, in altro tempo e in altro luogo, con larga mano, con premii e con suplicii sempiterni, riconosce i giusti dagli ingiusti," *ibid.*, libro VI, chapt. 4 (vol. II, p. 98).

correctness, and most important, he would focus on his particular area of investigation: constant change. Thus the historian gained his own peculiar function, and history took on an independent existence in the world of knowledge; there was no other place to look for the meaning of history than in history itself. The historian became both recorder and interpreter. Guicciardini's *History of Italy* is the last great work of history in the classical pattern, but it is also the first great work of modern historiography. Tanto operi nullum par elogium.

BIBLIOGRAPHICAL ESSAYS

A FLORENTINE

INSTITUTIONAL HISTORY IN

SCHOLARLY LITERATURE

The historical literature about Florence in the period of the Renaissance is abundant, and accordingly, the years between the fall of the Medici in 1494 and their return in 1512 have been frequently discussed. But every student of this period becomes soon aware that in describing Florentine political institutions writers are vague and often contradict each other. For example, Ferdinand Schevill's *History of Florence from the Founding of the City through the Renaissance*, New York, 1936, although a valuable book, reveals little about the nature of political institutions and how they functioned.

The principle of modern historical scholarship—that insofar as possible history should be based on documentary sources rather than on narrative accounts—has been only slowly and gradually applied to the history of Florentine institutions. The reasons for this are manifold. Since the fifteenth century, one might say since the times when Leonardo Bruni was writing his *Historiarum Florentini Populi Libri XII* (written between 1415 and 1444), Florentine citizens with a literary bent have regarded the writing of the history of their city as a task of primary importance. For the years 1494 to 1512 there are a number of histories written in the sixteenth century by men who were close to, or even contemporaneous with, the events they described. Filippo de' Nerli (1485-1556) devoted the fourth and fifth books of his *Commentarii de' Fatti civili occorsi nella città di Firenze dal 1215 al 1537* (first printed 1728) to the events of the years 1494-1512. While exiled from Florence, about 1553, Jacopo Nardi (1476-1563) wrote *Istorie della città di Firenze* (first printed 1582). His work begins with the year 1494, and over half of it deals with the republican period. Finally there is the *Storie fiorentine* by Francesco Guicciardini. This work, unknown before the middle of the nineteenth century, was published in 1859 by G. Canestrini in his edition of Guicciardini's *Opere inedite* (for details, see below, Appendix III). This *Storie fiorentine* was written in the years of the republic, and therefore it is nearly synchronous with the events it describes.

Although the authors of these three works held different political views—Nerli was an adherent of the Medici, Nardi an advocate of the popular regime, Guicciardini an aristocratic republican—all of them had an intimate knowledge of events, institutions, and personalities. The reputation of Nerli's and Nardi's histories can be indicated by the praise of young Ranke. In his work on modern historians (*Zur Kritik neuerer Geschichtschreiber*, Leipzig, 1824, pp. 82, 84), Ranke wrote that Nerli possessed "complete knowledge and a certain beauty"; Nerli, said Ranke, reminded him of an ancient historian. Of Nardi, Ranke predicted that his "convictions, originality and truthfulness of presentation will assure him of immortality as long as the Italian language is read." Because these accounts contain so much detailed and authentic information, scholars felt that it was unnecessary to turn to documentary sources as the basis for their work. Moreover, since the Italian Renaissance was usually treated as a cultural phenomenon rather than as a period of political change, scholars found the political documents in the archives of less interest than various writings which revealed the personalities of Renaissance figures. Writings of this sort had been preserved in Florence, and toward the end of the nineteenth century they were studied and published. The diaries of Luca Landucci (*Diario Fiorentino dal 1450 al 1516*, ed. Iodoco del Badia, Firenze, 1883) and Bartolomeo Masi (*Ricordanze dal 1478 al 1526*, ed. G. O. Corazzini, Firenze, 1906) were published in 1883 and 1906, respectively, in careful editions. Landucci's diary is available in an English translation; the German translation of Landucci, edited by Marie Herzfeld, Jena, 1927, is particularly useful because of its extensive notes. The lengthy diary of Giovanni Cambi (*Istorie*, ed. Fr. Ildefonso di San Luigi, Firenze, 1785-1786 [*Delizie degli Eruditi Toscani*, vols. XX-XXIII]) was published in the eighteenth century, but this is an uncritical edition, in which there is no distinction between the contemporary parts of the diary and later additions; moreover, certain passages were copied from other sources (see Nicolai Rubinstein, "The 'Storie Fiorentine' and the 'Memorie di Famiglia' by Francesco Guicciardini," *Rinascimento*, vol. IV [1953], p.216). To be certain of the authenticity of the entries in Cambi's diary one has to study the original manuscript, I.H.H.V.28 in the Biblioteca Nazionale di Firenze, which abounds in insertions.

Printed sources—the narrative accounts and the diaries of contemporaries—offered historians sufficient material for writing a full description of Florentine events during the republican period. But these sources did not provide much information about political institutions and their development. Contemporary historians and diarists were inclined to assume that the reader would be familiar with the institutional framework; moreover, the authors themselves were less interested in institutions than in men and events. Finally, these authors lacked printed collections of legislative measures, so they had to rely on their memory; often their references to laws and institutions were brief, and sometimes, misleading. For instance, Donato Giannotti, who in his *Libro della repubblica fiorentina* analyzed the Florentine government, occasionally ascribed to the republican regime of 1494-1512 features which were peculiar to the renewed republic of 1527 (For an example, see my article, "Florentine Political Assumptions in the Period of Savonarola and Soderini," *Journal of the Warburg and Courtauld Institutes*, vol. XII (1957), p. 188; in my article I have tried to describe the functions of the *Consulte e Pratiche* in the republican period).

It would be wrong, however, to convey the impression that nineteenth-century historians were entirely unaware of the need for placing the description of Florentine institutions on firmer ground than that provided by narrative accounts and diaries. The most prominent Italian historian of the second part of the nineteenth century, and the chief representative in Italy of the critical school of historical scholarship, was Pasquale Villari (1826-1917). For his studies in Florentine history at the beginning of the sixteenth century he undertook extended investigations in the archives. His two great works, *Storia di Girolamo Savonarola e dei suoi tempi* (first printed 1860), and *Niccolò Machiavelli e i suoi tempi* (3 vols., 1877-1882), both of which are available in English translations, are full of interesting new material and throw light on many aspects of Florentine institutions. But

Villari's approach was biographical, and he was concerned with Florentine institutions only insofar as they could help to explain facets of Savonarola's and Machiavelli's career. Since the publication of Villari's biographies others have continued to work on the careers of the two Florentines, and in so doing they have explored archival materials and thereby contributed to our knowledge of Florentine institutions. For Savonarola there are the biographies by J. Schnitzer, *Savonarola; ein Kulturbild aus der Zeit der Renaissance,* 2 vols., München, 1924 and Roberto Ridolfi, *Vita di Girolamo Savonarola,* 2 vols., Roma, 1952; the latter is available in English translation. A most comprehensive treatment is now available in Donald Weinstein, *Savonarola and Florence: Prophecy and Patriotism in the Renaissance,* Princeton 1970. For biographies of Machiavelli, which frequently contain references to the literature on Florentine institutional history, see Appendix II. Nicolai Rubinstein's article, "The Beginnings of Niccolò Machiavelli's Career in the Florentine Chancery," *Italian Studies,* vol. XI (1956), pp. 72-91, is important because it contains a succinct account of the organization of the Florentine Chancellery in this period.

Occasional investigations of specific institutions and particular institutional developments have not fulfilled the need for a systematic exploration of documents in the archives which are relevant to the history of Florentine institutions. It is perhaps slightly ironical that the vast amount of available material in the archives has been a deterrent rather than a stimulus to a thorough and comprehensive investigation. An impression of the extent of the holdings of the Archivio di Stato di Firenze can be gained from consulting the registers printed in Demetrio Marzi, *La Cancelleria della Repubblica Fiorentina,* Rocca S. Casciano, 1910, pp. 515-532. However, it should be mentioned that some of the files in the Archivio are incomplete; the material which one might expect to find there is sometimes in a quite different place. Moreover, many official documents have been incorporated in family archives, so that frequently research must extend beyond the Archivio di Stato and the Biblioteca Nazionale. On private archives in Florence, see Roberto Ridolfi, *Gli Archivi delle famiglie fiorentine*, Firenze, 1934. A systematic and comprehensive study of Florentine institutions based on archival materials demands almost unlimited time, exceptional paleographical training, and inexhaustible patience. It is therefore hardly surprising that until recently we have lacked the fundamental requirement for an understanding of Florentine history during the republican period: namely, an account of the government machinery and how it functioned. Amedeo Crivellucci's work, *Del Governo popolare di Firenze 1494-1512 e del suo Riordinamento secondo il Guicciardini (Annali della R. Scuola Normale Superiore di Pisa*, vol. III [1877], parte II: Filosofia e Filologia, pp. 225-338) is meritorious, but it is not precise and it is full of errors. A great step on the way to providing an analysis of Florentine institutions was made by Antonio Anzilotti whose book, *La Crisi Costituzionale della Repubblica Fiorentina*, Firenze, 1912, brilliantly illustrated the importance of material from the archives. Anzilotti examined the legislative measures of the Great Council, the decrees of the *Balìe* and the protocols of the *Consulte e Pratiche*. He showed that the divisions of Florentine politics in the republican period were irreconcilable because they reflected a fundamental contrast between those whose interests were best served by the maintenance of the city republic and those who sought to transform Florence into a territorial state. Anzilotti's book demonstrates that a precise analysis of institutional developments based on documentary sources is prerequisite for an understanding of the factors which determined Florentine politics in the republican period. From his researches in the history of sixteenth-century Florence Anzilotti turned to work on the Italian Risorgimento; and so unfortunately, for a long while his studies on the Renaissance remained isolated. Anzilotti's preference for more recent periods of Italian history might have been due, to some extent, to political considerations. Under Fascism the Renaissance, as well as social and economic history in general, was held in low esteem.

Anzilotti's suggestions for the investigation of Florentine history in the republican period were taken up only after the Second World War. To date the most impressive results of this approach are the two articles by Nicolai Rubinstein and the article by L. F. Marks, to which frequent reference is made in this book. Both Rubinstein and Marks have concentrated on institutional developments and both scholars have based their investigations on documentary sources. Since Crivellucci's work, Rubinstein in his article, "Politics and Constitution in Florence at the End of the Fifteenth Century," *Italian Renaissance Studies,* ed. E. F. Jacob, London, 1960, pp. 148-183, is the first to attempt to analyze the Florentine constitution in this period; in his article, "I Primi Anni del Consiglio Maggiore di Firenze (1494-99)," *Archivio Storico Italiano,* vol. CXII (1954), pp. 151-194, 321-347, Rubinstein gives the first precise description of the nature and function of the Great Council. L. F. Marks in his article, "La Crisi Finanziaria a Firenze dal 1494 al 1502," *Archivio Storico Italiano,* vol. CXII (1954), pp.

40-72, investigates thoroughly the financial problems which beset the republican regime in the early years. The excellence of these researches by Rubinstein and Marks indicates that the task of investigating Florentine institutions is so great that progress can be made only very slowly. Both scholars have concentrated on single aspects of Florentine institutions; Rubinstein's researches go to 1498, Marks's to 1502. We know little about the manner in which Soderini as *Gonfalonieri a vita* from 1502 to 1512 stabilized the finances of Florence. And we need to know more about the reasons for the violent opposition of the Florentine aristocrats to Soderini.

In the course of examining archival documents for this period the curious fact has emerged that the narrative accounts and diaries which have been published are not nearly as important as contemporary accounts and diaries which have not been printed—or only printed in part. In particular, there are two manuscripts: the *Storia Fiorentina* by Bartolomeo Cerretani and the diaries of Piero Parenti. Neither of these manuscripts has been unknown. In his essay on Savonarola, "Savonarola und die florentinische Republik" (printed in L. von Ranke, *Saemmtliche Werke*, vols. XL/XLI), Ranke recognized the importance of the accounts of both of these Florentines. And J. Schnitzer published excerpts from both (see J. Schnitzer, ed., *Quellen und Forschungen zur Geschichte Savonarolas*, vol. III, *Bartolomeo Cerretani*, München, 1904; vol. IV, *Piero Parenti*, Leipzig, 1910). Schnitzer's introduction contains biographies of Cerretani and Parenti, as well as a statement about the preservation of their manuscripts. (On Parenti, see also Guido Pampaloni, "Piero di Marco Parenti e la sua 'Historia' fiorentina," *Archivio Storico Italiano*, vol. CXIII [1959] pp. 147-153.)

Unfortunately, Schnitzer's publications have served to conceal the significance of both Cerretani and Parenti. Because Schnitzer selected from the manuscripts of Cerretani and Parenti only those sections which dealt with Savonarola and his times, the impression was created that both writers were only—or mainly—concerned with Savonarola. Such an impression is entirely false. Cerretani was a member of the Florentine ruling group and as such he possessed "inside" information; however, his *Storia Fiorentina*, which he wrote around 1509, is rather general. The continuation of this work, discussed above, pp. 147 et seq., which he wrote around 1520 is of greater value in detail as well as in approach. Parenti's diaries are more important for historians than Cerretani's works. Indeed Parenti's diaries are the fullest contemporary account we possess. Parenti, member of a rich Florentine family, played a modest part in politics, but his role was important enough to keep him fully informed about the proceedings in the Great Council, about the deliberations of the magistrates, and about the views of the leading Florentines. Moreover, he had an ear for the opinions of the people—he knew their hopes and fears—and he reported the rumors which spread through the city at every turn of events. Parenti's work is not a diary in the strictest sense, for it is not a day-by-day account; rather Parenti seems to have written down every two or three months all those occurrences which seemed to him to be worth recording. A critical edition with explanatory notes of Parenti's diaries would be most useful.

A full understanding of Florentine institutions in the republican period can be had only in the perspective of previous developments. As the articles of Guido Pampaloni, "Gli Organi della Repubblica fiorentina per le relazioni con l'estero," *Rivista di Studi Politici Internazionali*, vol. XX (1953), pp. 3-38, and Giovanni Antonelli, "La Magistratura degli Otto di Guardia a Firenze," *Archivio Storico Italiano*, vol. CXII (1954), pp. 3-39 illustrate, in the period of the republic the magistrates continued to work as they had in the past; thus the history of some institutions are vital for an understanding of their functioning during the republic. But such articles which are based on complete knowledge of the relevant documents are very rare.

There is a dearth of careful studies on Florentine institutions not only in the times of the republic but throughout the earlier periods of the city's history. A study—based on a systematic investigation of the archives —of the continuity of Florentine institutions would be most desirable. It is true indeed that Robert Davidsohn, in basing his *Geschichte von Florenz* almost exclusively on documentary sources, approached such a study. But when he died in 1937 he had not advanced his history beyond the Age of Dante. While Davidsohn was working to establish a secure basis for Florentine history up to the early fourteenth century, other scholars were subjecting to critical examination certain outstanding events of the late fourteenth and fifteenth centuries. For example, there are Niccolò Rodolico's works on *Il popolo minuto*, Bologna, 1899 and *La democrazia fiorentina nel suo tramonto*, Bologna, 1905, F. C. Pellegrini's *Sulla Repubblica Fiorentina al tempo di Cosimo Vecchio*, Pisa, 1899, and V. Ricchioni's *La Costituzione Politica di Firenze ai tempi di Lorenzo il Magnifico*, Siena, 1913. But a comprehensive study of Florentine institutions, continuing Davidsohn's great work, is still lacking.

Since the Second World War, however, an increasing

number of studies based on archival materials have appeared. It might be enough to refer to the bibliography by Gene A. Brucker in his *Florentine Politics and Society, 1343-1378*, Princeton, 1962. Brucker's book is a significant contribution to our understanding of Florentine political institutions in the second part of the fourteenth century. Less work has been done on institutions during the Medicean period; in part this is due to the fact that the filing of the documents of the *Mediceo avanti il principato* is not yet completed. Much of what we do know about institutions of the Medicean period has resulted from researches in economic history: L. F. Marks' article "The Financial Oligarchy in Florence under Lorenzo" in *Italian Renaissance Studies*, London, 1960, pp. 123-147 analyses the institution of the officials of the Monte, and Raymond de Roover's brilliant work, *The Rise and Decline of the Medici Bank 1397-1494*, Cambridge, 1963, has thrown light on the interrelationship of economic activities and political institutions.

Currently a number of scholars are working in the Archivio di Stato di Firenze on the institutions of the fifteenth century; a book by Nicolai Rubinstein on the government of the Medici in the fifteenth century will be published soon. But at present it remains true that as much as has been written about Florence, the history of its institutions is, in many respects, an unexplored area.

MACHIAVELLI

The most recent critical edition of Machiavelli's works is the one in the *Biblioteca di Classici Italiani*, Feltrinelli Editore; Sergio Bertelly is publishing a further complete critical edition, including all recently found manuscript material, in the Publishing House of Giovanni Salerno in Milano; a comprehensive edition of all of Machiavelli's official writings *Legazioni, Commissarie e Scritti di Governo*, has been undertaken by Fredi Chiappelli, and the first volume appeared in 1971. For Machiavelli's writings not yet printed in this edition I have used the earlier critical edition, Niccolò Machiavelli, *Tutte le opere storiche e letterarie*, ed. Guido Mazzoni e Mario Casella, Firenze, 1929. The principal works of Machiavelli are available in special editions with helpful commentaries: for the *Discourses*, see *The Discourses of Niccolò Machiavelli*, translated from the Italian with an introduction and notes by Leslie J. Walker, 2 vols., New Haven, 1950; for *Il Principe*, see *Niccolò Machiavelli, Il Principe e altri scritti*, introduzione e commento di Gennaro Sasso, Firenze, 1963 (until the appearance of Sasso's edition the edition by Burd, Oxford, 1891, was recognized as containing the most useful commentaries); for the *Istorie Fiorentine*, see Niccolò Machiavelli, *Istorie Fiorentine*, testo critico con introduzione e note per cura di Plinio Carli, 2 vols., Firenze, 1927. Of translations into English a recent edition of Machiavelli's literary works in the *Oxford Library of Italian Classics* (*The Literary Works of Machiavelli* edited and translated by J. R. Hale, London, 1961) is completely satisfactory. For *The Prince* and *The Discourse*s I refer to the Modern Library Edition of these works edited by Max Lerner and the edition of the *Discourses* by L. Walker, mentioned above.

The authoritative description of Machiavelli's life is the one by Roberto Ridolfi, *Vita di Niccolò Machiavelli*, Roma, 1954 (now available in English translation: *The Life of Niccolò Machiavelli*, transl. Cecil Grayson, New York, 1963). Ridolfi has done a magnificent job in eliminating errors and in broadening our knowledge of the facts of Machiavelli's life and career. Nonetheless, the classical biographies of Pasquale Villari, *Niccolò Machiavelli e i suoi tempi*, 3 vols., Milano, 1877-1882, and of Oreste Tommasini, *La vita e gli scritti di N. Machiavelli*, 2 vols., Torino-Roma, 1899, 1911, ought still to be consulted, mainly because of the rich source material which these authors discovered and published. Ridolfi is more interested in Machiavelli's life than in his thought; the book by Gennaro Sasso, *Niccolò Machiavelli, storia del suo pensiero politico*, Napoli, 1958, is the most recent intellectual biography of Machiavelli. A very readable account of Machiavelli's life and thought is J. R. Hale, *Machiavelli and Renaissance Italy*, New York 1960. Among the publications which appeared in celebration of the fifth centenary of Machiavelli's birth, *Studies on Machiavelli*, ed. Myron P. Gilmore, Firenze, 1972, contains essays dealing with all aspects of Machiavelli's political and literary activity.

Scholarly literature on Machiavelli fills many shelves; a complete bibliography is not only almost impossible but also unnecessary because a number of thorough and useful bibliographical essays have been published in recent times. First of all, each volume of Niccolò Machiavelli, *Opere*, in the Feltrinelli edition contains introductions and bibliographical notes which indicate the literature relevant to the works edited in the particular volume as well as analyze briefly the various opinions which have been expressed about this work. Then the *Journal of Modern History*, vol. XXXIII (1961), pp. 113-136, published an

article by Eric W. Cochrane, "Machiavelli 1940-1960."
One might not always agree with the author's evaluation,
but his thoroughness is unquestionable. Finally, Gennaro
Sasso, in the above-mentioned edition of *Il Principe*, pp.
40-44, provides a useful bibliographical note, and the most
recent scholarly literature is listed in Felix Gilbert, "Machiavelli in Modern Historical Scholarship," *Italian Quar-
terly*, volume XIV (1971). Thus the main purpose
of the following remarks is to explain and justify on the
basis of bibliographical material my statements on disputed issues.

• I •
Education

Little was known about Bernardo Machiavelli, Niccolò's father, until his *Libro di Ricordi* was published by
Cesare Olschki in Florence, 1954. Like other Florentine
writers of *ricordi* Bernardo jotted down only brief factual statements about the main events of his life in the
years 1474-1487. We hear about his daily activities: his
concern for his estates and his role as juris-consultant.
But the most interesting aspect of this book, rightly emphasized by the editor, is that it shows that Bernardo "è
anche umanista e partecipa alla intensa vita culturale
della Firenze a lui coeva ... " (p. XV). This point can be
further strengthened. The Archivio di Stato of Siena pos-
sesses a manuscript by Bartholomeus Scala, *De Legibus et
Judiciis Dialogus*, composed in 1483, which Lamberto
Borghi published in *La Bibliofilia*, vol. XLII (1940), pp.
256-282. This manuscript is a dialogue with two speakers,
one is the author, Bartolomeo Scala, the other is a Bernardo Machiavelli. This Bernardo Machiavelli must have
been Niccolò's father. According to the *Catasto* there
was only one other Bernardo Machiavelli living in Flor-

ence when Scala composed his dialogue, and this other Bernardo Machiavelli was without income, unable to pay taxes, a man of a very low stratum of society (see *A.S.F.*, Catasto 999, Campione 1480, Santo Spirito, Drago, c. 328). This was not a man whom Scala would have called "amicus et familiaris meus" (p. 257) and made a speaker in a dialogue. Moreover, Scala and Niccolò's father, Bernardo, were almost contemporaries (Bernardo was born 1428, Scala 1430) and both were trained in law so that the appearance of Niccolò's father in a dialogue concerned with legal problems was appropriate. The establishment of a close connection between Scala and Niccolò's father is of some significance. Scala, of course, was First Chancellor; he was very powerful under the Medici but also held his office under the Republic until his death in 1497. He was a man who could have opened the doors of the Chancellery to the son of an old friend. Niccolò Machiavelli became head of the second chancellery in 1498 (see Nicolai Rubinstein, "The Beginnings of Niccolò Machiavelli's Career in the Florentine Chancery," *Italian Studies,* vol. XI [1956], pp. 72-91) only after Scala's death, but it has been suggested that Niccolò received this position after some previous employment in the Chancellery because usually the higher positions in the Chancellery were given to men who had previously served in this office (on this question see Ridolfi, *op. cit.,* pp. 26-27).[1]

[1] After the manuscript of this book had gone to the press, I read the article by Sergio Bertelli, "Ancora su Lucrezio e Machiavelli", *Rivista Storica Italiana,* vol. LXXVI (1964), pp. 1-17; on pp. 12-13, Bertelli discusses Scala's dialogue; Bertelli acknowledges most generously that I directed his attention to Scala's work. Unfortunately, the footnote, recognizing my suggestion, is given at the end of a sentence, with which I can't fully agree. Like Bertelli, I consider it probable that Niccolò Machiavelli owed his appointment in the chancellery to the relations existing between Scala and Bernardo Machiavelli. But since Niccolò became second chancellor only after Scala's death, Bertelli assumes

Scala was not only a humanist himself but also a center of humanist society; his daughter Alessandra Scala, born 1475, was a poetess widely admired for her erudition. She learned Greek from Janus Lascaris who lived in Florence until 1494 and had brought back to Florence from his trips to the East numerous Greek manuscripts (for the literature on Bartolomeo Scala, Alessandra Scala, and Janus Lascaris, see M. E. Cosenza, *Biographical and Bibliographical Dictionary of the Italian Humanists and of the World of Classical Scholarship in Italy, 1300-1800,* Boston, 1962). (The appearance of Lascaris in Scala's circle is of some interest because the hypothesis has been put forth that Lascaris was the source for Machiavelli's knowledge of the Sixth Book of Polybius' History which he used in the *Discourses* and that Machiavelli and Lascaris met only around 1515; see J. Hexter, "Seyssel, Machiavelli and Polybius VI: the Mystery of the Missing Translation," *Studies in the Renaissance,* III (1956), pp. 75-96. But Machiavelli and Lascaris could have met in Florence before 1494 and a friendship between Scala and Bernardo Machiavelli would make such a meeting even likely; it might be added that, in 1504 in France, Machiavelli had long conversations with Claude de Seyssel, who, according to Hexter, had received knowledge of the Sixth Book of Polybius from Lascaris—no doubt before 1503, the year in which Lascaris left France for Italy.

---

a kind of "posthumous" influence of Scala. I find it more likely that Niccolò entered the chancellery during Scala's lifetime in a minor position, and his election to second chancellor in 1498 was due partly to his anti-Savonarolian attitude, but also a "natural" promotion. Bertelli presents in his article interesting new material on Machiavelli's role in the editing of Lucretius; this part of Bertelli's article confirms the assumption of a strongly humanist element in Machiavelli's education. It must be stated, however, that some scholars reject Bertelli's view that these manuscripts were copied by Machiavelli.

Thus, even if one assumes that Lascaris was the *only* person who could have given information about the Sixth Book of Polybius to Machiavelli, this assumption gives no reason to date the composition of the first chapters of the *Discourses* after 1515).

There is one further notice in Bernardo Machiavelli's *Libro di Ricordi* which might be regarded as an indication of his interest in humanist activities and of his concern for an education which would permit his sons an appreciation of intellectual endeavors. Bernardo wrote (p. 138) that, " . . . adì 5 di novembre 1481 Nicolò e Totto miei figliuoli cominciaron andare a imparare da ser Pagolo da Ronciglione maestro di grammatica." It seems not to have been noticed that this teacher is the priest Ser Paolo Sasso da Ronciglione who was a person of some standing in Florentine intellectual life. He was the teacher of the clerics of Santa Maria Reparata (for mentionings and literature about Ser Paolo Sasso da Ronciglione and his pupils, see Cosenza, *op. cit.*). Among the younger boys whom he taught were, in addition to Bernardo's sons, Pietro Crinito and Michele Verino (also born in 1469), both of whom achieved literary fame. Michele was the son of Ugolino Verino, another member of the Chancellery, one of Landino's foremost students, and a well-known writer and poet. Michele himself enjoyed great fame as a poet of Latin *disticha* and his death in 1487, at the age of eighteen, was regarded by leading humanists of the time such as Landino, Merula, and Pontano, as a great loss for Florentine intellectual life. Ugolino Verino dedicated a posthumous edition of his son's poems to Ser Paolo Sasso. Because there has been much discussion about the extent of Machiavelli's knowledge of classical writings, and because frequently he has been considered as being acquainted only superficially with the intellectual and scholarly achievements of his time, it ought to be stressed that the little we know about his father's interests and milieu and about Niccolò's education does not justify the assumption that Niccolò was less carefully educated than other young men of his time. If the thesis of Sergio Bertelli and Franco Gaeta, "Noterelle Machiavelliane," *Rivista Storica Italiana*, vol. LXXIII (1961), pp. 544-557, that Niccolò Machiavelli copied manuscripts of Lucretius and Terentius in his early years is correct, this view of a careful education directed towards humanist studies would be reinforced. In any case it is difficult to assume that the members of the Florentine Chancellery would have accepted and welcomed a colleague who was not thoroughly trained in the humanist corpus. The extent to which, in the later years of the fifteenth century, literary concerns prevailed over political aims in the Chancellery, which was of course, the permanent secretariat of the Florentine magistracies, emerges from the article by E. Garin, "I cancellieri umanisti della Repubblica Fiorentina da Coluccio Salutati a Bartolomeo Scala," *Rivista Storica Italiana*, vol. LXXI (1959), pp. 185-208.

• II •

Method

The best and almost only existing treatment of the methodical problems in Machiavelli's writings is contained in a lecture by Federico Chabod, which was published under the title "Niccolò Machiavelli" in the volume *Civiltà Fiorentina, Il Cinquecento*, Firenze, 1955, pp. 3-21, and is now available in English translation, with the more appropriate title "Machiavelli's Method and Style," in the volume Federico Chabod, *Machiavelli and the*

Renaissance, London, 1958, pp. 126-148.[2] It is worth quoting Chabod's statements about the relation of "intuition" and "reason" in Machiavelli's mind: Machiavelli "is not, then, primarily a logician, working from principles from which, by a continuous process of reasoning, rigorous and slavish, he deduces a complete 'system'. He is first and foremost a man of imagination, who sees *his* truth in a flash, with blinding clarity, and only afterwards trusts to reason to enable him to comment on that truth. . . . Supreme among the political thinkers of all time, Machiavelli, in common with the greatest politicians— who, like him, so resemble the artist in that their logic and their dogma are completely subordinate to their intuition—has what may literally be termed initial inner 'illuminations', immediate, intuitive visions of events and their significance. Only afterwards does he pass on to what we may call 'application by reasoning'." (pp. 142-143). In my opinion, these passages correctly point out the manner in which a reader should approach Machiavelli's writings. Chabod's article also contains penetrating remarks on particular aspects of Machiavelli's method, especially on "his dilemmatic technique of invariably putting forward the two extreme and antithetical solutions, . . . and employing a disjunctive style." (pp. 127-28).

Incidental remarks on Machiavelli's method can be found in most of the works dealing with his thought, but in general these questions have been raised in connection with Machiavelli's individual works rather than in a systematic manner. Thus, one must refer to a number of studies devoted to individual works for a discussion of

---

[2] Chabod's writings on Machiavelli are now collected in the volume Federico Chabod, *Opere*, vol. I: *Scritti su Machiavelli*, Torino, 1964.

Machiavelli's reliance on humanist patterns. The relation of the *Prince* to other books on princes, and particularly to the mirror-of-princes literature, has been analyzed by Allan H. Gilbert, *Machiavelli's Prince and Its Forerunners*, Durham, 1938 and F. Gilbert, "The Humanist Concept of the Prince and the 'Prince' of Machiavelli," *Journal of Modern History*, vol. XI (1939), pp. 449-483. Mr. A. H. Gilbert and I disagree insofar as he believes that Machiavelli follows the previous authors on princeship, whereas I suggest that he satirized this genre which idealizes rulers. But we both agree that these books served Machiavelli as a pattern. My article on "The Composition and Structure of Machiavelli's Discorsi," *Journal of the History of Ideas*, vol. XIV (1953), pp. 136-156, has shown the extent to which the *Discourses* were originally composed as a successive commentary on Livy, and may be considered as a contribution to the problem of elucidating Machiavelli's working methods; in addition the article raised certain questions about the dating of the composition of the *Discourses*, and this latter issue has aroused a lively discussion for which I refer to the above-mentioned bibliographies. The book by Marvin T. Herrick, *Italian Comedy in the Renaissance*, Urbana, 1960, provides a most helpful illustration of the role which the pattern of classical comedies played in the composition of Italian Renaissance comedies. On the relation of Machiavelli's *Florentine History* to the humanist prescriptions for the writing of history, see above, chapter 6, pp. 236 et seq. and my introduction to the English translation of Machiavelli's *History of Florence* (Harper Torchbook, New York, 1960). The most famous example of Machiavelli's method of stylizing events is his treatment of Cesare Borgia in the *Prince*. The contrast between Machiavelli's discussion of Cesare Borgia in his reports, and his discussion of Cesare Borgia in the seventh chapter of the *Prince* has been carefully analyzed by Gennaro Sasso, "Sul VII capitolo del Principe," *Rivista Storica Italiana*, vol. LXIV (1952), pp. 177-207. But here again a systematic discussion extending to all the writings of Machiavelli is lacking.

The question of the role which nationalism played in Machiavelli's political thought has been much debated; it may be appropriate to take up this problem at this place because the question is closely connected with Machiavelli's literary methods and procedures. For a general survey of the discussion on this problem see my article, "The Concept of Nationalism in Machiavelli's Prince," *Studies in the Renaissance*, vol. I (1954), pp. 38-48, and see also Vincent Ilardi, " 'Italianita' among some Italian Intellectuals in the Early Sixteenth Century," *Traditio*, vol. XII (1956), pp. 339-367. These two articles show that expressions of Italian nationalism in the sense of a feeling that all Italians belong together and ought to confederate against the outside world were quite common at this time. The issue therefore is reduced to the question whether Machiavelli went beyond such feelings and made out of them a program of practical politics: that Italy should become politically united. From this point of view the question of the significance of the last chapter of the *Prince* which contains the appeal to liberate Italy from the barbarians and is the strongest and clearest expression of Italian nationalism in Machiavelli's work is crucially important. Was this chapter envisaged by Machiavelli as an integral element of the treatise, as its conclusion to which all its discussions are pointed, or was this chapter added to the treatise as a kind of afterthought? The idea that this chapter did not belong to the treatise in its original form but was a later addition has been frequently advanced, although the adherents of this view seem to lose ground after the unified conception of *The Prince* had been strongly defended by Federico Chabod, "Sulla composizione de 'Il Principe' di Niccolò Machiavelli," *Archivum Romanicum*, vol. XI (1927), pp. 330-383. However, the question was never entirely settled, and recently, in the Feltrinelli edition, the editor Sergio Bertelli has made the persuasive point that, although the treatise itself might have been composed within a short time and emerged from a unified conception, the *dedicatio* at the beginning, and the *exhortatio* (the last chapter) were written at the same time, between September 1515 and September 1516, several years after the rest of the treatise.

• III •
Basic Concepts

No student of Machiavelli has been able to avoid discussion of terms like *virtù*, *fortuna*, or *stato*. These are key words, as Meinecke's says in his chapter on Machiavelli in his book on *Die Idee der Staatsräson*. There are only a few special studies on Machiavelli's terminology and the conclusions are frequently contradictory. The most comprehensive work on Machiavelli's vocabulary is by Francesco Ercole, *La Politica di Machiavelli*, Roma, 1926, but, although his investigation is helpful, Ercole is too much inclined to make Machiavelli a systematic philosopher. E. W. Mayer, *Machiavelli's Geschichtsauffassung und sein Begriff virtù*, München and Berlin, 1921, provides a still valuable, special study of Machiavelli's use of *virtù* although, like Ercole, he might be accused of over-systematizing Machiavelli's use of this term. The investigation of Fredi Chiappelli, *Studi sul Linguaggio del Machiavelli*, Firenze, 1952, is useful but it is limited to the *Prince* and its results regarding Machiavelli's use of the word *stato* have been attacked by J. H. Hexter, "Il Principe and lo stato," *Studies in the Renaissance*, vol. IV (1957), pp. 113-138. The reason for this inconclusive situation with regard to the determination of Machiavelli's key concepts is that, as several writers have pointed out, Machiavelli was not very much concerned with exactness in terminology. I may quote here a statement by J. H. Whitfield, who in his book on *Machiavelli*, Oxford, 1947, pp. 93-95, writes that an "unscientific use of terms is not untypical of Machiavelli." I would like to emphasize that, in my opinion, the chapter of Whitfield's book entitled, "The Anatomy of Virtù," from which this quotation is taken, is the best that has been written on Machiavelli's vocabulary. Agreeing with Whitfield, I consider it more appropriate to give a descriptive discussion of Machiavelli's terms than to attempt a precise definition.

I believe that the way in which I have described Machiavelli's use of *Fortuna* is generally accepted; of course, *Fortuna* has a two-fold meaning: it can be good or bad fortune which raises and destroys a man in the way that it raised and destroyed Cesare Borgia. Or it can be the *Fortuna* which *virtù* can overcome and make favorable. For a recent brief description of the various aspects of Machiavelli's concept of *Fortuna*, see Burleigh T. Wilkins, "Machiavelli on History and Fortune," *Bucknell Review*, vol. VIII (1959), pp. 225-245, particularly pp. 235-237, and for a subtle analysis of all its nuances I refer to Sasso, *Niccolò Machiavelli, Storia del suo Pensiero Politico*, pp. 247-280.

For *virtù* I would like to refer to Sasso, in his edition of *Niccolò Machiavelli, Il Principe e altri Scritti*, p. 10, as well as to Whitfield's above-mentioned chapter, "The Anatomy of Virtù," in his book *Machiavelli*, pp. 93-98. The decisive aspects of Machiavelli's concept of *virtù* were taken from Latin historians, particularly Sallust whose influence on Machiavelli seems to me to have been very important. But many other elements entered into Machiavelli's concept of *virtù:* "Several Latin senses, that of energy of the will, of bravery, of Ciceronian *virtù* or the post-classical sense of Christian virtue." (Whitfield, p. 98). Sometimes the word *virtù* is used in only one of these various senses; mostly, however, it combines several of these meanings and which one is dominant depends on the context of the sentence. The fact that Machiavelli ascribes *virtù* not only to individuals but to collective bodies has been particularly emphasized by E. W. Mayer, *op. cit.,* p. 86 et seq.; he may have overstated his case but the fact is correct and important because it points to the idea of political bodies as organic units. E. W. Mayer, *op. cit.,* p. 113, remarks correctly that "der Ansatz zu einem abstrakten Staatsbegriff findet sich bei Machiavelli weniger in dem Worte stato als in der Hypostasierung des Begriffs virtù zu einer das staatliche Leben tragenden Macht, an deren Wachstum und Vergehen das Schicksal eines Volks geknüpft ist."

I also agree with Whitfield in his remarks about Machiavelli's use of *stato:* "*Stato* has a whole gamut of meanings, ranging from the Latin one of *state, condition,* to something very near the modern conception of the State; but with a general tendency to convey something less than this last, *power, those that hold it, government* rather than *territory*—though this last is not absent. In any given passage the word *stato*—such is the uncertainty of Machiavelli's use of it—may have any one of this range of shades." (p. 93).

The above-mentioned studies by Chiappelli and Hexter appeared after the publication of Whitfield's book but apparently neither of these scholars has taken account of it. Hexter is undoubtedly right in criticizing Chiappelli for assuming too easily that Machiavelli's use is almost regularly *stato* in the modern sense of the word. I also agree with Hexter that in the *Prince* Machiavelli uses *stato* chiefly "in an exploitative way." But I have some reservations regarding Hexter's study. He says that Machiavelli "and no one else coupled *lo stato* as objective or passive subject with verbs of exploitative tonality." But this use of *stato* is quite common and it may be enough to refer to Guicciardini's famous Ricordo 48: "Non si può tenere stati secondo conscienza, perché—chi considera la origine loro—tutti sono violenti, da quelli delle republiche nella patria propria in fuora, e non altrove: e da questa regola non eccettuo lo imperadore e manco e preti, la violenza de' quali è doppia, perché ci sforzano con le arme temporale e con le spirituale." Moreover, Hexter's reduction of the use of the term *stato* in the *Prince* to an "exploitative" meaning is exaggerated. In order to explain my objections it would be necessary to go through all the uses of *stato*, particularly those mentioned by Hexter on p. 127. It may be enough here to say that an "exploitative" meaning cannot be attributed to the sentence in *Prince*, chapter 12: "Si divise la Italia in più stati." Nor does the reduction of the meaning *stato* to an "exploitative" term do justice to the meaning of the statement "E' principali fondamenti che abbino tutti li stati, così nuovi come vecchi o misti, sono le buone legge e le buone arme" if one considers that Machiavelli continues "e, perché non può essere buone legge dove non sono buone arme, e dove sono buone arme conviene sieno buone legge, io lascerò indrieto el ragionare delle legge e parlerò delle arme." We know from the *Discourses* that Machiavelli speaks of "stato libero" (for instance, Book II, Chapter 18) and gives to *stato* a meaning which is not "exploitative." It is entirely natural that the "exploitative" meaning plays a great role in the *Prince* because in the *Prince* Machiavelli considers politics from the point of view of the ruler. But since in other writings Machiavelli uses *stato* in quite different ways, it is artificial to force every meaning of *stato* in the *Prince* into an "exploitative" mold. Hexter's reason for this *tour de force* seems to be that he wants to say that the problem of reason of state existed for Machiavelli not in the *Prince* but only in the *Discourses*. I agree with C. J. Friedrich, *Constitutional Reason of State*, Providence, 1957, p. 23, that the problem did not exist for Machiavelli at all. This point is also implied in the discussion of Machiavelli's "filosofia naturalistica," which Vittorio de Caprariis gives in his introduction to *Il Principe*, Classici illustrati Laterza, p. 11. He says that states as well as men and the entire world of history were for Machiavelli elements of nature. The fourth chapter of this book on Machiavelli indicates the importance which I attribute to Machiavelli's "naturalistic" philosophy. Although it is questionable to draw serious conclusions from ideas expressed in Machiavelli's poems, it may not be out of place to cite the passage from Machiavelli's "Asino d'Oro," in which he contrasts an animal's closeness to nature with man's alienation from nature:

"Il mio parlar mai non verrebbe meno,
S'io volessi mostrar come infelici
Voi siete più ch'ogni animal terreno.

Noi a natura siam maggiori amici;
E par che in noi più sua virtù dispensi,
Facendo voi d'ogni suo ben mendici."

THE SCHOLARLY TREATMENT
OF RENAISSANCE HISTORIOGRAPHY

• I •

General Works

The one comprehensive work on the history of historiography is Eduard Fueter, *Geschichte der neueren Historiographie,* first edition, München and Berlin, 1911, rev. and enlarged edition, 1936. This book is now obsolete in many respects. It evaluates historical writings almost exclusively from the point of view of the critical historical method of the nineteenth century, and its factual statements contain many errors so that its data must be carefully checked. Nevertheless Fueter's book has its use as a kind of biographical dictionary of historians, and its bibliography provides a survey of the older literature on the history of history.

Of great general importance for the questions discussed in the second part of this book is the work by Rudolf von Albertini, *Das Florentinische Staatsbewusstsein im Uebergang von der Republik zum Prinzipat,* Bern, 1955. Albertini's chief attention is given to the developments after 1527, and, in contrast to the present book, Albertini is not primarily interested in the history of historiography, but in the evolution of a new concept of the state. Nevertheless, in analyzing the factors which led to the acceptance of Medicean absolutism, Albertini discusses changes in the intellectual climate which were significant for the development of historiography: for instance, he has interesting observations about the sixteenth-century views about the role of *Fortuna*. More-over, Albertini deals in detail with the political views and actions of several of the figures whose historical works we have analyzed and his bibliographical references are judicious and up-to-date.

In the book by Myron P. Gilmore, *Humanists and Jurists*, Cambridge, 1963, the first two essays, entitled "The Renaissance Conception of the Lessons of History" and "Individualism in Renaissance Historians," are devoted to problems of Renaissance Historiography; the second of these essays contains an interesting discussion of the question to what extent the assumption of a "human scheme of causation" is compatible with the assumption of the working of the "hand of God" in history.

• II •

Humanist Historiography

A special work on the humanist theory of history does not exist. The writings of P. O. Kristeller, by emphasizing the connection between rhetorics and humanism, have placed the study of Italian humanism on a new basis. But the consequences of Kristeller's views for the evaluation of humanist historical theory have not yet been drawn. Some general remarks on the position of history within humanist thought can be found in Eugenio Garin, *L'Umanesimo Italiano*, Bari, 1952, particularly Chapter 7, and in his *Medioevo e Rinascimento*, Bari, 1954, particularly the chapter on "La storia nel pensiero del Rinascimento." The above-mentioned article by M. P. Gilmore on "Individualism in Historians" has emphasized the importance of Pontano's dialogue *Actius* for the humanist theory of history.

For literature on individual humanists, see now M. E. Cosenza, *Biographical and Bibliographical Dictionary of the Italian Humanists and of the World of Classical Scholarship in Italy 1300-1800*, Boston, 1962. A helpful survey of historical writings in Latin including bibliographical references is given by Beatrice R. Reynolds, "Latin Historiography: A Survey 1400-1600," *Studies in the Renaissance*, vol. II (1955), pp. 7-66. There are a few studies on the historical works of prominent humanists. For Bruni see, E. Santini, "Leonardo Bruni Aretino e suoi 'Historiarum Florentini Populi Libri XII'," *Annali della R. Scuola Normale Superiore di Pisa*, vol. XXII (1910), Filosofia e Filologia, and B. L. Ullman "Leonardo Bruni and Humanistic Historiography," *Studies in the Italian Renaissance*, Roma, 1955, pp. 321-344; for Biondo see Denys Hay, "The Decades of Flavio Biondo," *Proceedings of the British Academy*, vol. XLV (1959); for Valla see Franco Gaeta, *Lorenzo Valla, Filologia e Storia nell' Umanesimo Italiano*, Napoli, 1955: for Scala see Nicolai Rubinstein, "Bartolomeo Scala's Historia Florentinorum," *Scritti in Onore di Tamaro de Marinis*, Verona, 1964; for Bembo see Carlo Lagomaggiore, "L'Istoria Veneziana di M. Pietro Bembo," *Nuovo Archivio Veneto*, N. S., vol. VII, (1904), vol. VIII (1904), vol. IX (1905).

Concerning general problems of humanist historiography, the question of their influence on changes in the chronological scheme of history has been examined by Wallace K. Ferguson in the first chapter of his well-known work on *The Renaissance in Historical Thought*, Boston, 1948.

The question to what extent the humanists used a critical method in the evaluation of sources needs further clarification. There is no doubt that several of them applied an advanced critical method in investigating the foundation of a city. See the various studies by Nicolai Rubinstein, "Beginnings of Political Thought in Florence," *Journal of the Warburg and Courtauld Institutes*, vol. V (1942), pp. 198-227; "Il Poliziano e la Questione delle Origini di Firenze," in *Il Poliziano e il suo tempo, Atti del IV Convegno Internazionale di Studi sul Rinascimento*, Firenze, 1957, pp. 101-110, and Hans Baron, *The Crisis of the Early Italian Renaissance*, 2 vols., Princeton, 1955, particularly vol. I, pp. 38-63.

But the chief question is whether the humanists applied a critical approach when they wrote histories of periods in which the sources came from the post-classical world. As far as I can see those who used documentary sources did so because they found them most easily accessible and not because they considered documentary sources of greater value. The only humanist for whom the claim has been made that he recognized the superiority of documentary sources over narrative accounts was Bruni. Hans Baron, our main authority on Bruni, has not dealt in any detail with Bruni as an historian, as the author of the *Historiae Florentini Populi Libri XII*. A special study of Bruni's Florentine History is the above-mentioned article by Santini, which has been accepted by B. L. Ullman and others. Santini seems to me to show that Bruni proceeded with unusual care and good critical sense. Although Bruni took a chronicle like Villani's as his guide, he considered other sources and checked his facts. Bruni used material from the archives; in particular, he seems to have relied on the archives for his description of the origin and development of Florentine magistracies. But the question remains open whether Bruni ascribed to archival sources a higher value than to narrative accounts. Also, although Santini proves that Bruni sometimes corrected mistakes made by Villani, Santini's article does not permit us to judge the extent to which Bruni remained dependent on Villani. As valuable as Santini's article is, he has opened up a number of questions about Bruni as historian rather than solving them.

• III •

Guicciardini

The literature on Francesco Guicciardini is extensive. The *Storia d'Italia* was published first in 1562; the authoritative critical edition is the one by Alessandro Gherardi, 4 vols., Firenze, 1919. (The most widely used edition of the *Storia d'Italia* is that of Constantino Panigada in the series *Scrittori d'Italia*, 5 vols., Bari, 1929). The rest of Guicciardini's writings were first published by G. Canestrini in ten volumes, 1859-1867, but better texts are now available in the edition which the publishing house Laterza in Bari published in its collection, *Scrittori d'Italia*, 1929-1936, and the volumes of this edition have been used in my text. For the *Ricordi* it is necessary to use the edition by Raffaele Spongano, Firenze, 1951; Spongano was the first to establish a correct text of this work. Guicciardini's second *Florentine History* was unknown until it was edited by Roberto Ridolfi under the title, *Le Cose Fiorentine*, Firenze, 1945. An edition of Guicciardini's correspondence is still under way. So far ten volumes reaching to 1526 have been published, the first four edited by Roberto Palmarocchi, the later volumes by G. P. Ricci. For the older literature on Guicciardini I refer to the bibliography given in André Otetea, *François Guicchardin, Sa vie publique et sa pensée politique*, Paris, 1926. A volume of essays on Guicciardini entitled *Francesco Guicciardini nel IV Centenario della Morte*, (*Supplemento* no 1 *di Rinascita*), Firenze, 1940 contains bibliographical data on pp. 231-303. A more recent bibliographical survey can be found in the article by Roberto Palmarocchi, "Cento anni di studi Guicciardiniani," *Studi Guicciardiniani*, Città di Castello, 1947. In recent years a number of works on Guicciardini have been published by Vito Vitale, *Francesco Guicciardini*, Torino, 1941; Luigi Malagoli, *Guicciardini*, Firenze, 1939; Paolo Treves, *Il Realismo Politico di Francesco Guicciardini*, Firenze, 1931, etc., but these works have been made obsolete by two important studies, the one is the biography by Roberto Ridolfi, *Vita di Francesco Guicciardini*, Roma, 1960; the other is by Vittorio de Caprariis, *Francesco Guicciardini dalla Politica alla Storia*, Bari, 1950. Based on careful researches in Guicciardini's papers and in the Florentine Archivio di Stato, Ridolfi presents the first full and authentic presentation of Guicciardini's life and career; if not stated otherwise, I have followed Ridolfi in the dating of Guicciardini's works and in the description of his career. Vittorio de Caprariis has given an outline of Guicciardini's intellectual development and has stressed the importance of the year 1527 when Guicciardini changed from a political theorist to an historian.

A number of studies on particular works of Guicciardini should be mentioned. The evolution of Guicciardini's first *Florentine History* has been described by Nicolai Rubinstein, "The 'Storie Fiorentine' and the 'Memorie di Famiglia' by Francesco Guicciardini," *Rinas-*

cimento, vol. IV (1953), pp. 173-225. The various stages of the development of the *Storia d'Italia* have been analyzed by Roberto Ridolfi, *Genesi della Storia d'Italia Guicciardiniana*, Firenze, 1938, and reprinted in Roberto Ridolfi, *Opuscoli di Storia Letteraria e di Erudizione*, 1942, pp. 175-201. Roberto Palmarocchi, in a study on Guicciardini's concept of Fortune, printed in *Studi Guicciardiniani*, Città di Castello, 1947, pp. 31-58, emphasizes that (p. 43) "il Guicciardini, a differenza di altri umanisti, riconosca alla fortuna un predominio quasi assoluto e non dia alla virtù dell' individuo neppure quella percentuale di autonomia che le assegnava il Machiavelli." The book by Raffaello Ramat, *Il Guicciardini e la Tragedia d'Italia*, Firenze, 1953, investigates the gradual development of Guicciardini's ideas about the tragic fate of Italy. Finally, it might be mentioned that the influence which Guicciardini's *Storia d'Italia* had on later times has been studied in Vincenzo Luciani, *Francesco Guicciardini and His European Reputation*, New York, 1936 (an enlarged Italian translation appeared under the title: *Francesco Guicciardini e la fortuna dell'opera sua*, Firenze, 1949). For the Florentine historians of the second part of the sixteenth century, see Rudolf von Albertini, *Das Florentinische Staatsbewusstsein im Uebergang von der Republik zum Prinzipat*, Bern, 1955; their writings disclose that there was a narrowing of historical interest after Guicciardini.

INDEX

Acciaiuoli, Giovanni, Florentine politician, 123, 124, 125

Acciaiuoli, Roberto, 1467-1539, Florentine politician, pro-Medicean, 125, 203, 204

Accoppiatori, 16, 17, 23, 52, 53, 133, 135

Adriani, Marcello Virgilio, 1464-1521, Florentine humanist, First Chancellor since 1498, 71, 83, 163

Aegidius Colonna, 208

Aiazzi, G., editor, see Rinuccini

Alamanni, Lodovico, 1488-1526, Florentine politician, pro-Medicean, 99, 101, 102, 103, 106, 107, 130, 136, 137, 138, 150, 151, 163

Alamanni, Luigi, 1495-1556, brother of Lodovico, Florentine republican and poet, 141

Alamanni, Piero, 1434-1519, Florentine politician, belonged to the circle of Lorenzo Magnifico, father of Lodovico and Luigi, 132

Alberti, Leon Battista, 50

Albertini, Rudolf von, 101, 102, 103, 106, 107, 130, 131, 133, 134, 136, 137, 138, 140, 141, 150, 151, 243, 331, 337

Albizzi, Rinaldo degli, leading Florentine statesman before the rise of the Medici, 245

Alexander VI (Roderigo Borgia), Pope from 1492 to 1503, 31, 56, 74, 169, 260, 262, 263, 266, 286

Alfonso, King of Aragon and Naples, 1416-1458, 261

Alfonso, King of Naples, 1494-1495, 261, 266, 267, 285

Alviano, Bartolomeo d', 1455-1515, 265, 272

Amboise, George d', Cardinal (of Rouen), 1460-1510, advisor of Louis XII, 125

Ambrogini, Francesco, Florentine politician, 11

America, 284

Anghiari, battle of, 1440, 10, 237

Antonelli, Giovanni, 313, 314

Anzilotti, Antonio, 58, 76, 133, 310, 311

Aragon, Aragonese, 255, 256; see also Alfonso, Ferdinand I, Ferdinand II

Arezzo, 14, 63, 64, 70, 169

Ariost, 163

Aristotle, 23, 205, 206, 218

Athens, Duke of (Walter of Brienne), tyrant of Florence, 1343, 232, 238

Badia, Jodoco del, editor, see Landucci

Baglioni, family ruling in Perugia, 126

Baron, Hans, 91, 93, 185, 220, 233, 334

Bayley, C. C., 92, 130, 154

Beloch, Karl Julius, 20

Bembo, Pietro, 1470-1547, Venetian humanist, secretary to Leo X, Cardinal in 1539, 219, 225, 226, 333

Bentivogli, family ruling in Bologna, 126

Beroaldus, Filippus (il Vecchio), 1453-1505, humanist from Bologna, 90

Bersi, Ruggero, 223

Bertelli, Sergio, 183, 319, 320, 322, 326

Bessarion, Cardinal, 1403-1472, 219